HINDU CULTURE IN ANCIENT INDIA

HINDU CULTURE IN ANCIENT INDIA

S. V. VISWANATHA

Hindu Culture in Ancient India

ISBN : 978-81-8205-490-5

Reprinted in 2009 in India by
Isha Books
B-63, 1st Floor
New Gupta Colony,
Near DDA Market,
Delhi - 110009
First Published in 1928

Printed at : **Vishal Kaushik Printers, Delhi**

CONTENTS

PREFACE

THIS book has grown out of what was delivered as University-Lectures at Mysore in 1925. Its scope and limitations are indicated in the Introductory chapter. I have dealt with the subject from the view-point of social and cultural anthropology and propose to dwell on the physical in a subsequent volume.

I have had to differ from accepted views in the treatment of certain topics. The indulgent attention of the reader is drawn to these as well as to the Appendices.

My thanks are due to my brother, Professor S. V. Venkateswara, of the University of Mysore, who has kindly read the proofs, and to my old pupil, Mr. N. S. Narasimhan, B.A., who has drawn for me the map of Ancient India.

S. V. VISWANATHA.

PART I

INTRODUCTION

INTRODUCTION

I

India is One

The ancient history of India teems with illustrations which go to prove its fundamental unity amidst large differences in detail which have not, however, affected the cultural development and the progress of her great and ancient civilization. The author of *The Early History of India* [1] exclaims that attention has been concentrated too long on the Indo-Aryan aspect of this culture, and that it is time that due regard should be paid to the non-Aryan element. There is in the following pages an attempt to present the history of Hindu society and culture, having due regard to the non-Aryan contribution to Indian civilization. I have ventured to show the blend in Indian culture, to narrate the unifying processes in the relations of the Aryas and the non-Aryas who have lived and worked together in India through the ages. The gradual fusion of the two is visible, evolving a type of civilization, common to the whole country in a manner sufficient to justify its treatment as a unit in the history of the social and intellectual development of mankind.

The subject of this study is the progress of the relations of the Indian Aryas with the other peoples of differing culture whom they met with in the course of their settlement and expansion over India. This topic is of especial interest, for the greatest mingling of the races of man has taken place exactly in those regions of the earth that have been occupied by the so-called Aryan race.[2] My endeavour is to show that the Aryas did not merely step into a void created by the expulsion of the conquered peoples, and that, though they may have been inferior in numbers, they were not lost in the ocean of the conquered population. Wherever they settled, they mixed with those they found, incorporated gradually their habits and ways of living, and took wives and domestic servants from among them. In fact, a policy of "give and take" is clearly in evidence, that led to the peaceful existence side by side and the unification of the divergent cultures in Ancient India. In this is an attempt to elucidate the harmony and concord among the conflicting interests and ideals of the various castes and tribes of India, the bridging of the disparities that existed between the Aryan and the non-Aryan, and the narrowing of the cleavage in respect of customs, manners, languages and functions that seemed to differentiate one class from another.

II

A Note on Sources

The sources of our information are chiefly works of Sanskrit literature. For the earliest period of the history of Indian culture, we have to rely on the data of the *mantras* of the *Rig-Veda* and some hymns of the *Atharvan*. The Brāhmaṇas and the Epics disclose the later phase of the struggle of the Aryas for dominion in non-Aryan territory. Detailed information about the changes in the last epoch is derived chiefly from the Buddhist and Jaina works. The Law-books and Purāṇas, some of which should be assigned to this period, indicate the results of the reaction against the heretical preachings of the Buddhists and the Jainas. To these should be added prehistoric archæology, comparative philology and ethnology and the evidence available in the old coins, inscriptions and foreign travellers' accounts. The non-Aryan sources are rare as such and require dexterous handling. There are not only the relics of the past in Dravidian folklore and linguistics, the primitive customs and usages, but evidence imbedded in Sanskrit literature itself of the civilization and modes of life of the non-Aryan peoples alike of the North and the South. What is even more important in this connexion is Pāḷi, Prākrit and Tamil literature, the accounts of foreign travellers and such of the traditions and practices as are extant among the aboriginal peoples like the Muṇḍas, Asuras and others of North India and the hill-tribes of the South.

The greatest difficulty of the Indian ethnologist has been that at the present day there is practically no non-Aryan people extant with all their pristine purity, and with their old institutions and habits unchanged by contact with the other people in the plains. The men of the hills have become so converted as to be classified with their brethren on the plain. The result is that, as Mr Thurston writes,[3] tribes which only a few years ago were living in a wild state, buried in the depths of the jungle subsisting on roots, fruits and other forest produce like other animals of God's creation, have been subjected to the domesticating and, in many cases, detrimental influence of civilization, resulting in large changes in their conditions of life, religion, morality and language. The Paṇiyans of Wynad and the Iruḷas of the Anamalai are regularly working for wages in coffee and pepper plantations on the hill-estates, and could not be distinguished very easily from their caste-brethren working along with them as labourers. It is therefore no wonder if a Toda boy was seen reading in the third standard of a village school, instead of tending the buffaloes of his *mand* (a Toda hut), a Toda lassie curling her ringlets with a cheap foreign looking-glass in hand, a Toda adult smeared with Hindu sect-marks and praying for prosperity at a Hindu shrine. It is a misfortune for the ethnologist that the Todas of the Nilgiris have now become practically extinct as an aboriginal race, while their brethren on the hills, the Badagas and the Kotas, have become thinned in numbers, besides becoming so profusely Hinduized as not to be distinguished from caste-Hindus. One of the urgent needs of the day, in the interests of the science of anthropology, is to reclaim and preserve what is left of this once representative type of the Dravidian peoples of South India, though we realize that in the larger and more unselfish interests of humanity, these primitive peoples should be made to partake more and more of the amenities of modern civilization.

India has been looked upon as a museum of ethnic curiosities; and various influences have been at work to produce a confused array of castes and creeds in this country.[4] Many tribes have become converted and included in one of the castes or sub-castes, and this change of tribe into caste has been effected in the following ways:—

(1) The prominent leaders of an aboriginal tribe, because of their wealth and status, have managed to get admission into one of the more distinguished castes.

(2) The members of an aboriginal tribe giving up their animistic religion embrace the tenets and observe the practices of a Hindu religious sect, and thus become converted to Hinduism to take a place among the castes.

(3) A whole tribe of aborigines enrol themselves as Hindus under the style of a new caste which may be readily distinguished from any of the standard or recognized castes. They form thus a separate caste.

(4) An aboriginal tribe or a section thereof abandon their tribal designation and become gradually converted to Hinduism.

Anthropometry is the first handmaid of anthropology, and in India the conditions are generally favourable for the application of the science. "Nowhere else in the world do we find the population of a large sub-continent broken up into an infinite number of mutually exclusive aggregates, the members of which are forbidden by an inexorable social law to marry outside the group to which they themselves belong. In a society thus organized, . . . differences of physical type . . . may be expected to manifest a high degree of persistence, while methods which seek to trace and express such differences find a peculiarly favourable field for their operation." [5] But because of the large crossings that have been effected, and the consequent admixture of blood and of institutions, even anthropometric data, such as cranial measurements, nasal indices, the colour of the skin, the iris and the hair, and the projection of the jaw, may cease to be the outstanding criteria for determining racial affinities. The castes and tribes of India have already shown a defiance of the measurements and calculations of anthropometrists. As Mr Dalton says, "There is a considerable admixture of Aryan blood (among the Kols). Many have high noses and oval faces and young girls are at times met with who have delicate and regular features, finely chiselled straight noses and perfectly formed mouths and chins . . . and I have met strongly marked Mongolian features." What Dalton observes about the Kols seems applicable to the other representatives of the primitive inhabitants of India.[6]

III

Divisions

The question of chronology has given room for considerable difference of opinion among oriental scholars.[7] In a subject like this it is not possible to say exactly when a particular change was effected in the relations of the two peoples. Social and religious changes evolve only gradually and slowly. We cannot point to a fixed date when the old order may have changed yielding place to the new. I have found it convenient to divide the whole course of the survey into three parts having regard to the antiquity of the sources of information and to the peculiar features prominent in each of these divisions. In the first—The

Age of the Mantras—the relations were mostly of a warlike and political character. In the second—The Epoch of the later Vedic Texts and the background of the Epics—remarkable changes in social life are also in evidence. In the third—The Period of Buddhism, the Smritis, the Purāṇas and the *Śangam* Texts of South India—the fusion of the social and the religious institutions of the Aryas and the non-Aryas had gone on apace. The political relations are not hostile now, and may be relegated to a subordinate position. The scope of the subject extends from the period of the *Rig-Veda* to about the fourth century after Christ.

IV

Limitations

It is not easy to distinguish the exact nature and extent of the influence of the one people over the other. The works of literature written by the Aryas define Aryan territory, at first, as the region of the Seven Rivers (*saptasindhavah*). Later, the sphere of Aryan influence was the Kuru-Pāñchāla country and adjacent tracts of land. The centre of activity is shifted from the Indus valley to the Ganges and the Jumna. In the Law-codes,[8] *Āryāvarta* is defined as the tract of territory lying between the Himālaya and the Vindhya mountains, and extending from the eastern to the western sea, the region where the black antelope roamed about freely. And like the Greeks who considered as barbarians all those who were alien to them, the Aryas held the lands different from theirs to be those of the *Mlechchas* (barbarians). Again, we read in the Smritis [9] that the inhabitants of Avanti, Aṅga, Magadha, Saurāshṭra, the Dekhan, Upāvrit, Sindh, and Sauvīra are of mixed origin. He who has visited the countries of the Āraṭṭas, Kāraskaras, Puṇḍras, Sauvīras, Vaṅgas, Kaliṅgas, or Praṇūnas shall offer a *punasthoma* or *sarvaprishṭa ishṭi* (sacrifice). In the literature of the *Śangam* age the land of the Tamils is described as bounded on the north by the Venkaṭa hill (Tirupati), on the south by Cape Comorin, and on the east and west by the southern seas.[10] Still further the culture of the Aryas got gradually extended over the lands that were uninhabited or inhabited by non-Aryan tribes of a different civilization which the Aryas looked down upon as being on a lower level than theirs. The various processes of this expansion were conquest, colonization and settlement, and the institution of protectorates or spheres of influence, as the Epic and the Purāṇa literature clearly tend to show.[11] From the age of the *Rig-Veda* the Aryas are seen to penetrate into the surrounding jungle tracts that were the abodes of the non-Aryan peoples. The *Rāmāyaṇa* tells the the story of the attempt at the colonization of South India by the Aryas of *Madhyadeśa*, and shows how they faced the resistance of the non-Aryan powers of the South in the process of advance into new tracts of territory. Before the age of the Epics the Aryas had been confined to the regions of the Jumna and the Ganges; and their onward movement is clearly illustrated by the greater geographical knowledge that is revealed in the Brāhmaṇas. Coming to later times, the colonization of Ceylon by Prince Vijaya from North India,[12] and that of Java and other foreign countries are historical examples of this process of acquisition of new territory. In the same manner, in the history of mediaeval South India we have instances of attempts made by some of her kings [13] to extend their influence over the princes of the North, in however feeble a way. *Digvijaya* or conquest of the four quarters, on which successful kings set out from time to time, is clearly illustrative of the fact that conquest was one of the most important methods of territorial expansion. In the *Arthaśāstra* [14] acquisition of new lands by conquest is considered very desirable, and later kings such as Samudragupta and Harsha were great conquerors. For example, in the

Allahabad Pillar Inscription of Samudragupta we read that the kings of *Dakshiṇāpatha* were "captured and liberated", the forest-kings were "violently exterminated", and impressed into the service of the emperor; and even the foreign dynasties in India had their ruling chieftains restored when they surrendered, and the imperial flag flew over their dominions. In this process of expansion of the Aryan dominion of the North or the non-Aryan kingdoms in the South, of which the most important in the Epic age was Lanka, we have the formation of spheres of influence or protectorates. Instances of these were Kishkindha, the realm of the Vānara tribe; and Khāṇḍava vana and Hiḍimba-vana inhabited by Nāgas and other aboriginal races.

The political divisions of India in the Buddhist age comprise the sixteen *mahājanapadāh*. The list of kingdoms does not contain any south of Avanti. South India and Ceylon are omitted and there is no mention of even Orissa or the Dekhan. "The horizon of those who drew up the list is strictly bounded on the north by the Himālayas and on the south by the Vindhya range, on the west by the mountains beyond the Indus, and on the east by the Ganges as it turns to the south." [15]

Thus in course of time the geographical horizon of the Aryas became widened until in some form or other it extended directly or indirectly over the whole of India. It is in some cases not possible to determine what features of a particular epoch are distinctively due to Aryan and what due to non-Aryan influences. The exact share of each in this common civilization is not easily fixed. As a great Dravidian scholar [16] wrote in the case of non-Aryan institutions, the process of Aryanization may have gone too far to enable the historian to distinguish the native warp from the foreign woof. A similar statement holds good, as will be shown in the sequel, in the case of many Aryan institutions as well. Hindu culture as it was developed in the early centuries of the Christian era was the result of such a complete amalgamation, that it is extremely difficult to draw the line of demarcation between the Aryan and the Dravidian and other non-Aryan elements in this compound civilization. As Colonel Hodson says, " there are many facts to indicate that the effects of the interpenetration of cultures which, by reason of its long history, characterizes Indian culture as a whole, are not less manifest in modifications of the social attitudes of the higher culture than in those of the lower culture." [17]

The treatment of the subject does not pretend to be exhaustive. Changes in religion and society take place almost unnoticed, and it is not therefore possible to cover all the processes of change in the evolution of Hindu culture. The field is so vast, the materials lie so scattered, the crossings in society that have taken place are so numerous, and have so largely modified the picture of Indian social life, that one can be expected to do little more than present the salient features and results in outline.

Lastly, there lay in South India a tract of non-Aryan territory larger than anywhere else in India; and very little, complains Dr Smith, is known concerning political events in the far south during the long period extending from 600 B.C. to 900 A.D. The materials for lifting the veil of secrecy are scanty. The paucity of authentic sources of information relating to the study of the social relations and religious influences of the North and the South must certainly be more striking. The account of the contribution of the Aryan to the Dravidian culture and *vice versa* has, of necessity, to be culled from stray and scattered references in the original sources of Indian history.[18]

V

The Aryas (Origin and Affinities)

Recent excavations have made it necessary to go once more over the ground that has been traversed many times by competent authorities. Divergent views have been held as to the geographical position, the origin and the racial affinities of the Aryas. The latest is what has been projected by Dr Giles in the *Cambridge History of India*.[19] He uses the word *Wiros* to denote the speakers of the Indo-European or Indo-Germanic languages, this being the word for men in the great majority of the languages in question; and places the original habitat of his Wiros in the areas which cover modern Hungary, Austria and Bohemia. He holds that the great similarity between the various languages spoken by the so-called Aryan races would lead us to infer that they must have lived for ages in a severely circumscribed centre, so that their peculiarities developed for many generations in common. Such a confined and close area must have been separated from the outer world either by great waters or mountains; and the climate in which they lived belonged to the temperate zone. The original Aryas were not a nomad but a settled people, and they were familiar with corn and the domestication of animals. The animals best known to them were the ox and the cow, the sheep, the horse, the dog, the pig, and probably some species of deer. Of birds they knew the goose and the duck, and the most familiar bird of prey among them was the eagle. The wild animals wolf and bear were known, but not the lion and the tiger.

After presenting the above data as the basis of his study, Giles asks the question: Is there any part of Europe which combines pastoral and agricultural country in close connexion which has in combination hot low-lying plains suitable for the growth of grain and rich upland pasture suitable for flocks and herds, and at the same time trees and birds of the character already described? He says it is not likely to be India, for neither the fauna nor the flora as detailed above are characteristic of this area. His conclusion is that there is apparently only one such area in Europe, that which is bounded on the eastern side by the Carpathians, on its south by the Balkans, on its western side by the Austrian Alps and the Bohmer Wald, and on the north by the Erzebirge and the mountains which link them up with the Carpathians. This is a fertile and well-watered land with great corn plains in the low-lying levels of Hungary, but also possessing steppe-like tracts which make it one of the best horse-breeding areas in Europe.

One may very well agree with the line of inquiry adopted above and consider how far the conclusions are warranted by the facts that are known. It may be pointed out that the Himālayan-tracts admirably satisfy all the conditions set forth above. A study of the birds and beasts known to the people of the Rig-Vedic age, and of the habits and institutions of the Aryas of India, clearly tends to show that the flora and the fauna which are held to be peculiarly characteristic of the Balkan region were exactly those with which the Vedic Aryas were most familiar. The bull and the cow have been the favourite animals of Indians from the Vedic period onwards. The sheep and the dog are indicative of the pastoral life of the Vedic Indians. Saramā, the dog in the Veda, is made the subject of one whole hymn.[20] It is a known fact that the Aryas of the *Rig-Veda* were good cavalry men, and depended for their success on their horses, like the Dadhikra, in praise of which a good number of hymns are to be found. The *krishṇa* and other kinds of deer have always played, and still continue to play, a large part in the religious and social life of the Aryas. The *ajina* or deer-skin was used by the Aryas in daily rituals and ceremonies. The region of Kashmir and tracts of land round the lake of Manasarowar have been sung as the sacred spots where the *hamsa* birds abounded. The *śyena* (eagle or hawk) is described in the Veda as a swift and rapacious bird. There is reference to the hungry hawk in one of the hymns.[21]

The climate of the region is temperate, or even cold, though India as a whole may be in the Tropics, and was specially conducive to the growth and rearing of horses. That the Aryas of India were accustomed to a cool climate is clear from the following prayer: "Let there be no extreme heat on our way."[22] This shows that the Vedic Aryas were not used to much heat and loved the cool and temperate climate of the uplands of India. In ancient literature and tradition the region of North India extending over Kambhoja and Gandhāra was essentially favourable for horses. The horses of these tracts were considered famous as late as the period of Kauṭilya's *Arthaśāstra.*[23] As Giles himself admits, forest trees like the birch are more magnificent on the Kinchinjinga than in any part of the western world,[24] and there are besides well-watered plains in the lowlands for cultivation, and steppe-like areas affording good grazing ground for cattle and horses in the land which is proposed to be marked as the original habitat of the Aryan race.

Colonel Waddell in his book *Indo-Sumerian Seals Deciphered* writes that the Sumerians were the Aryas, and the ancient Vedic sages and kings wrote and spoke in the Sumerian tongue; for he found that over 50 per cent of the basic words in Sanskrit and Hindi are clearly derived from Sumerian. According to him the early Sumerians of the Indus valley appear from the testimony of their own seals to have been merely a temporary wave of Sumerian (Vedic Aryan) sea-faring traders who penetrated to the Indus valley, and holding it as a colony of Mesopotamia, settled there for several centuries, accompanied by their families and family-priests. They were an advance guard of the so-called Aryan invasion of India. The Phoenicians properly so called were Aryas in race and speech and were the leading pioneers of Aryan civilization over the world and, in particular, the introducers of Aryan civilization into ancient India. He is of the opinion that the Indo-Phoenician Sumerians whose seals he has attempted to decipher were not the same as the Aryas of "the Aryan Invasion of India", which he says took place in the seventh century B.C. by sea. Waddell says further that the term Akkad was only a Semitic word for the land called by the Sumerians Ariki or Uriki, i.e. the land of the Aryas. About the religion of the Phoenicians, the precursors of the Aryas, Waddell is of the opinion that it was a monotheism with the worship of Indra (In-duru), and the name of this god is derived from *daro* or *darya*, which means sea or water, and this, he says, is identical with Sumerian *duru*.

Waddell's identification of the Aryas with the Sumerians or the Phoenicians rests on the similarity of names and little more. Linguistic resemblances constitute no certain guides for the determination of racial affinities, apart from the validity or otherwise of the identification made by Waddell. The question whether the Sumerians of Western Asia or the Aryas of India were the progenitors of Vedic civilization is easily disposed of by him with the verdict that the Aryan invasion of India took place in the seventh century B.C. May not one, following the line of research that Waddell takes, based on linguistic inferences, point out the close resemblance of Sumerian to mount Sumeru? Is it untenable to hold that the Sumerians, a branch of the Aryan race, were the people that migrated from the region of Sumeru in the Western Himālayan country?

As regards the origin of the Akkadian religion and civilization there are two distinct schools of opinion. The German school led by Schraeder and Delitsch hold that it was due to the Semitic people of the west, while the school led by Lenormant seek to establish that it was borrowed from the Vedic Aryas.

It is highly probable that the western peoples like the Phoenicians and the Sumerians had already known of Vedic Indra as the god of rain or waters, and had adapted the word, thus giving the meaning sea or water to *duru* or *daro*, if Waddell's surmise be right.

That the Sumerian civilization with which Waddell deals was later than Vedic civilization is clear from his own statement that the Khattiyo (Kshatriyas) were the chief and ruling caste in the Sumerian social structure and that in Sumerian literature there is indication of the exaltation of the Baramas (Brāhmans) to the first rank by Bur-Sin (Paraśurāma). This latter event belongs to the Post-Vedic Epic age in Indian history.

The westerly movement of the Vedic Aryas and their culture is indicated in a reference in one passage in the *Rig-Veda* [25] to Indra and Nāsatyas having fled into far-off lands. " O, Indra, if you are not regaling yourself in Ruma, Ruśama, Śyavaka and Kripa, come." Ruma reminds us of Rūm, i.e. Byzantine Empire or modern Turkey.[26] Kripa (Krivi) is the same as the land of the Syrio-Phoenicians.[27] Śyavaka is suggestive of Slavaka. This migration is perhaps corroborated by the names of the deities mentioned in the Boghaz-Keui inscription, viz. Indra, Varuṇa, Mitra and Nāsatya. These are invoked to witness a treaty between a Mitannic and a Hittite prince and appear as Indar, Uruvṇa, Mitra, Nasaattiia. The interesting point to be noticed here is that the gods mentioned in the inscription are two of them identical with the gods (Indra and Nāsatya) who, the Vedic bard complains, had fled to foreign lands. It is also remarkable that Agni is not mentioned in the epigraph. Giles himself admits [28] that the Boghaz-Keui inscription may be an argument for deriving the origin of these tribes from India rather than the West.

In another passage [29] of the *Rig-Veda* Indra's migration to the West is indicated thus : O Indra, you crossed the *Samudra* and brought Turvaśa and Yadu from afar! The geographical details in the *Rig-Veda* show that the Turvaśas and the Yadus were occupying the lands to the west of the River Indus, and *samudra* in this passage may simply refer to the Indus.[30] The order of the rivers mentioned in the *Rig-Veda* runs from the East to the West. This circumstance, taken along with the migration of Saramā, a messenger of Indra, to the region of the Paṇis, after crossing the impassable river Rasā, may indicate a westward move of the Aryas from India.[31]

The story of Nābhānedishṭha, a son of Manu, who was left out by his father while partitioning his property, and who got cows from Angiras for having acted as a priest, is also illustrative of the fact that the Vedic Aryas were split up into two sections. The word Nābhānedishṭha is etymologically connected with Nabhanazdishta in the *Avesta*. Lassen saw in this incident the reminiscence of an Indo-Aryan split. The further question is, what was the place of this split? Was it in India or elsewhere? According to the genealogical table given on page 221 [32] *Manu was one of the earliest Prajāpatis*, being the fourth in descent from the Creator, and Nābhānedishṭha was a son of Manu. So it is more likely that the division took place in India than that it was effected in western lands. The story is perhaps indicative of the migration of a section of the Vedic Aryas who took with them the worship of the fire (Angiras).

In the cuneiform tablets at Tel-el-Amarna we find the names of the following kings tributary to the Pharaohs: Artamanya, Bavarzana, Subandu or Subandi, Suvardata, Sutarna, Yasdata, etc. The names of the Mitannic kings found are: Sa-uṣ-sa-tar, Artatama, Suttarna, Dusratta, Artassumara, and Matiuaza. Two things are noteworthy in connexion with these names. They look like names of Indian princes, where *S* appears as such without undergoing a change into *H* as in later times.

In the Kassite records of Babylon such names occur as Suria, Marut and Simālaya. Dr Sten Konow [33] explains these terms by saying, "I think that the explanation of these facts has been given by Professor Bloomfield who considers it possible that the Mitanni and other western Asiatic Iranoid proper names came from a dialect closely allied to the Iranian, but not yet exactly Iranian, i.e. a dialect which did not change *S* into *H*." What is this dialect? *The word Simālaya must give the clue.* It leads to the inevitable conclusion that the religion supposed in these names must have migrated from the region of the Himālayas, and the language of these names was apparently derived from the Vedic Aryan language.[34]

Further, the Akkadian prayers to the Sun and Fire quoted below among others seem to be exact reproductions of Vedic passages [35] :—

> "O Sun, thou hast stept forth from the background of heaven, thou hast pushed back the bolt of the brilliant sky; above the land thou hast raised thy head. O Sun, thou hast covered the immeasurable space of heaven and countries."
>
> "Thou who drivest away the evil *Markim*, who furtherest the well-being of life, who strikest the breast of the wicked with terror, Fire, the destroyer of foes, dread weapon, which drivest away pestilence."

It is interesting to note that the word *Marka* is found in the Veda only, as a *guru* of the Asuras, and it is strange that the Assyrians and the Akkads should speak of *Marka* as an evil god.[36] Thus, these passages, besides containing similarity of sentiments with those found in the Veda, contain a name that is clearly a direct borrowing from Vedic language and thought.

Professor Keith,[37] one of the exponents of the invasion of India by the Aryas from the west, is constrained to admit that the Mitannic evidence indicates that the entry of the Aryas into Iran took place from the north-east. The tripolic culture of southern Russia marks the advance of Indo-European tribes westwards in the third millennium B.C. This will explain the close similarity between the accounts of the nomadic tribes among the Indo-Europeans and the Mongols in far later times. As regards manner of life, religion and funeral customs, similarity of circumstance would produce similarity of results. Dr J. H. Moulton [38] observes that "we know nothing about the movements of Indian or Iranian tribes in the second millennium" and that "we could postulate an ebb from India without compromising anything that is really established". G. Boni, the Italian archæologist and antiquarian, has shown from the remarkable similarities between Indo-Aryan and Roman funeral and other practices "that the earliest Latins were of Aryan stock who had reached Europe from northern India through Persia and Asia Minor ". In the Vedas alone could he hope to find the key to the " Forum riddle ".[39]

It becomes clear in the light of the foregoing evidence that the views about an Aryan invasion of India have to be given up,[40] and that there is nothing in prehistoric archæology, philology or ethnology that militates against the cradle of the Aryas being in the Himālayan region, roughly extending from the valleys of the Seven Rivers to the place where the Ganges and the Jumna are seen to have their rise. The sight of this region made the travel-diarist exclaim :—" In the midst of a nature, which builds up such mountains, a Mahābhāratam may very well be created. All the grandeur of Indian mythology is preconceived in her. How well can I understand to-day the significance which the Himālayas possess for the Indian consciousness! Within their domain lies Śiva's paradise; even there the holiest of rivers rises. In the Himālayas, the *munis* and the *rishis* dwell, and all those who thirst for wisdom strive up towards them irrepressibly in an unending chain. From the Himālayas the Vedas have come, so have the Upanishads; all inspiration emanates from them even to-day." [41] From this central position in Asia the Vedic Aryas appear to have expanded outwards.

The chronological stages in this expansion can at present be only roughly indicated. The history of ancient Aryan religion and culture discloses the following general landmarks :—

(1) Agni worship—fourth millennium B.C.

(2) Indra worship—third millennium B.C. The transition from the worship of Agni to that of Indra and the prominence attached to the latter is indicated in the following hymn [42] :—

"Agni, Soma and Varuṇa must give way. The power goes to another, I see it come. In choosing Indra, I give up the father, though I have lived with him many years in friendship."

(3) The spread of Indra-worship into the regions of the Mitanni, Hittites, Kassites, etc., as well as the Iranian or Zoroastrian offshoot from India may be placed in the second millennium B.C.

VI

The Non-Aryan Peoples

As regards the origin and ethnic affinities of the non-Aryan peoples also ethnologists have differed in opinion. The non-Aryan problem is as perplexing as that of Aryan origins. We may here attempt only a brief resumé of the various views held on the subject.[43] The non-Aryan element in the population of India has run in two main streams that may be designated the Kolarian and the Dravidian. It was held by a school of ethnologists that the former migrated to India from the north-east, while the latter invaded India through the north-west passes, leaving a branch in the Brahui. Neither of these theories is feasible, nor are they necessary.

VII

The Origin of the Dravidians

About the Dravidians, Haeckel writes in his *History of Creation* "at present the primeval species, Homo Dravida, is only represented by the Dekhan tribes in the southern part of Hindustan, and by the neighbouring inhabitants of the mountains on the north-east of Ceylon. But in earlier times, this race seems to have occupied the whole of Hindustan, and to have spread even further. It shows on the one hand traits of relationship to the Australians and the Malays; on the other to the Mongols and the Mediterranese. The Indian Ocean formed a continent, which extended from the Sunda islands along the southern coast of Asia to the east coast of Africa. This large submerged continent of former times Sclater has called *Lemuria*." Sir William Crooke says that the Dravidians represent an invasion from the African continent. Topinard is inclined to establish the affinity of the Dravidians of South India to the Jats. Mr A. H. Keene is of the opinion that although the Dravidians "preceded the Aryan speaking Hindus, they are not the true aborigines of the Dekhan, for they were themselves preceded by dark peoples, probably of aberrant negrito type", and that Indian ethnologists like Risley have confused the Dravidian with the negrito races.

Against the Lemurian theory of Dravidian origins Sir William Turner [44] asserts that "by a careful comparison of Australian and Dravidian crania, there ought not to be much difficulty in distinguishing one from the other". A comparative study of the characters of the crania of the Australians and the South Indian aborigines has not led him to the conclusion that these characteristics can be adduced in support of the theory of the unity of the two peoples.

Dr Haddon [45] has no doubt that, "so far as is known, the bulk of the population of India has been stationary." The jungle tribes probably represent the oldest existing substratum. The Dravidians have always been in India, the Brahui being only a case of cultural drift. This may be taken to be the last word on the subject so far as our knowledge of the Dravidian institutions goes at present. "Taking them as we find them now, it may safely be said that their present geographical distribution, the marked uniformity of physical characters among the more primitive members of the group, their animistic religion, their distinctive languages, their stone monuments, and their retention of a primitive system of totemism justify us in regarding them as the earliest inhabitants of India of whom we have any knowledge." [46] It is desirable, taking the caution suggested by Keene, to remember that there is a great admixture of the negrito element in the aboriginal population of India, and it would be wrong if we place, as Risley does, the Paṇiyans of Wynad, the Kadirs of the Ānamalai, and the Santals of Chota Nagpur, in the same category with the Todas of the Nilgiris and the Khonds of Central India.

VIII

The Kolarians

The main representatives of the Kolarian type have been taken to be the aboriginal hill-people of Central India, such as the Asuras, Muṇḍas, Śavaras, Oraons, etc. The chief of these is the Muṇḍa tribe. In general, the Kolarians are for North India what the Dravidians are for the South, and the Muṇḍas resemble the Dravidians so closely as not to be distinguished from them, and appear to have been the original inhabitants of the valley of the Ganges and Western Bengal. Very probably, these are the remnants of the non-Aryan races that were pushed into the interior and driven eastward by the Aryas in the course of their expansion over the valleys of the Ganges and the Jumna. The Asurs of the Muṇḍa tradition are perhaps the descendants of the Asuras who appear as the foes of the Aryas in the *Rig-Veda*.[47] The Śavaras put us in mind of a tribe of the same name which finds mention in the *Rāmāyaṇa*.

IX

The Adicchanallur Ruins

A large mass of evidence has been accumulating in recent years which has thrown remarkable light on the civilization of India in palæolithic and neolithic times. Various prehistoric objects have been secured such as palæolithic and neolithic implements, pottery, beads and bangles, cromlechs and dolmens and remains of the dead buried in caves, jars and urns with some of the ornaments and implements used by the deceased.

The prehistoric remains of Adicchanallur in the Tinnevelly district of the Madras presidency were excavated by the Archaeological Department in the year 1902.[48] The most remarkable of the ruins was the *panḍukuḻi* (antique caverns). In these were found entire skeletons of human bodies in terra cotta sarcophagi which contained beside the bodies some articles of food and garments kept in small pots. They enclosed also articles made of pure bronze or iron, viz. beautiful vases and utensils, figures of animals, and weapons and implements. It has been supposed that the culture disclosed by these ruins was that of the Early Dravidians of South India.

X

The Finds at Mohenjo Daro and Harappa

Though the discoveries in the Punjab and Sindh valley have not been exhausted, and the finds not fully subjected to examination, we may hazard one or two conclusions at this stage of excavation. The ruins extend over a very large area. So far as the results of the discovery have been published by Sir John Marshall, they may be briefly stated thus :—

Layers of buried sites have been unearthed, and the one nearest the surface is taken to belong to the chalcolithic period. The ruins point to the existence of temples and houses, made of sun-burnt bricks or kiln-burnt clay. The houses seem to have been provided with wells, bathrooms and good drainage. At Harappa were found long, large and thick walls, one separated from the other by broad aisles of 24 ft. The walls are said to be 52 ft. long. Among the ruins were ring-stones of huge size and of varying shapes. There was a tablet of blue faience, which contained a figure seated cross-legged, with men to the right and the left, a Nāga (serpent) and a pictograph. Beneath the floor of one of the houses were copper vessels and implements, jewellery of carnelian and other stones, a necklace, talismanic stones, needles, and bangles of silver. Every house was seen to contain engraved seals. The seals disclose the figures of bulls with or without the hump, and twin-heads of antelopes shooting from a tree like the peepul. There were, besides, the figures of tigers, elephants and crocodiles. The bodies that were buried in these sites had on them shell-bangles, copper rings and bracelets. Stone knives and other implements abound. A costly necklace of fifty-five gold beads with agate pendants was also among the finds.

At Mohenjo Daro statues of men were exhumed, and they were found to be brachycephalic, with prominent nose, low forehead, narrow oblique eyes and fleshy lips. The dead were cremated in these places, according to the latest statement of Marshall.

"The usual method of disposing of the dead in the latest cities of Mohenjo Daro and Harappa was by cremation, a few fragments of the burnt bone being subsequently collected and placed in a large earthenware jar along with a number of medium-sized and miniature vessels, or in small brick structures resembling Hindu *samādhis*. Examples of these 'cinerary' urns have been found at both Harappa and Mohenjo Daro. But at Mohenjo Daro also, it is true some complete skeletons in excellent preservation are now being unearthed, but these appear to have been interred at a much later age, probably about the beginning of the Christian era."

"At a spot called Nal, about 250 miles south of Quetta in the Jhahalavan country of Baluchistan, Mr Hargreaves has discovered a burial ground of the same chalcolithic period, where the dead were buried either in caves of sun-dried bricks or directly in the ground. In the former case the skeleton was complete; in the latter, only a few bones and the skull of each body were found instead of a whole skeleton, and they were accompanied by numerous earthenware vases, copper implements, beads, grindstones and other small objects. All of these objects are analogous to those found at Mohenjo Daro and Harappa." [49]

Various opinions have been held as regards the antiquity and the affinities of these finds. In the earliest view of Marshall,[50] "it is possible, though unlikely, that this civilization of the Indus valley was an intrusive civilization emanating from further west. Painted pottery and other objects somewhat analogous to those found at Mohenjo Daro and Harappa have been found in Baluchistan, and there are linguistic reasons for believing that it was by way of Baluchistan that the Dravidian races entered India." Later he changes his opinion, and declares that the civilization as disclosed by the ruins may have been indigenous, and "there is no reason to assume that the culture of this region was imported from other lands, or that its character was profoundly modified by outside influences".[51] Professor Sayce points out the close resemblance between the seals and plaques found at Harappa and those found at Susa, which may indicate intercourse between North-west India and Susa as far back as 3000 B.C.[52] Mr R. D. Bannerji, one of the archæologists engaged in the excavation, is inclined to establish the affinity between the people whose civilization is in evidence in the ruins, with the Dravidians of India. He goes further, and holds the opinion that this culture was closely related to the Cretan and Mycenæan culture of the Greeks. He speaks of an Indo-Cretan cultural homogeneity at about 3000 B.C.[53] Messrs Gadd and Smith of the British Museum say that the Indian articles got from the ruins were similar to those of the Sumerians, e.g. pottery, seals, figures of the bull design, ornaments and even the brickwork of the structures. They are inclined also to establish the identity of most of the characters in the Indian seals with those of the Sumerian seals dating from 3000 to 2400 B.C.[54] They are not sure whether they belong to the Aryan or the Dravidian. Waddell in his book holds the view that the characters on the Indian seals have to be read in the light of those on the Sumerian seals, and that they belong to the Aryas. He also says that the

Sumerians were the Aryas, and that the Vedic Aryas were a branch of the Sumerians.

So far as the systems of the disposing of the dead go, it seems impossible to assign these remains to the Dravidians with whom the prevalent form of interring the dead was burial of some kind or other. The burial practices found in the remains at Adicchanallur agree with those found at Nal, and those described of the non-Aryan tribes of India in the Epic age like the Vānaras and the Rākshasas, and of the Dravidian tribes in South India as disclosed in the *Śangam* literature like the *Maṇimekalai*.[55]

Among the Vedic Aryas cremation was the rule, though there were also exceptions. In the *Rig-Veda* [56] we read of "corpses burnt by fire" (*agnidagdha*) and "unburnt" (*anagnidagdha*). Other methods allowed in exceptional circumstances are *paropta* (cast away—for example in the battlefield) and *utthita*, which the authors of the *Vedic Index* render as "exposure".[57] This term would more properly mean "burying in the erect posture". The term *vailasthānam* in the Vedic hymns seems to indicate the practice of burial in caves.[58] Sacrificial utensils and other articles were placed along with the dead body, as the Grihya Sūtras distinctly show. The charred bones of burnt bodies seem also to have been deposited in sepulchral mounds (*śmaśānachiti*). It is thus highly probable that the ruins belonged to the Aryas on this ground alone.

The rectangular aisles, separated from each other by long walls, bring to our minds the Aryan sacrificial altar of a rectangular shape in which were made the offerings to Fire and the other gods. The bricks were the *ishṭika* which we find used for the Nachiketas fire-altar in the Brāhmaṇas, and which should have been used for making the fire-pits in Vedic India.

The humped bull [59] is peculiarly Indian, and the *kakut* of the bull finds mention in the Vedic texts. The figure of the antelope is certainly indicative of the Aryan affinity of the finds, for the deer has been from the Vedic times onwards an animal favoured by the Aryas for their religious functions. In fact, the bounds of *Āryāvarta* were given as the regions over which the antelope roamed about freely. Thus, the Arya country could not be separated from the antelope. The peepul tree (*aśvattha*) has been an object of worship from the Vedic age onwards, as will be shown in the sequel.

The brick flooring and the drainage system are in conformity with the description of houses in the Vedic texts. Though generally, houses were made of timber and covered with grass, we find "four-walled" houses of the rich and well-built mansions, which had rooms paved with stone. The hall for Fire (*Agniśāla*) was paved with bricks.

Among the articles found in the ruins are knives (see *R.V.* i, 166, 10; viii, 4, 6), needles (*sūchī* in *R.V.* i, 191, 7). Silver articles are not mentioned in the *Rig-Veda*, and find mention in the other Vedas. Silver is rarely met with in the finds. The beautiful necklet of fifty-five pieces of gold shows great similarity to a garland of *nishka* (gold pieces) with which the Aryas of the Vedic age were familiar.[60]

Of the ethnic features of the statues that have been unearthed, the prominent nose is characteristic of the Aryan race, if ethnological features can at all be taken as safe guides in determining racial affinities. The narrow oblique eyes and the round head, which are some other features of the human figures found among the ruins, are Mongolian in character according to the ethnological ideas of modern times.

The writing on the seals shows that it may have been Aryan, if we accept Waddell's conclusions in this respect. His identification is based on the characters on the Sumerian seals, which show great resemblance to those on the Indian seals, as Gadd and Smith also have said. Fresh examination of the seals and the characters on them seems to be necessary.

The figure seated cross-legged with worshippers to the right and left is an Indian god. The figure of the Nāga shows that this find has to be assigned to a time when the Aryan religious features had been blended with the non-Aryan ones. The clay figurines of men and animals recall the figures of elephants and horses dedicated to the village gods of South India, and should be referred to the later Vedic period, when images were fashionable and image making had become a fine art.

The talismanic stones echo the magic and religion of the *Atharva-Veda*, which again is in some important respects the outcome of a commingling of the cultures, Aryan and non-Aryan. The shell bangles and pottery of a finished kind prove the relation of the culture of these finds to that of Adicchanallur.

The buildings believed to be temples storeys high bring to our minds the *gopura* of South India. They apparently belong to an age when temples had been elaborately built for the worship of Indian gods, probably to the period of the later Vedic texts.

Thus, the discoveries tend to show features of both cultures—Aryan and non-Aryan or Dravidian, and perhaps point to a period in Indian cultural history when the Aryan and non-Aryan had begun to get coalesced into one culture, the heritage of India.

The age of the ruins seems to lie between that of the earliest Vedic Mantras and the time when the Atharva practices had come to be recognized as part and parcel of the religion of the Hindus.

If, as specialists in archæology hold the view, these ruins belong to the chalcolithic period, i.e. 3000 B.C., the age of the *Rig-Veda* will have to be pushed up to about 4000 or 5000 B.C.

NOTES TO PART I

[1] V. A. Smith, *Early History of India*, p. 5.
[2] G. E. Boxall, *The Awakening of a Race*, pp. 26 f.
[3] *Castes and Tribes of India*, Introduction.
[4] *Imperial Gazetteer of India*, vol. i, chapter on Ethnology.
[5] *Impl. Gaz. of Ind.*, i, 287–8.
[6] *Descriptive Ethnology of Bengal*, p. 190.
[7] The Rig-Vedic Age has been assigned the following dates :—

4th Mill. B.C.	Tilak in *Orion*.
2780–1820 B.C.	Weber in *History of Indian Literature*, i, 2.
2400–2000 B.C.	Haug in *Aitareya Brāhmaṇa*, i, 47.
2050–1600–1000 B.C.	Pargiter in *Ancient Indian Historical Tradition*, p. 301.
1400–1000 B.C.	Keith in the *Cambridge History of India*.
1200–1000 B.C.	Max Müller.
700 B.C.	Waddell.

The *Brāhmaṇas* are given the date 1400–1200 by Haug and 600 B.C. by Pargiter.

The *Mahābhārata* War

1400 B.C.	Colebrooke and Wilson.
1370 B.C.	Wilford.
1424 B.C.	Jayasval.
950 B.C.	Pargiter.

Mr Pargiter holds that ancient tradition was compiled into the original Purāṇa about ninth century B.C., and the tradition was carried down to A.D. 400. By the end of the seventh century B.C. the original Purāṇas had been compiled.—*Anc. Ind. Hist. Tr.*, pp. 326 and 334.

[8] *Himavadvindhyayormadhyam yatprāgvinaśanādapi* |
Pratyageva Prayāgāccha Madhyadeśah prakīrtitah ||
Āsamudrāttu vai pūrvāt āsamudrāttu paśchimāt |
Tayorevāntaram giryoh Āryāvartam viduh budhāh ||
Krishṇasārah tu charati mrigo yatra svabhāvatah |
Sa jñeyo yajñiyo deśo Mlechchadeśah tatah parah ||
(*Manusmriti*, ii, 21–3.)

It seems to me that in the above passage, the *pūrva* and *paśchima samudra* refer respectively to the large collection of waters by the confluence of the Ganges and its tributaries in the extreme east, and by that of the Indus and its tributaries in the west. The passage apparently does not refer to the "eastern and western seas", as it is generally understood to mean, especially as Aṅga, Vaṅga, Magadha, and Vaiśāli were not included within the Āryan pale in the sacred texts. These countries will fall within the area of *Āryāvarta* if by *samudra* we mean the "sea".

[9] *Baudhāyana*, i, 1, 2, 13 f.
[10] *Vaḍavenkaṭam tenkumari yāyiḍai kūṟu Tamiḻ nallulakam* (*Tolkāppiyam*)
Neḍiyōnkuṉṟamum Toḍiyōlpauvamum
Tamiḻ varamparutta taṉpunnāḍu (*Śilappadikāram*).
[11] S. V. Viswanatha, *International Law in Ancient India*, pp. 25 and 45.
[12] Turnour, *Mahāvamśa*, chapters 6–8.

[13] E.g. Gangaikoṇḍa chōḷa. [14] p. 293.

[15] Rhys Davids, *Buddhist India*, p. 29. The expression *Dakshiṇāpatha* occurring in the *Sutta Nipātā* 976 is used to describe a settlement or colony on the Upper Godavari (*Vinaya*, i, 195, 196, and ii, 298). The *Majjhima Nikāya* (i, 378) mentions the Kalinga forest. Barukachcha and Suppāraka are perhaps referred to in *Vinaya*, iii, 39, and *Udāna*, i, 10.

[16] P. Sundaram Pillai in *Tamil Antiquary*, for 1908, p. 4.

[17] *Primitive Culture of India*, p. 13.

[18] I hope to issue before long a study of the culture of the Dravidians of the South, as is made from the original sources of literature—the *Śangam*.

[19] *Camb. Hist. of India*, i, pp. 66 ff. The reader may be referred to the *JRAS.*, vol. xvi, pp. 172–200, for a fairly exhaustive study of the Aryan problem. Arguments are adduced here for a theory of the "Punjab-Cradle" of the Aryan race. Canon Isaac Taylor long ago postulated in *The Origin of the Aryans* an Asiatic origin for the Aryas on the ground of their being tall, blonde and brachycephalic.

[20] *R.V.*, x, 105.

[21] Ibid., iv, 38, 5. The sun is addressed as the "eagle" in *R.V.*, iv, 20, 3; Agni is like the "hawk" in *R.V.*, vii, 15, 4, and *A.V.*, vi, 48, 1.

[22] *R.V.*, i, 42, 8. [23] *Arthaśāstra*, p. 298.

[24] *Camb. Hist. of Ind.*, p. 68.

[25] *R.V.*, viii, 4, 2. [26] See Alberuni, *India*, i, 303.

[27] Waddell, *Indo-Sumerian Seals Deciphered*, p. 8. The King of the Ruśama is Riṇanchaya in *R.V.*, v, 30, 12–15.

[28] *Camb. Hist. of India*, p. 72. Mr Pargiter summarizes his views on the Aryan invasion of India thus :—

1. That there was an outflow of people from India before the fifteenth century B.C.
2. That they brought Aryan gods from India.
3. That therefore Āryas and their gods existed in India before at least the sixteenth century.
4. That the Āryas had entered India earlier still from the Mid-Himālayan region.
5. *Iḷāvrita* is, according to Mr Pargiter, the original seat of the Aryas, for, this has been the sacred spot in Indian Historical Tradition. It is described as the centre of the universe (*Iḷā prithivī vritā yena*).

We read in Alberuni's *India* that *Iḷāvrita* was the "highest of all" (i, 248). The relation of *Iḷāvrita* to Mount Everest is striking.

[29] *R.V.*, viii, 20, 12; cf. vi, 41, 1.

[30] *Infra*, chap. i.

[31] The Purāṇas say that Gandhāra was a son of Druhyu, whose migration to the West is indicated in "*Prachetasah putraśatam rājānah sarva eva te | Mlechcharāshṭrādhipāh sarve hi udīchīm diśamāśritāh ||*".

[32] See App. i.

[33] *JRAS.* for 1901, pp. 44 and 45.

[34] A view that was held by scholars like Schlegel and Sergi.

[35] *R.V.*, iii, 59, 19; ii, 6.

[36] The word Marka is mentioned with Śaṇḍa as a demon that harasses children, in the *Grihya Sūtras*. He is *Asurāṇām Purohita* in *Taittirīya Samhitā*. See also *Mantrapāṭha* of the Āpastambins, Ed. of Winternitz, ii, 13, 9. Among the Oraons the term is used in the sense of "heaven" or seat of the gods. (*Memoirs of the Asiatic Society of Bengal*, i, No. 9, p. 135.)

[37] *Bhandarkar Commemoration Volume*, p. 92.

[38] *Early Zoroastrianism*, p. 7.

[39] *Review of Reviews*, Aug.–Sept., 1925, pp. 135 f.

[40] Since writing the above, I have come across the careful and comprehensive account of the Aryan prob'em by Mr Childe, based mainly on linguistic palaeontology, but I do not see any reason for changing my view about the cradle of the Aryan race. The discovery of MSS. written in the Tocharian language with its two distinct dialects in close proximity to Tibet, seems plausibly to lend a little more weight to my conclusion. The *centum* language of Tocharian would point to the orginal home of the Aryas as somewhere near the region of Tocharia, rather than in distant Scandinavia or anywhere else.

[41] Keyserling, *The Travel Diary of a Philosopher*, i, pp. 310 f.

[42] *R.V.*, x, 124.

[43] I would refer the reader to the introductory chapter in Thurston's *Castes and Tribes of South India*, as well as Risley's *The People of India*, for a clear exposition of the origins of the Dravidians.

[44] *Contributions to the Craniology of the People of the Empire of India*, pt. ii.

[45] *Wanderings of Peoples*, p. 26.

[46] *Impl. Gaz. of India*, i, 299.

[47] See S. C. Roy in *Journal of the Bihar and Orissa Research Society*, ix, pp. 380 f.

[48] Some of the antiquities are exhibited in the Madras Museum. See Archæological and Ethnological Sections.

[49] *Times of India, Illustrated Weekly* for 7th March, 1926, p. 15.

[50] *Illustrated London News*, 20th September, 1924.

[51] *Ill. Lond. News* for 27th Sept., 1924.

[52] Ibid.

[53] *Modern Review* of 1924, p. 673. Professor Hunter notes in the *Times of India, Illustrated Weekly* one main difference between the plaques and seals found at Susa and those that were discovered at Mohenjo Daro and Harappa, viz., that the former are of a curved or undulating shape, while the latter are flat.

[54] *Ill. Lond. News* for 14th Oct., 1924.

[55] *Śuḍuvōr iḍuvōr toḍukuḷippaḍuppōr*
tāḻvāyinaḍaippōr tāḻiyirkavippōr.

[56] *R.V.*, x, 15, 14; x, 18, 10. [57] *A.V.*, xviii, 2, 34.

[58] *R.V.*, i, 133, 1.

[59] The good bull is described in Indian tradition as having a high and big hump, broad shoulder and loin and a straight tail. His eyes resemble the *vaiḍūrya*.

Unnataskandhakakut ṛijulāngūlabhūshaṇah
Mahākaṭitaṭaskandho vaiḍūryamaṇilochanah
(Haradatta.)

This description tallies well with the features of the bull as are in evidence in the seals of the Indus valley.

[60] Even to-day it is held that the neck-ornament (South Indian *Kāśumālā* —the string of gold pieces) should contain only 55 pieces. The magic of the number 55 is therefore continued in India through the ages.

India is peculiarly a land of symbolism, and there is a distinct and separate symbolic significance attached to odd numbers as against even numbers. It is interesting that in the Boghaz-Keui inscription (see Moret and Davy, *From Tribe to Empire*, p. 241) there is mention of the numerals in Sanskrit, 1, 3, 5, 7 and 9 (*aika, tera, panza, satta, nāv*). Is it possible that this enumeration is in any way connected with the symbolism of numbers which we find some evidence of in the *Chamakādhyāya* of the *Taittirīya Samhitā*?

PART II

THE AGE OF THE MANTRAS

THE AGE OF THE MANTRAS

I

ARYA AND DASYU

In the *Rig-Veda*, which contains the earliest description of the Aryan civilization, we come across two kinds of people who stand in marked contrast to each other in social and religious institutions, in language and habits of daily life. These are on the one hand the Aryas, and on the other, those who were looked upon by them as enemies, comprised under the terms Dasyu, Vritra, Krishṇa, Paṇi, etc., all being brought under the general category Dasyu. Indra is said to slay the Vritras and win and gather their riches.[1] He smites the Vritras and gains spoils of war and high renown.[2] The word occurs in some places as the demon of drought who was overcome by Indra to make the water-courses flow freely with water for the fields of the Arya. The Paṇis, who are also frequently mentioned, appear to have been a trading people.[3] One non-Aryan tribe was called the Ahi, and Indra is addressed as, "Thou art the slayer of those who are called serpents; thou art the slayer of every Dasyu."[4] The word Krishṇa is used in various senses. It denotes a non-Aryan black tribe, a chief, and a sage in the *Rig-Veda*.[5]

The Aryas are described as performing sacrifices to bright and friendly gods—the Powers of Nature. The Dasyus were, on the other hand, irreligious, sensual and non-sacrificing, were enemies that disturbed Aryan religious rites and worshipped strange gods, such as trees, snakes and perhaps the "phallus".[6] This difference in religious observances is brought out in the *gāthā Usthavaiti* where Zārathushtra asks:[7] "That I will ask thee, tell me it right, thou living god, who is the religious man and who impious; with whom of both is the black spirit and with whom the bright one? Is it not right to consider the impious man who attacks me or thee to be a black one?" The Aryas depict themselves as sociable and civilized, noble and of good birth.[8] They always ate cooked food as is clear from the hymn which says, "even though a man may be forced to eat dog's flesh, he cooks it."[9] The Dasyus are *kravyāda* or *amāda*, i.e. eating uncooked meat.[10] Aryan social and family life was *in general* monogomous, and the social and political organization of the age rested on the patriarchal family in which the relationship was reckoned through the father. In the Vedic family the father was easy of approach to the son, who prostrated before him and was treated with affection; and it was the duty of the son to tend the father in old age.[11] Polygamy seems also to have been prevalent, as references to a "doubly-wedded" man and "rival wives" clearly show.[12] The Dasyus are treated as marauders, eating raw flesh and, according to the estimate of the Vedic hymnists, as being certainly in a lower order of civilization. The Aryas spoke a refined language[13]; their accent and enunciation were clear and well defined, while the Dasyus spoke a strange and vulgar tongue. The *Śatapatha Brāhmaṇa*[14] describes the speech of the Asuras as follows: "The Asuras being deprived of speech, were undone crying, *He'lavah, He'lavah.*" This is in keeping with the passage in the *Rig-Veda* which prays to the Aśvins for destroying those who are yelling hideously like dogs.[15]

II

Dasyus, the Non-Aryas

Who were these Dasyus of the *Rig-Veda*? It was once considered that the word Dasyu in the Veda refers only to superhuman beings. Indeed, Roth observes, "it is but seldom, if at all, that the explanation of Dasyu as referring to the non-

Aryans, the barbarians is advisable."[16] He relies on the passages where the Dasyus are referred as *amānusha*. This word may as well be taken to mean "inhuman" as "superhuman".[17] If the Dasyus were non-human, the epithets applied to them such as non-sacrificing, dedicated to strange gods, doers of evil deeds, etc., would be meaningless. Secondly, Roth cites the names Śambara, Sushṇa, Chumuri, etc., of Dasyus as applying only to the demons subdued by Indra. But some of these names are met with among the aboriginal race of the Muṇḍas to this day.[18] One may mention Śambara, Kuyava, Ongha, Bala, Danu, Karañja and Parṇeya, which correspond to the Muṇḍari names Sumber, Kuba, Ongha, Balia, Danu, Kalang and Parna. These and similar names of Dasyus are depicted as those of demons, for as the hostile races were subdued by the Aryas and were brought gradually under the civilization of the latter, the names became opprobrious, until they ceased to possess any ethnological force and were in the eyes of the Aryas purely evil appellations, just like the word Asura, and synonymous with the meaning "demon".[19]

A close examination of the texts leads one to the conclusion that in most, if not in all, passages the Dasyus referred to the non-Aryan peoples with whom the Aryas came into contact. The hymns represent them as dwelling in mountain fastnesses and strong fortresses.[20] Śambara is said to have possessed a hundred castles of stone which were destroyed by Indra.[21] The autumnal castles of the Dasyus (*śāradī*) are mentioned, besides other varieties of dwellings of earth (*urvī*), stone (*aśmanmayī*), and iron—perhaps only strong (*āyasī*).[22] We have in the Rig-Vedic texts "palaces with a thousand doors", "stately mansions", "lowly buildings" and "three-storied dwellings".[23] One wonders how, in spite of these references, Keith can hold the opinion that "the *pura* which is often referred to was probably no more than a mere earthwork fortification". His explanation of the autumnal castles of the Dasyus is ingenious.

He writes, "by far the most probable explanation of this epithet, is that it refers to the flooding of the plains by the rising of the rivers in the autumn when the cultivators and the herdsmen had to take refuge within the earthworks which at other times served as defences against human foes." [34] The wealth in land and cows, gold and jewels, that the Dasyus possessed is also frequently referred to. One stanza reads thus [25]: "May we divide his accumulated treasure despoiled by Indra." Thus, it is clear that the Dasyus had attained to a high degree of civilization and were not a barbarous race. In a few passages the word may have the etymological sense of "an enemy fit to be destroyed" as interpreted by Yāska.[26] There is one verse which says, "it is for this fate that the Dasyus were born," [27] and this meaning of the term seems to have been continued to the age of the *Mahābhārata* where we read, "Warfare was necessary for the destruction of the Dasyus and Indra created the instruments and weapons for this purpose." [28]

The Dasyus have in certain passages of the Veda been referred to as Piśāchas and Rākshasas, e.g. one runs thus [29]: "O Indra, destroy the Piśāchis who are reddish in appearance and utter fearful yells. Destroy all these Rākshasas." Rākshasa is explained by Yāska as "one against whom we should protect ourselves".[30] The term is used in one passage merely in the sense of enemy.[31] In another place the dreadful eyes of the Rākshasas are mentioned.[32] That Dasyu had become a term of reproach becomes quite clear from the following passages where the appellation yātudhāna is applied to Vasishṭha, the most perfect and orthodox of the *rishis*, by Viśvāmitra and his party. Vasishṭha says [33]:

> "May I die at once if I be a yātudhāna, or if I hurt the life of any man. But may he be cut off from his ten friends who falsely called me a yātudhāna."

"He who called me a yātudhāna when I am not so, or who said, I am bright devil, may Indra strike him down with his great weapon; may he fall the lowest of all beings."

In these two texts, yātudhāna is a hateful word used by Viśvāmitra against his rival Vasishṭha. The sense of a cannibal is also intended to be conveyed in the first of these two extracts, a meaning that becomes clear in other passages of the *Rig-Veda*. Some Vedic texts themselves show that Piśācha and Rākshasa are used to denote names of tribes. One is a passage in the *Atharva-Veda* [34] which runs to the following effect: "Show me the hiding place of the Piśāchas." Another is in the *Taittirīya Āraṇyaka*,[35] "The messengers of the Rākshasas are come." In fact, the words Rākshasa, Piśācha, Yātudhāna, Asura, and Dānava were originally names of tribes. The growth of the Paiśāchi language [36] in later times is another proof of the non-Aryan ancestry of the people among whom it was spoken, as the prevalence of the Paiśācha form of marriage in the Aryan social system during the age of the Smritis points perhaps to the same conclusion.

III

Ethnic Differences

A few hymns seem to point to ethnic distinctions between the Aryas and the Dasyus. The latter are spoken of as "black-skinned" and "noseless".[37] In contrast with this there is reference to the white complexion of the Aryas and their friends.[38] A tribe of the Dasyus is called the Krishṇa,[39] and there is reference to an aboriginal or non-Aryan chief by name Krishṇa in the following [40]:—

"The fleet Krishṇa lived on the banks of the Amśumatī with ten thousand troops. Indra became cognisant of this loud-yelling chief. He destroyed the marauding host for the benefit of the Aryas."

Krishṇa is spoken of in another context[41] as lurking in the hidden region of waters like the sun under a cloud. There are two hymns where the black colour of the Dasyus is described as congenital.[42] In one passage they are described as reddish black (*piśanga*),[43] perhaps the same as the colour of coffee unmixed with milk which has been considered by ethnologists as the colour of the Dravidians of South India. It would appear, however, that some Aryas of the *Rig-Veda* were also dark in complexion, e.g. Kaṇwa the *rishi* is represented as *śvāva* or *krishṇa*.[44] But it has to be noted that Kaṇwa appears as a *rishi* of the "mixed" tribes in the Veda, and this reference shows probably that the colour of some of the Aryas had changed a little, due certainly to the climate and possibly also to miscegenation even in the period when the Rig-Vedic hymns were composed and sung.

The Dasyus are referred to in a single hymn as *anāsa*. Max Müller has taken this word to mean literally noseless. But this may be only an exaggeration for inconspicuous or flat nose in contrast with the prominent and aquiline nose of the Aryas. Another epithet that is applied to the Dasyus is *viśipra* (prognathous) as against *suśipra* applied to the Aryas.[45] Ethnologists are agreed that the Dravidian type is platyrrhine, i.e. characterized by flat nose. As ethnological data regarding nose, colour, hair, etc., are no sure tests, we may, following the interpretation of Sāyaṇa, take *anāsa* to mean *āsyarahita* (devoid of words or crude-speaking), for the Dasyu is called *mridhravāk*. Sāyaṇa interprets this word as "of injurious speech and forms".[46]

It is clear that the two peoples stood for two different cults and cultures, though there is not sufficient evidence to prove that the ethnical differences between them were marked. Great stress has been laid in the hymns on the religious differences between the Aryas and the non-Aryas of the age. The fundamental point of distinction lay in the worship of Fire and Indra by the Aryan tribes, while the non-Aryan offerings to their deities were fireless. The kindling of the sacred fire and the invocation to the Fire-God preceded any ceremony or sacrifice performed by the Aryas.[47] The differences pertained primarily to matters of cult. The gods that the Aryas worshipped were the bright and benevolent Beings of heaven and earth, but the non-Aryan deities consisted of spirits of trees and stones, of mountains and ravines. To the Aryas, again, the language spoken by their non-Aryan foes appeared unintelligible and queer, as their customs and manners looked strange and vulgar.

IV

Relations in War

The *Rig-Veda Samhitā* bears witness to the fact that there was constant warfare between the two peoples. Some of the important features of warfare may be considered. That there were organized hosts on either side is clear in the evidence. We read of the following prayers [48] :—

> "O Destroyer of foes, collect together the heads of these marauding troops and crush them with thy wide foot. Thy foot is wide."
>
> "O Indra, destroy the power of these marauding troops. Throw them into the vile pit, the vast vile pit."
>
> "O Indra, thou hast slain three times fifty such troops and people extol thy deed." "Indra slew fifty thousand black-coloured enemies in battle." [49]

The Dasyus had women who may also have done the fighting. One hymn runs thus: "The Dāsa Namuchi made women his weapons. What could his female hosts do unto me?" [50]

They also possessed efficient weapons for use in war—we know not exactly of what description—but perhaps the same as the Aryas employed, for we read, "thou hast bent the weapons of those who worship no gods," addressed to Indra.[51] Another prayer of a *rishi* is :—

"O Indra and Varuṇa, the weapons of the enemy assail me in all directions, save us in the day of battle." [52]

The Paṇis, a non-Aryan people, are seen to tell Saramā, "we have many sharp weapons with us." [53]

The excellent war-horses which the Aryas possessed gave them a position of advantage in warfare.

"Enemies fear the horse Dadhikra, who is radiant and ravaging like a thunderbolt. When he beats back a thousand men around him, he becomes excited and his might invincible." [54]

"The horses raise the dust with their hoofs and sweep over the fields with loud neighings. They do not retreat, but trample the marauding enemies under foot." [55]

Apparently, the non-Aryas of the age were not acquainted with cavalry warfare. Horses in war were a surprise to them as the extract below will show :—

"As people raise a hue and cry after a thief who has stolen a garment, even so the enemies do at the sight of Dadhikra. As tiny birds scream at the sight of the hungry hawk on its descent, so the enemies shout at the sight of the war-horse careering over the fields in quest of plunder, of food and of cattle." [56]

The Aryas appear in this manner to have achieved a military superiority over their foes by means of their cavalry force which must have facilitated their rapid and concerted marches. The coats of mail which the conquerors wore and which also struck the Dasyus with surprise, made them invincible in defence.

"When heroes rest their persons (until abandoning the pleasant abode of their progenitors), grant us for ourselves and our posterity an unsuspected defence (armour) and scatter our enemies." [57]

"When the battle is nigh and the warrior marches in his armour, he appears like a cloud. Warrior, let not thy person be pierced; be victorious, let thy armour protect thee." [58]

In another hymn there is reference to an army of three thousand mailed warriors marching to do the fighting.[59]

"The leather guard protects the arm from the abrasion of the bow-string, and coils round the arm like a snake in its convulsions. It knows its work, is efficient and protects the warrior in every way." [60]

Among the instruments used in warfare were bows and arrows, axes, javelins, and swords.

"The string of the bow when pulled approaches the ear of the archer. It whispers words of consolation to him and with a hiss it clasps the arrow."

"The quiver is like the parent of many arrows, the arrows are like its children." [61]

In other passages javelins, sharp-edged swords and battle-axes are compared to lightning in their speed and effect.[62] There were, besides, banners and flags which were designed to distinguish the Aryas from their enemy-ranks.[63] There were also drums and musical instruments.

"The *dundubhi* (drum) sounds loud to proclaim to all men the hour of battle. Our leaders have mounted their steeds and have collected together. O Indra, let our warriors who fight in chariots win victory." [64]

The fighting was mostly on foot and soldiers engaged in hand-to-hand scuffles.[65] Chariots drawn by horses appear as other agents used in warfare.

"The expert charioteer stands on his chariot and drives his horses wheresoever he will. The reins restrain the horses from behind. Sing of their glory." [66]

Elephants also seem to have been used in the battle-field, though not so frequently.[67] Thus all the main divisions of fighters—the *chaturangasena* of India—infantry, cavalry, chariots and elephants appear in the warfare of India in the Rig-Vedic age.

No fair fighting could be expected on either side in this primitive age. Even Aryas used poisoned arrows to slay their adversaries in battle:—"We extol the arrow that is poisoned, whose face is of iron."[68] The Dasyus on their side harassed the Aryan homesteads, lifted their cattle and ravaged their fields. Indra is invoked to slaughter the foes and win back from them the kine that were stolen from the Aryas.[69] They disturbed the Aryan religious rites, waylaid travellers and robbed them of their wealth.[70] Invasions of Aryan villages by Dasyus were beaten back, and the latter are described as hiding behind forests and mountains and prowling in unknown regions. In one hymn the Vedic bard exclaims:—

> "We have travelled and lost our way and come to a region where there is no grazing ground for cattle. The extensive region gives shelter to Dasyus only. O Brihaspati, lead us in our search for kine. O Indra, show the way for your worshippers who have lost their way."[71]

The Aryas pursued their foes into the forest-retreats, and these when cleared added to the extent of the Aryan dominion.[72] The conquered Dasyus were either driven away or reduced to slavery. They were driven westward and eastward and are referred to as Dāsas.[73] In one hymn we have a prayer to Indra for protection against the *bhritya*.[74] Elsewhere a Vedic *rishi* asks for a hundred asses, goats and Dāsas.[75] Aryan victory had therefore two main effects—the expansion of *Āryāvarta* at the expense of non-Aryan territory and the gradual reduction of some at least of the aboriginal population to the condition of serfs. Dāsīs, probably Dasyu women conquered in war, were employed in the Aryan households for husking rice and churning milk.[76]

V

Diplomatic Relations

But the relations were by no means of an entirely hostile character. Aryan conquest of the non-Aryan element in India was essentially intellectual and spiritual—more social than racial—and we have traces of this tendency even in the earliest times. The Aryan tribes had bitter jealousies and quarrels among themselves which often broke out into internecine wars. These naturally led the way for the friendly relations of some Aryan tribes with the Dasyus against their fellow Aryas; and we find the Aryan bards call down the wrath of their deities on their enemies, Arya and Dasyu alike.

> "Crush, O Indra and Varuṇa, your enemies, whether Dāsas or Aryas, and defend Sudās with your protection." [77]
>
> "Whoever, be they Dāsas or Aryas, do battle against us, give us easy victory over them. The warriors who leagued together against us, whether kindred or strange, break their might." [78]

In course of time such alliances of the Aryas and the Dasyus must have assumed a permanent character.

VI

The Pañchajana

The *Rig-Veda* mentions the "Five Peoples" or "Tribes" variously styled as Pañchajanāh, Pañchajātāh, Pañchabhūmāh,

Pañchacharshaṇīh, Pañchakrishṭīh, and Pañchakshitayah. These were the Pūrus or the Bharatas whose territory lay north of the Parushṇī (Rāvī); the Tritsus who were perhaps the later Pāñchālas on the south bank of the Śatadru (Sutlej) as far north as the Himālayas; the Turvaśas and the Yadus to the south and south-west of the Tritsus, and the Anus whose land lay west of the Indus to include probably modern Baluchistan. Yāska [79] explains the term Pañchajana as Gandharvas, Manes, Gods, Demons and Monsters. But this explanation cannot account for such synonyms as Pañchabhūma and Pañchakrishṭi. These words clearly show a reference to a definite extent of territory. Sāyaṇa suggests that the word means the four castes and the Nishadas. Pañchakrishṭi is rendered by him as *pañchamanushyajātāni*.[80] This also seems inadmissible for the reason that there is, in many of these words, reference to a defined territory or land. The terms are not used in the sense of *jāti*, caste or class. *Jāti* is a comparatively modern word. It is used in the *Kātyāyana Śrauta Sūtra* [81] in the sense of a family and not of caste. The word does not occur used earlier even in this sense. The distinguishing word found in all the Vedic texts is *varṇa*. Further, there are other tribes mentioned in the Veda beside the Nishada, e.g. Nāga, Paṇi, etc. Why should the Nishada be chosen in preference to these, to be included as the fifth in the "five *jātis*"? In one passage in the *Rig-Veda*, Yadu and Turvaśa are condemned as Dāsas.[82] In the *Mahābhārata* [83] the descendants of Yadu, Turvaśa, Druhyu and Anu are respectively known as Yādava, Yavana, Bhoja and Mleccha, and are included in the same category. The Purāṇas [84] relate that Yadu and Turvaśa were the sons of Yayāti by Devayānī, while Druhyu and Anu were his sons by Śarmishṭā, the daughter of the Daitya king Vrishaparvan. These are found to take part in the "Battle of the Ten Kings" which was fought between the Tritsus, a pure Aryan race, under their leader Sudās and a confederacy of non-Aryan and mixed tribes.

VI.

The Battle of the Ten Kings

The Battle of the Ten Kings was the first battle fought in ancient India between the Aryas and the non-Aryan and mixed tribes that dwelt in the region of the "Seven Rivers". We find that against the confederacy of ten kings, the Tritsus were assisted in this battle by the Prithus and the Parsus who may be identified with the ancestors of the historical Parthians and the Persians. Viśvāmitra appears as the bard of the confederates led by Purukutsa, while Vasishṭha is the priest of the Aryas under Sudās. The battle was fought on the banks of the Parushṇī. The confederates must have made very effective preparation for the fight as will be clear from the following:—

> "The sixty-six thousand six hundred and sixty-six warriors of Anu and Druhyu, who had desired for cattle, and were hostile to Sudās were laid low." [85]

The bards of both parties invoked Indra and Varuṇa for wealth to be used in war.

> "The wily foes planned destruction and broke down the embankment," but "the waters of the river Parushṇī flowed through the old channel and did not take a new course". [86]

Thus, the plan of the enemies of Sudās to cut away the Tritsus ended in failure. The aim of the confederates appears to have been to cross the river and surprise in the rear the Tritsus who had encamped on the northern bank of the river Rāvī. At first, the success seemed to lie on their side. The river was crossed because of the efficacy of the prayers of Viśvāmitra. But the final result of the battle was that the Bharatas were forced to retreat, being severely routed, and on their way back they fell into the river and perished. They hoped to cross the river as easily as they would march on land, and many were drowned in the waters. "Sudās filled the earth with his prowess," "his horse marched over the country," and "he earned glory by killing twenty-one men *of both regions*. As the young priest cuts the *kuśa* grass in the house of sacrifice, even so Sudās cut his enemies".[87] The victory was claimed by Vasishṭha; "the ten kings who did not perform sacrifices were unable though combined to beat Sudās."[88] "It was Indra who enabled poor Sudās to achieve these deeds. Indra enabled the goat to kill the strong lion. Indra felled the sacrificial post with a needle. He bestowed all the wealth on Sudās."[89]

VIII

Social Life

It is rather difficult to estimate exactly the ways in which the two peoples influenced each other in their social and religious life. Some of the non-Aryas appear to have been incorporated into the Aryan fold. It is believed that the struggle between Viśvāmitra and Vasishṭha was really one between the liberal and conservative parties of the Aryas. Ragozin goes so far as to hold the opinion that the *gāyatrī*, a hymn ascribed to Viśvāmitra, recorded the confession of faith required of non-Aryan converts to the Aryan religion.[90] This is fanciful, but it is clear that Viśvāmitra was a friend and civilizer of the non-Aryas. A hymn runs to the effect[91] that the Kīkaṭas, a non-Aryan people according to Yāska,[92] and other low branches of the community brought their offerings to Viśvāmitra. It has been already noted that Viśvāmitra took sides with the non-Aryan confederates in the Battle of the Ten Kings, against Vasishṭha and the Tritsus. There are at least two hymns in the *Rig-Veda* which seem to contain references to Aryan attempts at proselytism, and to elevate the non-Aryas. The Aśvins are said to have lifted Rebha from a well into which he had been thrown. Kaṇwa and Vandana were set free into the light of day from a dark dungeon in which they had been confined. The Aśvins are likewise praised for having relieved from misfortunes Antaka and Bhujyu and the two Asuras Karkandhu and Vayya.[93] In the former two cases, as the *Nītimañjarī* has it, the *rishis* brought the misfortune on themselves by maintaining friendly intercourse with the Asuras. "In these and similar instances . . . we may possibly have allusions to the dangers undergone by some of the first teachers of Hinduism among the people whom they sought to civilize."[94] In the same way the dialogue between Saramā the messenger of Indra and the Paṇis (probably the Phoenicians) seems to allude to some attempt that may have been made by the Aryas to introduce the worship of Indra among non-Aryan tribes. The Paṇis, however, are seen to resist the intrusion and would try to convert the messenger of Indra to their faith rather than accept the Aryan cult.[95]

PAṆIS: O Saramā, what brought you here? It is a good long way. What have we with us that may be of service to you? How long has been your journey? How did you cross the waters of the Rasā?[96]

SARAMĀ: I come as the messenger of Indra. It is my object to recover the prodigious wealth you have hidden. The waters helped me; they felt a fear at my coming, and thus I crossed the Rasā.

P.: What is that Indra like, as whose messenger thou hast come from so far? How does he look? (Let her come; we will own her as a friend; let her take charge of our cows.)

S.: I know not any one who can conquer Indra whose messenger I am. Verily he is invincible. It is he who conquers everybody. The deep rivers cannot restrain his course. You will surely be slain by Indra and will lie prostrate.

P.: O beautiful Saramā, here are the cows thou desirest, coming from the ends of space. Who else would have given the cattle without a strife? We have many sharp weapons, too, with us.

P.: O Saramā, thou hast come here because the god threatened thee and sent thee here. We will accept thee as a sister. Do not return. We will give thee a share of this cattle.

S.: I do not understand what you mean by your prattle about brothers and sisters. Indra and the powerful sons of Angiras know all. They have commissioned me to guard the cattle; and I have come here under their shelter. O Paṇis, run for your lives.

IX

The Germs of Caste

The word "caste" as it is now understood was first used by the Portuguese who derived it from Latin *castus*, meaning purity of blood. The earliest mention of the institution in the Portuguese chronicles is in a Decree of the Sacred Council of Goa of A.D. 1567, where it is stated "the Gentoos divide themselves into distinct races or castes (*castas*) of greater or less dignity, holding the Christians as of lower degree, and keep these so superstitiously that no one of a higher caste can eat or drink with those of a lower".[97] The term has been defined as a collection of families or groups of families bearing a common name which usually denotes or is associated with a specific occupation; claiming common descent from a mythical ancestor, human or divine; professing to follow the same calling, and . . . as forming a single homogenous community. A caste is almost invariably endogamous in the sense that a member of the large circle denoted by the common name may not marry outside that circle, but within this circle there are usually a number of small circles each of which is also endogamous. Thus it is not enough to say that a Brāhmaṇa at the present day cannot marry any woman who is not a Brāhmaṇa; his wife must also belong to the same endogamous division of the Brāhmaṇa caste. It may be questioned whether the principles of the system, as have been indicated above, ever existed in the Vedic age of Indian history. It is doubtful if even the basic principles are in evidence in Rig-Vedic literature. A Vedic *rishi* says,[98] "I am a composer of hymns, my father is a physician, my mother grinds corn on stone. We are all of different occupations." Occupation was therefore not a criterion of caste. It was never accepted as a rule in this period that the members of the same caste should pursue the same occupation; e.g. a Brāhmaṇa is seen as a physician.[99] Max Müller writes,[100] "if then with all the documents before us we ask the question, does caste as we find it in Manu and at the present day form part of the most ancient religious teaching of the Vedas, we can answer with a decided 'no'." It may be remarked that the caste system in India has made progressive development and one cannot find in the *Rig-Veda* the features of *jāti* even as it was developed in the period of the *Yajur-Veda*.[101] It is indeed an exaggeration to say "it is impossible to deny that in the Vedic period *much* of the groundwork upon which the later elaborate structure was based was already in existence".[102] The word *varṇa* in Vedic literature has been taken to be the basis of the later caste system.

X

Varṇa

In the evolution of *varṇa* which cannot be taken to be identical with "caste" we may note the following stages in general outline. There is mention of *ubhau varṇau* [103] referring perhaps only to the two colours Aryan as against Dasyu—white and dark. Mention of the three distinct occupations of the three Aryan castes (*traivarṇika*) in one of the hymns[104] shows that the division of Indian society into four classes was a later feature. Lastly, *chāturvarṇyam*, as we find it described in the *Purusha-sūkta* hymn and in later works, secular and religious, included within the fold Śūdras also. But there is absolutely no evidence to show that in this early age there was the prohibition in regard to marriage which is the most important criterion of caste as it is now understood, among the three higher classes. Interclass marriages among the *dvija* or "twice-born" were prevalent and were legalized as late as the age of the *Mahābhārata* and the Law-books.

The introduction of the non-Aryan element, which was effected in the course of the wars and conquests brought in a novel feature. The three original classes of the Aryas, though there may not have existed among them restrictions regarding occupation and marriage in the age of the Mantras, should have at first detested the connexion with the women of the conquered non-Aryan peoples whose colour, speech and general habits of living were very different from their own. The introduction of the Dāsas into the Aryan social fold, slowly effected by illicit connexion of the masses of the Aryas, especially of the Viś or Vaiśya, with non-Aryan women, was probably responsible for the formation of caste restrictions. Only in this sense does Dr Slater's statement "caste is of Dravidian rather than of Aryan origin"[105] seem to be warranted by the evidence in Indian literature regarding the evolution of caste. Hence we meet with the term *Śūdrāryau*, i.e. Śūdra used in contrast with Arya. Arya is sometimes used to denote Brāhmaṇa, Kshatriya and Vaiśya, and in a few cases the last class alone. In the *Atharva-Veda*[106] we read, "with it do I see every one, both who is Śūdra and who is Arya." Similarly in the *Vājasaneyi Samhitā*[107] we find the word Arya used as the opposite of Śūdra. These citations show that the Śūdras had not been included at one particular stage in the Aryan social system.

XI

The Sūdra

The authors of the *Vedic Index* hold that it is reasonable to reckon the Śūdra of the later Vedic texts as belonging to the aboriginal people who had been reduced to subjection by the Aryas. This is only partly right, in my view, for it is not reasonable to suppose that the Aryas would have readily included all the conquered non-Aryan population in their social fold even so early as the age of the *Rig-Veda*, to form a very important division of it. Further, it will not satisfactorily explain the difference between the words "Dāsa" and "Śūdra", which is in evidence in later ages and which is continued to this day. It is essential that we should examine carefully the origin of the term "Dāsa" and inquire into the exact relation between "Dāsa" and "Śūdra" in the early history of Indian social and cultural life. The view of Keith given in the *Cambridge History of India* that "probably enough this word was originally the name of some prominent tribe conquered by the Aryans" cannot be easily substantiated. Possibly, he got the idea from Ptolemy's identification of a town on the Lower Indus or Arachosia, which seems to have some resemblance to the word.[108] This theory cannot explain how the name of this insignificant tribe (the word occurs only about half a dozen times in the Veda), even if it be granted to denote a tribe, should have been used by the Aryas to denote such a large and important section of the Indian people.

As we have seen, wars were waged not only between the Aryas and the non-Aryas but among the Aryan tribes themselves, and the Vedic *mantras* speak of Dasyu foes as well as Aryan foes. There were consequently Dasyu captives taken in war as well as Aryas captured as prisoners. It is quite possible, on considerations of humanity and communal feeling in those distant ages, that the conquering Aryas may have given differential treatment to the two sets of the conquered people. This seems more likely in view of the fact that the Aryas were comparatively small in numbers. They should have discerned the danger of the reduction in strength and the consequent loss of the power of resistance, if the members of their community that had been captured in war were excommunicated from the Aryan fold. It is probable that the term Dāsa was used to denote the enslaved Dasyu population; while the word Śūdra was applied to the Aryas that had fallen. Aryan captives counted less in number than Dasyu captives, and this is very probably the reason why the word Śūdra occurs so rarely in the Vedic texts. The Aryan prisoners of war were more readily included in the Aryan ranks, but could certainly not be allowed the same status with the general class of Aryas. Therefore, they were relegated to a subordinate position, the fourth order in the society. The Dāsas were "slaves" captured in war, and were not taken into the ranks along with the Śūdra. Dāsa thus meant a *bhritya* (a slave fit to be swayed),[109] while Śūdra came to mean only a *karmakara* (servant). Nowhere in the *Rig-Veda* does the word Dāsa appear to have been used where Śūdra was meant, while Dāsa appears as a synonym for Dasyu. In this way the four classes of the Aryan population came to be formed and, as we read in *Manusmriti*, "all those that were outside the pale of people born from the mouth, the arm, the thigh and the foot of Brahma were Dasyus (outcastes), whether they speak the language of the Arya or of the Mlechcha."[110]

But, as time passed, the "Dāsas" must have gone to swell the ranks of the Śūdra class, because of the similarity of their occupation, both the classes being employed for menial work. Gradual admixture of blood should have been effected between the fourth class of the Aryan population and those outside their pale, especially as Dāsīs or Dasyu women were engaged in menial occupations in the Aryan households.[111] Hence, as Yāska says, the *varṇa* of the Dāsas came to be looked upon as identical with that of the Śūdras and others.[112] The word Dāsa was identified with *karmakara* (servant) which in its turn was what was implied by Śūdra.[113]

The word Dāsa in the exclusive sense of "slave" as distinct from Śūdra seems to have survived in its old meaning in the time of Kauṭilya in whose *Arthaśāstra* we have the following [114] :—

> "Never shall an Arya be subjected to slavery." "The selling or mortgaging by kinsmen of the life of a Śūdra who is not a born slave and has not attained majority, but is the son of an Arya shall be punished with a fine of twelve paṇas ; of a Vaiśya, twenty-four paṇas ; of a Kshatriya, thirty-six paṇas ; and of a Brāhmaṇa, forty-eight paṇas." But the Mlechchas can sell or mortgage the life of their offspring.

The points that become clear from the above are :—

(1) Śūdra born of an Arya could not be reduced to the position of a Dāsa, i.e. could not be enslaved.

(2) The distinction may be noted between a man enslaved by capture or mortgage and one that was a "born" Dāsa. A Śūdra was not a "born" Dāsa, though it was possible that he may have been looked upon as a Dāsa because of his occupation.

(3) All Mlechchas, i.e. those outside the four classes (*vide* Manu) were at liberty to sell or mortgage their offspring because they were born slaves.

(4) Throughout the work Śūdra was distinct from Dāsa whether used in the sense of "born" or "pledged" (*udaradāsahitakau*).

In the *Miḷinda Praśna* [115] we note that servants were treated differently from "slaves". Similarly in the Hindu law-codes the rules regulating the conduct and treatment of Dāsas (slaves) are quite different from those of Śūdras (servants).

In this way the distinction between Arya and Śūdra, losing in course of time its old significance, was reducing itself to that between a "twice-born" and Śūdra.[116] Later still, the contrast is brought out between Brāhmaṇa and Śūdra, as is clearly illustrated in the Buddhist works and the Hindu law-codes to which we shall advert later.

XII

Connubial Relations

As regards connubial relations, there are a few passages which show that there was illicit connexion not only of Aryan men with non-Aryan women, but of non-Aryan men with Aryan women. It is reasonable to expect the conquering race to take to wives women of the conquered population, but it is rather strange that even so early in their career of conquest there should be any evidence of the connexion of non-Aryan men with the women of the conquering Aryas, as a passage in the *Vājasaneyi Samhitā*[117] tends to show. A hymn of the *Atharva-Veda* has been interpreted as referring to the seduction of Indra by an Āsurī (Asura woman).[118] Vilistengā the Āsurī was able by her spells to draw Indra from his place, and he is said to have lived in the company of the Asuras for some time. Passages to the same effect are found in the *Taittirīya Samhitā* as well.[119] On the strength of these texts alone one may agree with the view of Macdonell and Keith that "it is not unlikely that, if illicit unions took place, legal marriage was quite possible".[120] But we cannot find any evidence of Aryas in this period having entered into *marriage* relations with the non-Aryas.

There were obviously no restrictions in regard to marriages among the members of the three higher classes, Brāhmaṇa, Kshatriya and Vaiśya. The law-code of Baudhāyana says that the offspring of a Brāhmaṇa by a Kshatriya woman is a Brāhmaṇa, that of a Kshatriya by a Vaiśya woman is a Kshatriya. But as time went on, there was apparently the tendency among the Vaiśyas to get merged in the Śūdra class because of the large marriage connexions between the two classes. Therefore, we find that the old principle of connubial freedom was done away with and, "though a Brāhmaṇa, for example, could take wives from all the four castes, only the progeny from the first two in order are entitled to Brāhmanhood." "From the two others sons less pure taking the mother's caste are born." This is perhaps the reason why some of the law-codes, e.g. Manu, would not assign any definite name to the offspring of a Vaiśya by a Śūdra woman; while Vishṇu would classify them as Śūdras.

XIII

Agrarian Foundations

Next we may note the relations of the two peoples in the fields of industry and commerce. The non-Aryan influence on Aryan agriculture and rural organization is thus dwelt on by Sir William Hunter.[121] Throughout five-sixths of the continent the actual work of tillage remained in the hands of the non-Aryan and Śūdra classes. As the Kandh hamlet in Orissa exhibits the four essential characteristics of a Hindu village, Hunter suggests the possibility that the rural organization of India was based less upon Aryan types than upon the institutions of the pre-existing Indian races. The above statement as regards the basis of rural organization appears to be founded on an erroneous assumption. The main characteristics of an Indian village as described by Hunter are :—

(1) A community of agricultural families in the village with rights in the soil.

(2) A headman for the village, half-elective and half-hereditary, to lead its members.

(3) The village lands that lie round and form a territorial jurisdiction of which the associated homesteads are the nucleus.

(4) Certain low castes attached to the village, who carry on the work of tillage but are destitute of any right in the soil.

But these features seem to have characterized the Aryan village of the earliest times as is clear from the evidence of the *Rig-Veda*.[122] The *grāma* of the Vedic times may be regarded as an aggregate of several families, not necessarily forming a clan. The Brāhmans or Kshatriyas held interest in the village by royal grant or usage. At the head of the village was the *grāmaṇi* who was in some cases hereditary, sometimes nominated or elected. Vedic Indians dwelt in villages scattered over the country, some close together, some far apart and connected by roads and tracks. The villages were probably open and, no doubt, as in later times, included as their members various menials besides the cultivating owners. These features of the village community, therefore, could not be safely adduced to show that the village organization in India was originally non-Aryan. On the other hand, a considerable number of Muṇḍari and Santali words [123] relating to agriculture seem to be connected with Vedic Sanskrit, such as the words for plough, sickle, cotton and cattle, etc.

	Muṇḍari.	*Santali.*	*Sanskrit.*
Plough	*si, siu*	*si*	*si* in *sītā* (*R.V.*, iv, 57, 6 and 7)
Sickle	*datrom*	*datra*	*dātra* (*R.V.*, viii, 78, 10)
Cattle	*go*	*go*	*go*
Cattle-shed	*goḍha*	—	*goshṭha*
Cotton	*ka-asom*	*kasakom*	*kārpāsa* (later Sanskrit)
Yoke	*ārārā*	—	*arara*
Rice	*māṇḍi*	—	*maṇḍa*
Straw	*būsu*	—	*būsa*
Sheep	*miṇḍi*	—	*menḍha*
Milk	*toya*	—	*toya*
Tree	*dāru*	—	*dāru*

But these Aryan words have been inflected and constructed according to Santali grammar, the grammatical system in Sanskrit having greater power of resistance.[124] If, as Sir Henry Maine says, " the occasional removal of the arable mark from one point of the village to another is in India a feature of non-Aryan rather than of Aryan tillage,"[125] the Aryas had brought into use a variety of agricultural products such as millets, barley, wheat, beans and sesamum and supplemented the rice crops of the non-Aryan agriculturists in the plains of India.[126] Our conclusion is that the main features of Indian agricultural organization may have been common to both, and that Indian agriculture as it developed in later times may be the result of influences both Aryan and non-Aryan.[127]

XIV

Features of Indian Agriculture

Some of the important features of Aryan agricultural organization will become clear from the following passages in the *Rig-Veda*[128] :—

"We will cultivate this field with the grace of the Lord. May He nourish our cattle and our horses. May He bless us."

"O Lord of the field, bestow on us copious rain, sweet and pure, even as cows yield us milk. May the Lords of the sweet waters bless us."

"Let the cattle work merrily; let the men work in joy; let the plough move on easily; fasten the traces well and ply the goad."

"O Śuna and Sīra, accept this prayer. Moisten the sod with the rain you have created in the sky."

"O Furrow, proceed onwards; we bow to thee; bestow on us wealth and abundant crop."

"May Indra protect the furrow; may Pūshan improve it; may she be filled with water that she may yield us heaps and heaps of corn year after year."

The Vedic Indians dug channels for the irrigation of fields, and wells were sunk for the same purpose. The fields were measured with rods. Bulls and horses were used to plough the soil and there were granaries where the corn was stored. The lands were kept free from birds, locusts and other insects by watchmen who raised loud shouts. Some other features of Aryan agriculture will become clear in the following [129] :—

"Fasten the ploughs, yoke the cattle and sow the seed on the prepared plots; let us cut with our sickle corn that is ripe in the neighbouring field."

"Prepare water-troughs and fill them with water for use by the cattle. Fasten the leather string and let us take water in pots from the deep well that never dries up."

"Refresh the horses; collect the corn stacked in the field; make a cart for conveying it easily."

"This well full of water for the drinking of animals is one *droṇa* in extent and there is a stone-wheel (*aśmachakra*) near it. The reservoir for men's use is one *kośa*. Fill it also with water."

It is obvious from these passages that the Indian agricultural operations as are at present conducted, bear great similarity to the methods in vogue in Indian rural life in the age of the Mantras.

XV

Seafaring and Commerce

India had commercial relations with the countries of the West from very ancient times, and there is evidence for the maritime commerce of India with the West reaching to the very earliest period of humanity.

Professor Perry says [130] that the Egyptians visited the Indian shores for trade at least from 2600 B.C. Mr Kennedy's statement that one "can find no architectural or literary evidence for a maritime trade between India and Babylon prior to the seventh century B.C., but that for the sixth century direct evidence is forthcoming" has to be modified in the light of the recent discoveries made in the Punjab and Sindh valley, among which have been found writing in pictographs and bitumen which is peculiarly a Babylonian commodity. A piece of timber identified by some with teak was discovered among the ruins of the Akkadian temple at Ur [131] and blackwood was found among those of Jamjama.[132] Among the recent Egyptian discoveries in Tutankh-Amen's tomb are ivory carved tables and furniture and articles made of some wood, ebony or teak. The presence of indigo here is positive proof of the connexion with India. "Even in the Mosaic period (1500–1400 B.C.) precious stones which were to a great extent a speciality of India and the neighbouring countries appear to have been well-known and were already highly valued in the West. It is probable that some of the stones in the breast-plate of the High Priest may have come from the far east." [133] Ktesias says expressly that these came from India, and that onyxes, sardincs and the other stones used for seals were obtained in the mountains bordering on the sandy desert. "The passage of Ktesias contains some indications which, relatively to the onyxes, appear to refer to the Ghat mountains, since he speaks of a country not far from the sea. . . . Also, the Babylonians imported Indian dogs. The native country of these animals was that whence the precious stones were obtained." [134] Again, it was towards the close of this period that Indian commodities, some of them peculiarly South Indian, such as sandal-wood, ivory, apes and peacocks, were transhipped to Palestine for use among the Jews.[135] Sandal-wood was the *almug* or *algum* which may be related to Sanskrit *valguka* and Malayāḷam *valgum*. It is grown now primarily in Mysore and certain tracts of Malabar. The Hebrew word *hebin shen* (elephant's teeth) may be derived from the Sanskrit *ibhadanta*. The word for peacock in Hebrew is *tuki*, while the ancient Tamil-Malayāḷam has *tokai*. Hebrew *kof* can be easily identified with Sanskrit *kapi* or Tamil-Malayāḷam *kavi*. Hebrew *ahalin* or *ahaloth* is derived apparently from Dravidian *aghil*. Besides, it has been found that there are a great number of Batak and

Javanese numerals in traders' slang in South India, which may also point to very ancient commerce between South India and the East.[136] As Rev Foulkes says,[137] "the fact is now scarcely to be doubted that the rich oriental merchandise of the days of king Hiram and king Solomon had its starting place in the ports of the Dekhan." These commodities may either have been South Indian products conveyed to the west with their Dravidian names, or North Indian commodities which were known only by their Tamil names, or articles produced in South India the names for which may have been borrowed from Sanskrit.[138] The traditional fame of South India as the seat of the precious metals and gems seems to have been carried down to the time of the *Arthaśāstra*,[139] where we read that "with the exception of blankets, skins and horses, other articles of merchandise, such as conchshells, diamonds, precious stones, pearls, and gold are available in plenty in the South".

The South Indian Dravidians were a great maritime people in antiquity. It is no wonder, being surrounded by the sea on three sides, that they should have developed the arts of shipbuilding and sea-borne commerce. In the *Maṇimekalai*, one of the most ancient pieces of literature of the Tamils, there are a good number of original words denoting the sea: *kaḍal*, *paravai*, *Puṇari*, *arkaḻi*, and *munnīr*. The waves of the sea were known to the Tamils as *ōḷa*.[140] The only word in the *Rig-Veda* which has been interpreted to contain a reference to the sea is *samudra*. The word *ōḍa* meaning a boat is an original term, and there are words which denote a ship in *Śangam* literature, e.g. *kalam*, *marakalam*, *mitavai* and *kappal*, which are independent of outside influences; while in Rig-Vedic literature we have only *nau*, *duroṇa*, and *plava* to denote a boat, sometimes with many oars.[141] What we have in earliest Tamil literature is certainly reminiscent of the life that was led by the Dravidians of South India in much earlier times. Among the daily occupations of the Tamils, sailing and fishing find a prominent place, especially for the pearls of the surrounding seas. South India and Ceylon have been from times immemorial centres of the Indian pearl industry, and the Sanskrit word *mugdha* (pearl) is apparently a borrowing from Tamil *muttu*. The Vedic word for pearl is *krisana* which is perhaps only artificial pearl got from the earth, and cut, chiselled and polished, as the word *kriṣ* from which *krisana* is derived tends to show.[142] This pearl is distinguished from *śangha kriṣana*, which we find only in the *Atharva-Veda*.[143] On these grounds we may adduce that the people of South India should have been the main carriers of the commerce between India and the west in this distant antiquity.

But our evidence does not enable us to determine the exact part played by each of these peoples in this sea-borne trade of India, though the Aryas also appear to have taken some part in the commercial activities of the age. The existence of a peaceful internal trade in which the Aryas and the non-Aryas are seen to have taken part is brought out in certain passages of the *Atharva-Veda*,[144] which say that the Aryas purchased drugs from Kirāta girls who got in exchange clothes, mats and skins. As Caldwell says,[145] " it seems probable also that Aryan merchants from the mouth of the river Indus must have accompanied the Phoenicians and Solomon's servants in their voyages down the Malabar coast towards Ophir, or at least have taken part in the trade." The Babylonian word for axe is the same as the Greek and Sanskrit word *paraśu*.[146] The name of muslin in Babylonia was *sindhu* and the word for measure was *manā*, the same as what we find in the Vedic passage,[147] " O Indra, bring to us a brilliant jewel, a cow, a horse, an ornament together with a golden *manā*." This word has been identified with the Latin *mina*, the Greek *mna*, the Phoenician *manah*, " the well-known weight brought from Nineveh to the British Museum." Max Müller has got some doubt about this identification and renders *manā hiraṇyayā* as " two golden armlets ". But the following verse

prayaditthā ṛ rāvatah śochirna mānamasyatha[148]

shows distinctly reference to a measure in *māna*, the connexion between which and the *manā* or *mina* of Babylon is apparent. If Babylonian *manah* is the same as *manā* of the *Rig-Veda*, it would be irrefragable evidence of at all events a commercial intercourse between Babylon and India, at a very early time.[149]

XVI

Shipping in the Vedic Age

The evidence is not clear that in the Rig-Vedic period the Aryas were much acquainted with the sea or the construction of sea-going ships. Max Müller and Wilson hold that *samudra* in the Veda means the sea.[150] The latter discovers the details of a distant voyage across the ocean. The authors of the *Vedic Index* are not apparently so sure, and they declare guardedly that there are references to the treasures of the ocean, perhaps pearls or the gains of trade, and the story of Bhujyu seems to allude to marine navigation.[151] The word *samudra* appears in the texts to have other meanings besides the sea. We have indication to the effect that the word when it is used to denote extensive watery region refers rather to the Indus than to the ocean. The river Sarasvatī is described as flowing from the mountains as far as the *Samudra*.[152] This river comes between the Yamuna and the Śatadru in the enumeration of rivers apparently from the east to the west.[153] Probably it corresponds to the modern Sarsuti which is lost in the desert at Bhatnair. But a dry river-bed can be traced from that point to the river Indus. It is thus probable that the old Sarasvatī flowed into the Indus which in the hymn is denoted by *samudra*. The expression *samudre antarikshe* is used in the sense of the "watery sky".[154] The word means only full of water in *duroṇe yo vām samudrāntsaritah piparti* (He who carries you across the rivers full of water in a *duroṇa*).[155] *Samudra* in the sense of "watery cloud" is seen in *na samudraih parvataih Indra te rathah.*[156] It may likewise be pointed out that in some cases *samudra* is metaphorically used as of the two—"upper" and "lower", e.g. *ubhau samudrau āksheti yaścha pūrvah yaśchāparah.* These refer in the passage to the course of the river Indus. It is not appropriate to take them to mean the "eastern" and the "western" seas, for the Aryas of this period being confined mostly to the region of the *Sapta Sindhavah* could not reasonably be expected to refer to the Bay of Bengal and the Arabian Sea. Similarly, proceeding on *argumentum ex silentia*, there is no mention of the ebb and flow or the waves of the sea in the Veda; fish has been very rarely mentioned as an article of diet; and salt is mentioned nowhere in the Vedic passages.[157]

There is thus not much evidence to prove that the Aryas used ships in the Vedic times or that they may have carried on direct sea-borne trade with the west in these ancient ages. The story of the rescuing of Bhujyu[158] who was caught in troubled waters has been taken to indicate that the Aryas had known of voyages on the seas and had also been acquainted with the art of ship-building. It cannot help us to show, as will be clear from the passages quoted below, that there were Aryan ships plying on the seas and that the Aryas of the Vedic period were familiar with the arts of seamanship. It was either a story of navigation that the Aryas had only heard of, or it only illustrates the woes of a stray Aryan *rishi* caught in the troubled sea (*samudra*), who found it difficult to get out of it except with the help the Aśvins gave him in the shape of a boat with a hundred oars, chariots and horses. If Bhujyu were identical with Barmyazwa of the Indus valley seals, as Waddell holds,[159] it is possible that this adventurous Arya was one of the earliest to think of colonizing new lands taking the sea-route. Perhaps the story may allude to the first dire experience of some of the Aryas who may have attempted a passage across the sea to foreign lands. The story clearly shows that the Aryas were not much acquainted with seafaring, or at any rate, could not have been experts in the art. There is, however, little evidence to prove that the commerce may have been carried on between India and the western world by the land-route, as Smith suggests.[160] If Aryan articles found their way to the west, or western influences flowed into India at this stage, why should they not have been through the non-Aryas?

NOTES TO PART II

[1] *Rig-Veda*, x, 89, 18. [2] *R.V.*, viii, 15, 3.

[3] *R.V.*, i, 83, 4; vi, 51, 14; vii, 22, 6; x, 108, etc. *Paṇi* is derived from *paṇ*—to barter or trade (see St. Petersburg Dict.). Ludwig thinks, " References to fights with Paṇis are to be explained by their having been aboriginal traders who went in caravans—as in Arabia and North Africa—prepared to fight, if need be, to protect their goods against attacks " (*Der Rig-Veda*, iii, 213–15). Probably they were the Phœnicians famous as traders in distant antiquity.

[4] *R.V.*, ix, 88, 4. [5] *R.V.*, viii, 85, 3 and 4.

[6] e.g. *abrahman* in *R.V.*, iv, 16, 9; *avrata* in i, 51, 8; *akarman* in x, 22, 8; *brahmadvisha* in vii, 104, 2; *apavrata* in v, 52, 9; *ayajvāna* in viii, 59, 11; *paripanthi* (waylaying) in i, 103, 6. *Śiśnadevāh* in *R.V.*, vii, 21, 5, is explained by Sāyaṇa as *abrahmacharyāh*, while Macdonell and Keith render it as " those who have the phallus for their deity " (*Vedic Index*, ii, 382).

[7] Haug, *Essays*, p. 7.

[8] Yāska, *Nirukta*, vi, 26. *Airya* in the *Avesta* means " noble ".

[9] *R.V.*, iv, 18, 13. [10] *R.V.*, x, 87, 2.

[11] *R.V.*, i, 1, 9; i, 38, 1; ii, 33, 2; vi, 3, 7.

[12] *R.V.*, x, 101, 1; i, 105, 8; x, 141, 1–3.

[13] They took pride in calling it alone *vāk*. *Aitareya Āraṇyaka*, iii, 2, 5.

[14] *Śatapatha Brāhmaṇa*, iii, 2, 1, 23. Cf. what Dr Rivers says about the people that speak the Melanesian languages. He writes that phonetic differences among these " must be due to definite structural differences in the organs of speech, and it is most unlikely that these could be produced by such differences of environment as exist within the regions ". *History of Melanesian Society*, ii, p. 471.

[15] *R.V.*, i, 182, 4; viii, 96, 13. [16] Roth's *Lexicon*, *s.v. Dasyu*.

[17] *R.V.*, x, 22, 8. *Akarmā dasyuh abhino amantuh anyavrato amānushah.*

[18] *R.V.*, ii, 12, 11; ii, 11, 6; i, 63, 7; ii, 12, 3; i, 32, 9; i, 53, 8. For the Muṇḍari names I am indebted to S. C. Roy's *The Mundas and their Country*, pp. 47–9.

[19] See Pargiter, *Ancient Indian Historical Tradition*, p. 290.

[20] *Śambaram parvateshu kshiyantam* (*R.V.*, ii, 12, 11).
Avagireh Dāsam Śambaram han (*R.V.*, vi, 26, 5).

[21] *Śatamaśmanmayīnām purāmindro vyāsyat* in *R.V.*, iv, 30, 20.

[22] *R.V.*, i, 189, 2; i, 58, 8; iv, 30, 20.

[23] *R.V.*, vii, 88, 5; i, 101, 8; v, 101, 2.

[24] *Cambridge History of India*, i, p. 99.

[25] *R.V.*, viii, 40, 6; i, 33, 8. In i, 100, 18, fields taken in war from the enemies were distributed by Indra among the white-hued Aryas.

[26] *Dasyuh dasyate kshayārthāt* in *Nirukta*, iii, 89.

[27] *R.V.*, x, 49, 7.

[28] *Mahābhārata*, Udyoga, 29, 30, and 31.

[29] *R.V.*, i, 133, 5. *Piśangabhrishṭim abhṛṇam Piśāchim Indra sammṛṇa | sarvam Raksho nibarhaya ||*

[30] Yāska: *Nirukta*, iv, 18.

[31] *R.V.*, iii, 15, 1. [32] *R.V.*, vii, 104, 2. [33] *R.V.*, ii, 104, 16 and 17.

[34] Whitney's Tr. *Atharva-Veda*, iv, 2, 6.
[35] *Taittirīya Āraṇyaka*, iv, 33. 3.
[36] *JRAS.* for 1905, pp. 285–8. The peculiarity of the Piśāchas was perhaps the deformity of their facial features (*Rāmāyaṇa*, Āraṇya Kāṇḍa, 35, 6). They are eaters of carcasses in *A.V.*, v, 29, 9. *Piśācha veda* or *vidyā* refers perhaps to surgery in *Gopatha Brāhmaṇa*, i, 1, 10, and *Āśvalāyana Śrauta Sūtra*, x, 8, 6.
[37] *R.V.*, i, 130, 8; ix, 41, 1. *Anāsa* in v, 29, 10.
[38] *R.V.*, i, 100, 18.
[39] *R.V.*, iv, 16, 13.
[40] *R.V.*, viii, 96, 13.
[41] *R.V.*, viii, 96, 14.
[42] *Krishṇa yoniḥ* in ii, 20, 7; *Krishṇa garbhāḥ* in i, 101, 1.
[43] *R.V.*, i, 133, 5. See Risley, *The People of India*, pp. 12 f.
[44] *R.V.*, x, 31, 1.
[45] *R.V.*, v, 29, 10; v, 45, 6.
[46] *Himsitavāgindriyān.* Sāyaṇa on *R.V.*, v, 29, 10.
[47] The importance of Agni in the Aryan religion is nowhere so clearly brought out as in the first mention of this god in the opening hymns of the *Rig* and *Sāma Vedas*.
[48] *R.V.*, i, 133, 2, 3 and 4.
[49] *R.V.*, iv, 16, 13.
[50] *R.V.*, v, 30, 9.
[51] *R.V.*, i, 174, 7 and 8.
[52] *R.V.*, vii, 83, 5.
[53] *R.V.*, x, 108, 5.
[54] *R.V.*, iv, 38, 8.
[55] *R.V.*, vi, 57, 7.
[56] *R.V.*, iv, 38, 5.
[57] *Chchardirachittam.* *Chchardiḥ* = *chchādanam* = *āyudhānām nivārakam*. *Achittam* = *śatrubhirajñātam* (armour unknown to enemies). *Varma* (mailed armour) in *R.V.*, vi, 75, 18; *varūtha* (shield) in *A.V.*, v, 5, 4; *kavacha* in *Vājasaneyi Samhitā*, xvi, 1.
[58] *R.V.*, vi, 75, 1 and 2.
[59] *R.V.*, vi, 27, 6. *Trimśat śatam varmiṇā' Indra sākamyavyā vatyām Puruhūtaśravasya* |
[60] *R.V.*, vi, 75, 14.
[61] *R.V.*, vi, 75, 3.
[62] *R.V.*, v, 52, 6; vi, 47, 10; v, 57, 2.
[63] Banner in *R.V.*, v, 79, 2; flag (*ketu*) in i, 103, 1, for example.
[64] *R.V.*, vi, 47, 29.
[65] *Mushṭihā* in *R.V.*, v, 58, 4; *A.V.*, v, 22, 4.
[66] *R.V.*, vi, 75, 6.
[67] *R.V.*, i, 84, 17; *A.V.*, iii, 22, 4.
[68] *R.V.*, vi, 75, 15.
[69] *R.V.*, iii, 47, 4; vii, 18, 7. *Gavishṭau* has been interpreted by Sāyaṇa as *Asuraiḥ saha gavārthe yuddhe.*
[70] *R.V.*, i, 51, 8. *Anushṭātṛṇām upakshapayitāraḥ śatravaḥ* |
[71] *R.V.*, vi, 47, 20.
[72] *R.V.*, i, 165, 16, "*vṛjana.*"
[73] *R.V.*, vii, 6, 3 and 4. As a general rule, the word *Dāsa* is used in connexion with particular chiefs of non-Aryas who are defeated by Indra, and against whom his aid is sought. The word *Dasyu* is used when the non-Aryan foes *as a class* are referred to. There is more indiscriminate use of the two words in the tenth *maṇḍala* than in others.
[74] *R.V.*, iv, 20, 4.
[75] *R.V.*, viii, 46, 31.
[76] *A.V.*, iii, 10, 8; xii, 3, 13.
[77] *R.V.*, vii, 83, 1.
[78] *R.V.*, x, 38, 3.
[79] *Nirukta*, iii, 8.
[80] "It is an age-long tradition with great sanctity attached to it that there were only four castes, never a fifth."

Smritāścha varṇāśchatvāraḥ pañchamo nādhigamyate |
(*Mahābhārata*: Anuśāsana, 44.)

[81] *Kātyāyana Śrauta Sūtra*, xv, 4, 14.
[82] *R.V.*, x, 62, 10.
[83] *Mahābhārata*: Ādi, 79, 42.

[84] *Vishṇu Purāṇa*, i, 21, 6. Professor Hopkins suggests that *Turvaśa* means fleet, from *tura* (*Journal of the American Oriental Society*, xv, 264). The town *Anau* found in the Caspian Sea region perhaps suggests that the Anus may have migrated westward through that region.

[85] *R.V.*, vii, 18, 14.

[86] *R.V.*, vii, 83, 6; vii, 18, 8.

[87] *R.V.*, vii, 18, 8, 9, 11.

[88] *R.V.*, vii, 83, 7.

[89] *R.V.*, vii, 18, 17.

[90] *Vedic India*, p. 316.

[91] *R.V.*, iii, 53, 14.

[92] *Nirukta*, vi, 32.

[93] *R.V.*, i, 112, 5 and 6.

[94] Wilson's Tr., i, 289, note *a*.

[95] *R.V.*, x, 108.

[96] Rasā along with Trishṭāma and Susartu is one of the first tributaries of the Indus in the extreme north-west.

[97] *Imperial Gazetteer of India*, i, 311 f.

[98] *R.V.*, ix, 112, 3. *Kāruraham tato bhishak upalaprakshiṇīnanā nānādhiyah etc* | Yāska renders *Upalaprakshiṇī* as maker of groats (*saktukārika*), *Nirukta*, vi, 5.

[99] *R.V.*, x, 97, 6. *Viprah sa uchyate bhishak.*

[100] *Chips from a German Workshop*, ii, 307.

[101] *Vedic Index*, ii, 81.

[102] *Camb. Hist. of Ind.*, i, 94.

[103] *R.V.*, i, 176, 1.

[104] *R.V.*, i, 113, 6. *Kshatrāya tvam śravase tvam mahīya' ishṭaye tvam arthamivatvamītyai* | *visadṛśā jīvitābhi prachaksha ushā.*

[105] *The Dravidian Element in Indian Culture*, pp. 53 and 150.

[106] *A.V.*, iv, 20, 4; v, 11, 3.

[107] *Śūdro yadāryāyai jārah* and *Śūdrā yadāryajārā* in *Vājasaneyi Samhitā*, 23, 31, and 14, 30. See Bloomfield, *Vedic Concordance*, *s.v. Śūdra.*

[108] Cunningham, *Ancient Geography of India*, pp. 246 and 247. *Ptolemy*, vi, 20. Suratdes recalls the Surakousoe of Diodorus and the Śūdrakoe and the Oxudrakoe of the Greek writers.

[109] e.g. *R.V.*, iv, 20, 4.

[110] *Manusmriti*, x, 45. *Mukhabāhurupajjānām yā loke jātayo bahih* | *mlechchavāchaśchāryavāchaścha sarve te dasyavah smritāh* || That language was no sure test of racial affinities is clear in the above passage, for it is indicated that there may be Dasyus speaking the Aryan tongue, and that, that fact alone was not enough to bring them into the Aryan fold.

[111] *A.V.*, iii, 10, 8; xiii, 3, 13.

[112] *Dāsam varṇam Śūdrādikam.*

[113] *Dāsah karmakarah Śūdrah.*

[114] *Arthaśāstra*, iii, 13 and 25. *Na tveva Aryasya dāsabhāvah* | *udaradāsavarjam Aryaprāṇam aprāptavyavahāram Śūdram vikrayādānam nayatsvajanasya dvādaśapaṇo daṇḍah* | *Vaiśyam dviguṇah* | *Kshatriyam triguṇah* | *Brāhmaṇam chaturguṇah* | *Mlechchānām adoshah prajām vikretum ādhātum vā* |

[115] *Milinda Praśna*, 39, 209 and 210. A *Dāsī* girl is different from a *Śūdra* girl in *A.V.*, v, 22, 6 and 7.

[116] The word *dvija* occurs for the first time in the *A.V.* (19, 71, 1) and probably not before. In *Vāj. Sam.* (20, 17) we have *yacchūdre yādārye yādēnaskurmā vayam.*

[117] 23, 31, and 14, 30, op. cit.

[118] *A.V.*, vii, 38, 2. Whitney's Tr., i, 413.

[119] *Taittirīya Samhitā*, vii, 4, 19, 3 and 4.

[120] *Vedic Index*, ii, 259.

[121] *Orissa*, ii, 206.

[122] *Vedic Index*, *s.v. grāma.* There were also *mahāgrāmāh.*

[123] *Bihar and Orissa Research Society's Journal*, vol. iv, parts 3 and 4, pp. 384 f.

[124] Sten Konow in *Viśwabhārati Quarterly*, Jan., 1925.

[125] *Village Communities*, p. 109.

[126] Havell, *History of Aryan Rule in India*, p. 15.

[127] "The first men in the world were a gardener, a ploughman, and a grazier" (*Old Saying*).

[128] *R.V.*, iv, 57, 1, 2, 4, 5, 6, and 7. [129] *R.V.*, x, 101, 3, 5, and 7.

[130] *The Children of the Sun*, p. 560.

[131] Sayce, *Empires of the East*, p. 178. Though Mr Rassam is disposed to identify with cedar a similar piece of wood found in the palace of Nebuchadnezar, which Taylor says was teak, "there is no doubt that this wood was imported into Babylon from India," *JRAS.*, 1898, p. 267. The ruins of Mugheir have been said to belong to 3000 B.C., when Ur Bagas, the first king of Babylonia, ruled in Ur of Chaldæa.

[132] Birdwood and Foster, *The First Letter-Book of the East India Co.*, p. xxix.

[133] *Indian Antiquary*, for 1884, "A geologist's contribution to the History of Anc. Ind."

[134] *Historians History of the World*, i, pp. 484–90.

[135] Caldwell, *Comparative Grammar of Dravidian Languages*, pp. 91 f.

> "Quinquiremes of Nineveh from distant Ophir
> Rowing home to haven in sunny Palestine:
> With cargoes of ivory, and apes and peacocks,
> Sandalwood, cedarwood and sweet, white wine."
>
> John Masefield.

[136] *Ind. Ant.*, 23, 49–52, and 24, 82. [137] Ibid., 8.

[138] The word for peacock in Vedic Sanskrit is *mayūra* (*R.V.*, i, 191, 4, and iii, 45, 1). Another word for monkey is *markaṭa* in *Tait. Sam.*, v, 5, 11, 1.

[139] *Arthaśāstra*, p. 298.

[140] Cf. *Ōḷiyar*, a name given in Tamil literature to a section of the Nāgas, the seafaring people in South India.

[141] Boats with many oars in *R.V.*, i, 116, 3; i. 131, 2; i, 101, 2.

[142] *R.V.*, i, 35, 4.

[143] *A.V.*, iv., 10, 123. [144] *A.V.*, iv, 7, 6; x, 4, 14.

[145] *Comp. Gr.*, p. 122.

[146] Bury, *Hist. of Greece*, chap. i.

[147] *R.V.*, viii, 67, 2. *Ānobharavyañjanam gāmaśvamabhyañjanam sa chā manā hiraṇyayā* |

[148] *R.V.*, i, 39, 1.

[149] Max Müller, *India, What Can it Teach Us*, p. 125.

[150] *Sacred Books of the East*, xxxii, pp. 60 and 61.

[151] *Vedic Index*, ii, 432.

[152] *Ekatchetat Sarasvatī nadīnām śuchiryati giribhya' āsamudrāt* (*R.V.*, vii, 95, 2).

[153] *R.V.*, x, 75, 5. *Imam me Gange Yamune Sarasvati Śutudri stomam sa cha tā parushṇyā Asiknyā Marudvridhe Vitastaya' rjīkīyiye Śrṇuhyāsushomayā* |

[154] *R.V.*, vi, 58, 3. [155] *R.V.*, vii, 70, 2. [156] *R.V.*, ii, 16, 3.

[157] Matsya is mentioned only once in *R.V.*, x, 68, 8, and here, too, it is what belongs to the river rather than to the sea.

[158] *R.V.*, i, 116, 3 ff.

[159] *Indo-Sumerian Seals Deciphered*, p. 44.

[160] *Impl. Gaz. of India*, ii, 106.

PART III

THE LATER VEDIC AND HEROIC PERIOD

THE LATER VEDIC AND HEROIC PERIOD

The cult and culture of the Dasyus, as the non-Aryan population in the age of the Mantras was called, were different from those of the Aryas. There were differences dividing them into hostile camps, differences more profound perhaps than the clash of political interests and the fighting of agrarian feuds. It was a struggle of the refined palate accustomed to delicious cooked dishes against the vulgar and aboriginal habit of eating raw venison. It was a struggle of a refined and well-enunciated language against one of uncouth exclamations and awful yells. It was a struggle of monogamy, chastity and continence against sensuality, promiscuity and barbarism. It was a struggle between the age-long military system with the *chaturangasena*, the mailed armour, the helmet and the shield, against primitive methods of warfare with brute force, crude weapons and swift sweeping dashes in battle. It was a struggle of a developed system of religion and advanced conceptions of metaphysics against impiety, superstition, fetishism, animism and shamanism. It looked as if Aryan and Dasyu cultures ran along divergent lines which, running straight and parallel, were destined never to meet.

The relations of the Aryas and the non-Aryas in the previous period were mostly political, entailing internecine strifes and resulting ultimately in the expansion of the bounds of *Āryāvarta* and the gradual reduction of some of the non-Aryan population to the condition of slaves. But alliances of the Aryas and the Dasyus are in evidence in the period, and some of the latter should have been included in the Aryan fold. Gradually, the conquering Aryas married the women of the conquered, and thus was engendered and fostered the gradual and steady acquaintance of the two peoples. In the prehistoric commerce between India and the western world the non-Aryas appear to have been the main carriers of the trade, and the Aryas are seen peacefully to co-operate with them. The foundations of Indian agriculture were firmly laid, and Indian village and agricultural life prospered through the ages due to the relative contribution and peaceful co-operation of the Aryas and the non-Aryas.

I

Aryan Expansion

Our evidence shows that the Aryas expanded eastward from the Indo-Gangetic basin, northward along the foot of the Himālayas, and southward along the Indus to its mouth and far down to Cutch. The expansion of the Aryas in the easterly direction is illustrated in the following story in the *Śatapatha Brāhmaṇa*[1]:—

"Mādhava the Videha carried Agni Vaiśvānara in his mouth. The *rishi* Gotama Rāhūgaṇa was his family priest. When addressed by the latter he declined to answer, lest Agni should escape from his mouth. The priest prayed to Agni, 'O ghee-sprinkled god, we invoke thee.' Agni flashed forth from the king's mouth as soon as mention was made of ghee and he could not be kept under control. He fell down on the earth. Mādhava was now on the banks of the Sarasvatī. Agni pushed blazing along to the east, followed by the prince and the priest. Mādhava then asked Agni where his abode was to be. 'Thou shalt reside to the east of this river,' was the ready answer. Even now this river forms the boundary of the Kosalas and the Videhas."

The purport of this story is that Mādhava, son of Videha, was jealously guarding the sacred fire Vaiśvānara on the banks of the Sarasvatī. His family priest Gotama Rāhūgaṇa invoked the fire on regions to the east and offered him oblations of ghee. As Agni-worship thus came into existence in the far east, Mādhava betook himself to these regions, and his race led the worship of Fire in the lands of the Kosalas and the Videhas. The story illustrates how the Aryas introduced the worship of Agni wherever they went. The migration of the Aryas was denoted by the migration of Fire.

The last wave of invasion to the South along the course of the Indus is proved by the fact that an Aryan king Śvanaya, son of Bhāvya, is mentioned as the lord of Indus (Sindhu) region and is praised by the sage Kakshīvant Auśija for the presents that were made to him, of a hundred horses, *nishkas* (gold coins or jewels), chariots, girls, cows and bulls.[2] This is also illustrated in the legend of Haryaśva. "He was a son of Ikshvāku, and married Madhumatī, a daughter of the 'demon' Madhu. He was driven out of Ayodhyā by his brother Mādhava and took shelter at Madhupura with his father-in-law. In a short time the country of his adoption known as Ānarta and Saurāshṭra which were rich in cattle, and Ānupa adorned by the sea, beach and forests, became very prosperous." [3]

In every case the non-Aryas were driven for the most part, and such of them as remained were captured and converted into serfs. The traditional history of the Muṇḍas discloses the migration of these aboriginal people apparently under the pressure of the Aryan invaders.

II

Aryan Kingdoms

In the Epic period the Aryas had formed into nations or states, each with territory and organization of its own. The Kauravas ruled over Indraprastha and the surrounding country. The Pāñchālas held sway round about Kanouj. The Videhas established themselves between the Guntak and the Kūsī. The Kosalas were supreme in the tract of territory between the Ganges and the Guntak. The Kāśis settled round Benares. It is not clear that the non-Aryas had kingdoms among those of the Aryas. The heart and centre of *Āryāvarta* was the Kuru-Pāñchāla country. We find a belt of non-Aryan kingdoms and tribes of a mixed nature on the confines of the Aryan world, whose kings are said to have taken part in the Mahābhārata War.[4] Chief of these were the Uttara Kuru, Uttara Mādra, Gandhāra and Bāhḷīka in the north; Anga, Magadha and Kīkaṭa in the east; Nīchya, Apachya, Bhīl, Kambhoja and Tangana in the west; and Bhoja, Āndhra, Draviḍa and Satva in the south. In the *Atharva-Veda*[5] in the hymns about *Takman*, the fever, we read of the following: Mūjavant, Mahāvrisha, Bāhḷīka, Gandhāra, Anga, and Magadha to whom the fever is "delivered like a servant, like a treasure". The countries mentioned by Sugrīva, while giving the order to proceed in the various directions to his Vānara armies, are also interesting as disclosing some of the important kingdoms of the Aryas and the non-Aryas in the period.[6]

III

The Nishadas

In the Epics we meet with the names of at least five prominent non-Aryan tribes with whom the Aryas entered into relations either in war or in peace—Nāga, Nishada, Vānara, Rākshasa, and Gandharva. The following description of a Nishada[7] is interesting as showing ethnic characteristics similar to those of the present-day Indian aboriginal population inhabiting the hills. "His nose was flat, his lower lip thick, his chin low, his jaws full, his forehead and cheek-bones protruding." They were hill-tribes possessing negro characteristics. The origin of these is thus given in the *Mahābhārata*[8]: Vena was the son of Atibala by Sunīthā, a daughter of Mrityu. The *rishis* pierced the right thigh of the king Vena, and from there came out a short, unclean person resembling a charred pole, with reddish eyes and black hair. This new-born child was asked to sit (*nishīda*). Hence he was Nishada, and from him were born the Nishadas, a cruel mountaineering tribe, and other Mlechchas that inhabit the Vindhya hills. In the *Vishṇu Purāṇa*,[9] a Nishada is described as of the complexion of a charred stake, with flattened features and dwarfish stature, short-armed, having high cheek-bones, inconspicuous nose, red eyes and tawny hair. He is depicted as black like a crow in the *Bhāgavata Purāṇa*.[10] The descendants of Nishada are the wicked tribes that are settled in the hills and forests, such as the Nishadas, Kirātas, Bhillas, Nāhalakas, Bhramaras, Pulindas and others given up to vicious and strange habits.[11] Guha was the chieftain of the Nishadas in the *Rāmāyaṇa*. His capital city was Śringiberapura.

IV

The Nāgas

It would appear that there were at least two branches of the Nāga race, the northern and the southern. Those in the North had perhaps originally established themselves at Takshaśila. The chief of these was Vāsuki. They killed Parikshit, and his son Janamejaya is said to have performed a "serpent sacrifice". This only illustrates that Janamejaya avenged the death of his father, and in a war that ensued, the Nāgas were defeated and destroyed. Yakshas, Rākshasas, Piśāchas and Nāgas appear, according to Indian tradition, to have belonged to the same family. The story of their origin is narrated below.[12] The valley of Kashmir was once a big lake. The god Śiva drained the water in the lake, and Kaśyapa, one of the progenitors of the "Indian Man", was asked to people the land thus reclaimed. He had several wives, Khadrū, Krodhavaśā and Khasā. These latter are said to have been the mothers respectively of the Nāgas, Piśāchas and Yaksha-Rākshasas. The Nāgas were the original inhabitants of North-West India. But owing to the internecine quarrels among the brothers, they were superseded in that region by the Piśāchas. Sir George Grierson[13] is inclined to believe that they may have been the ancestors of the non-Aryan inhabitants of Hunza-Nagar whose language Barusaski has not been identified as belonging to any known family of speech.

In later times the Nāgas spread through the whole of North India, as the modern races of the hills, who style themselves by the name seem to indicate. At present, philologically and geographically, the northern Nāgas fall into four groups. (1) Nāga Bodo (northern), comprising the Kaccha and the Kabui. (2) Western Nāgas, including Angamis, Kezamas, Rengmas and Semas. (3) Central Nāgas, chief of whom are Ao's and Lhotas. (4) Eastern Nāgas, known as Nāga-Kuki, the chief tribes being Mao and Tangkhul. In the Buddhist scriptures the Nāgas play a remarkable part, and are depicted as a highly civilized race. Many of them were converted by the Buddha to his faith,[14] and are, according to the Chinese chronicles, the friends and allies of the Buddha. The erection of ancient monuments is attributed to them, for they were regarded as clever architects and artificers.[15] They are spoken of as the custodians of the relics of the Buddha, and the following story of a contest between two Nāga kings over the sacred spot of the Buddha in Maṇipallavam is narrated in the *Maṇimekalai*[16] :—

" In the nether regions two kings who ruled the Nāga country contended for the seat, but neither was able to lift it off the ground ; loathe to give it up, with eyes all aflame, and breathing fury, they led their great armies and fought a bloody battle. The great teacher, the Buddha, then appeared before them and said, 'Cease your strife, this seat is mine.' Then he sat upon it and preached the law." In the *Buddhacharita* they are spoken of as the guardians of treasures. The land of the Nāgas is thus described in the Jātaka : " Filled with troops of Nāga maidens, gladdened constantly with their sports day and night, abounding with garlands and covered with flowers, it shines like the lightning in the sky. Filled with food and drink, with dance and song and instruments of music, with maidens richly attired, it shines with dresses and ornaments."[17] In another place their palaces are mentioned as being in water or near trees or in the Vindhya hills.[18]

The Nāgas are a semi-mythological people in the Sanskrit texts, and are referred to as islanders who had their seat in the waters in the nether regions. The Purāṇas consider *Nāgadvīpa*[19] as one of the divisions of *Bhārata Varsha*. The river Narmadā is spoken of as their sister, and there is a legend to the effect that king Pratarddana assisted them and went to war with the Gandharvas at the instance of Narmadā. In the *Rāmāyaṇa* we read that Rāvaṇa, the king of the Rākshasas, conquered their capital seat Bhogavatī, and the town is thus described[20] :—

" Near Bhogavati stands the place
Where dwell the hosts of the serpent-race,
A broad-wayed city, walled and barred,
Which watchful legions keep and guard.
The fiercest of the serpent youth,
Each awful for his venomed tooth;
And throned in his imperial hall
Is Vāsuki who rules them all."

They are frequently mentioned in connexion with the tribes in South India. Tamil grammarians have divided the early south Indian races under *Makkal*, *Tevar* and *Nāgar*. The southern Nāgas are mentioned as a very hardy and warlike race in the period of the *Śāngam* texts. They are described as "having curved lips, large bright teeth and a voice like thunder". They delighted in mischief and were always armed with the noose. That they had well-built cities becomes clear from the statement in the *Śilappadikāram* that Kāverippaṭṭaṇam, the Chōḷa capital, was as famous and ancient as the metropolis of the Nāgas and the *Nāganāḍu*.[21] They were a civilized people, and were, some of them, expert weavers, as is clear from the evidence afforded by the Tamil work *Śirupāṇārruppaḍai*,[22] where we read of the cloth of very fine texture presented by the Nāga, Nīla by name. The following names of Nāgas appear in the Mahābalipuram inscription of Rajendra Chōḷa: Ōḷi, Mugaḷi and Śanka were perhaps the three septs among them. The inscription reads as follows [23] :—

Ōḷi Nāgan Maḍaiyan Aḷagiya Chōḷa
Āmūr nāṭṭu Mūvenda Velan
Ōḷi Nāgan Chandraśekaran
Ōḷi Nāgan Nārāyaṇan
Indu Puravan Śankanāgan
Ucchari Kiḷavan Mugaḷi Nāgan.

The Nāgas are seen in Tamil literature divided into Maravar, Eyinar, Ōḷiyar, Ōviyar, Paratavar, and Aṛuvāḷar. The Maravars are represented as the fighting clan of South India, characterized by great vigour and hardihood and powers of fighting. "Of strong limbs and hardy frame, fierce-looking like the tiger, wearing long and curled locks of hair, the bloodthirsty Maravan armed with the bow, ever ready to injure others, shoots his arrows at poor and helpless travellers, only to feast his eyes with the quivering limbs of his victims." "The loud twang of their powerful bow-string, and the stirring sound of their double-headed drums, compel even kings with large armies to fly."[24] The Maravars seem thus to have made very successful soldiers, and the commander of the forces of one of the Pāṇḍya kings was a Marava by name Nalai Kiḷavan Nāgan. Eyinar or Veḍar corresponded in those old times to the Kaḷḷars of Tinnevelly, and were a band of free-booters, engaged in clearing the forests, and hunting and catching wild birds and beasts. Cattle-lifting and plunder were their main occupation. They were adepts in the black arts and the secret sciences of witchcraft and sorcery, and were particularly acquainted with the science of omens and signs. They indulged in buffalo sacrifices, and this animal was perhaps their totem, as, for example, it is seen to be of the Todas of the Nilgiris. The Paratavar were the fishing class; and the Ōḷiyars [25] appear to have been the seafaring section among them. The latter are spoken of in the *Mahāvaṃśa* [26] as having succeeded the Kōḷs, and wrested the domination of the sea from them. They were fairly dispersed over the coasts of South India, as may be inferred from place-names like Nāgapaṭṭaṇam and Nāgarkoil.

The women of the Nāgas should have been looked upon as beautiful, as is evidenced by the marriage of Arjuna the Pāṇḍava with Ulūpī the Nāga princess and the frequent marriage-relations of the Nāga women and South Indian princes. The Pallava Vīra Kūrcha married a Nāga princess. Kiḷḷi Chōḷa married the Nāga maiden Pīlivaḷai, the daughter of Valai Vāṇan by Vāsa Mailai, and had a son by her.[27] As Mr Venkayya says,[28] "the account of the Epic hero Arjuna marrying a Nāga queen, and similar stories current about the early Chōḷa kings in Tamil literature, combined with what is stated of Nāga connexions with the first Pallava kings . . . confirm the accepted belief that the Nāgas were the indigenous rulers of South India, and that they were subdued in course of time by the powerful kings from the North, eventually losing their individuality by intermarriage with the foreigners." We may conclude from what has been stated above, "that the Nāgas developed their sea-power, allied themselves with the Aryans of Hindustan and with the Chōḷas and the Pallavas in the South, entered into matrimonial relations with these princes, and expanded from the sea-coast into the interior of India in later times." [29]

VI

The Gandharvas

The Gandharvas were a tribe inhabiting the Himālayan region round the Uttara-Kuru. The Purāṇas contain stories of frequent fighting between the Gandharvas and the Nāgas. The cities of the Gandharvas are referred to as magnificent, as the women of the Nāgas were considered handsome. These are also mythicized in Sanskrit literature, are described as having their abode in the sky and aiding the gods by procuring for them *soma* for sacrifice. They are depicted variously as medicine-mongers and surgeons and as skilled musicians attending on the gods. They seem to have also had prevalent among them a system of marriage—the *gāndharva*—which was adapted by the Aryas and of which there is good evidence in the Indian Epic and Purāṇa stories.

VII

The Rākshasas

The Rākshasas were a colony of people inhabiting the region extending from Janasthāna, which may be placed somewhere in the delta of the river Godāvarī, to Lanka or Ceylon. They were a civilized people, and are said to have descended from the royal family of Vaiśāli.[30] Their sphere of influence lay over the whole of the triangular portion of South India from Nasik on the west, the mouths of the Godāvarī on the east to Lanka far in the south that was the capital of their king. The tribes Daitya, Dānava, and Rākshasa were kith and kin.[31] The Rākshasas were also known in Indian tradition as *Brahma-rākshasas*. They disturbed the Aryan ceremonies and sacrifices, and some of the tribe are described as cannibals.[32]

VIII

The Vānaras

The Vānaras were akin to the Rākshasas, both being descendants of Pulastya.[33] In the *Rāmāyaṇa*, for this reason, perhaps, Rāvaṇa and Sugrīva are spoken of as "brothers",[34] or at least as of the same family. The *Jaina Rāmāyaṇa* calls the kingdom of Sugrīva the kingdom of the monkey-flag. This device on the tribal banner may have, among other reasons, led to the forces being called the monkey-army.[35] The Vānaras are seen classified in the *Rāmāyaṇa* into various septs, Hari, Pḷavanga, Kapi, Ṛkshas and Golāngūlas, all these names being taken as synonyms for " monkey ". They were forest-dwellers and had Kishkindha as the seat of their king. They were closely allied to the Śabaras, another non-Aryan tribe that also welcomed the Aryan civilizing influences.

IX

Causes of Collision

Mutual rivalry among the Aryas and the non-Aryas formed the cause of wars in the previous period. The conception of war as an engine for destroying the heathen or barbarian, which prevailed in ancient Greece and Rome, is seen to operate in India also. The *Mahābhārata* says[36]: " War was invented by Indra for destroying the barbarians, and weapons and armour were created for the same end. Hence merit is acquired by the destruction of these." The hostile relations of the two peoples varied according to circumstances. Hardy colonists would certainly have penetrated into the thick jungles and shown their non-Aryan brethren features of their civilization and culture. The plot of the *Rāmāyaṇa*, for example, shows the attempt of the Aryas of the North to expand into the non-Aryan regions lying in the South. It is the first literary record of the crossing by the Aryas of north India beyond the Vindhya mountain, which was in this period the southern boundary of *Āryāvarta*, and their armed invasion into south India.[37]

Hunting excursions, which were a pastime with members of the rich families of the Aryas, may have similarly helped on the acquaintance of the two peoples resulting in war or peace. Of such the Epics abound in innumerable instances.

Next, it was customary for Aryan sages to choose the jungle

for their penance,[38] and there were complaints from *rishis* performing austerities that the non-Aryas interrupted their religious rites. Viśvāmitra requested Daśaratha for the loan of Rāma's services to put down the Rākshasas who shot at his sacrificial altar balls of flesh and clots of blood, and against whom all his curses were in vain.[39] While Rāma was residing in the summit of Chitrakūṭa during his exile, the hermits living round piteously complained to him of the harassment to which the *anārya* savages so frequently subjected them.[40] Khara the Rākshasa chief was bent on molesting the sages that had chosen Janasthāna for their austerities. Surrounded by others of his tribe, of horrid forms and features, he destroyed the ceremonies of the Aryan priests, cast away in confusion the sacrificial utensils and extinguished the sacred fire with water. Another instance is seen in the occasion for fight between the Pāṇḍava prince Arjuna and the Nishada chief Ekalavya.[41] Arjuna is said to have visited the country of Ekalavya, and conquered in battle a son of the Nishada king. This resulted in a war in which Arjuna fought furiously. The undaunted Pāṇḍava took the Nishada king himself and protected the sacrifices performed by the Aryan priests.

The sensuality and lust of some of the non-Aryan chiefs afforded another ground of quarrel. Rāvaṇa's attempt to seduce Sītā and Kīchaka's effort to outrage Draupadī are classical instances in point. We have a third where Jayadratha, the king of the mixed tribes Sindhu-Sauviras, tries to carry off Draupadī to the forest in the absence of her husbands during the period of their exile, and "commits therefore an act unworthy of an Arya". He is pursued and confronted by Bhīma and Arjuna, forced to submit and finally put to death.[42]

The frequent quarrels among the non-Aryas themselves invited no doubt the intervention of the Aryas. This finds a glorious instance in Rāma's alliance with the Vānara king Sugrīva against his brother Vāli.[43]

X

Non-Aryan Resistance

The Aryan colonization of new lands could have gone on not without a hard and serious attempt at resistance on the part of the non-Aryan tribes and chiefs. The wars which Bhīma had to wage with Hiḍimba and Baka, and those that were fought with Khara and Dūshaṇa by Rāma illustrate the extension of Aryan supremacy into the regions of non-Aryan tribes, who resisted the advance of the Aryas, but were at last vanquished. The Pāṇḍavas are said to have burnt the Khāṇḍava forest inhabited by Nāgas and other forest-tribes who obstructed the advance of the Aryan conquerors and objected to the conflagration which was ultimately carried out by the Pāṇḍavas, on the advice of their friend and guide Krishṇa. The latter had apparently to fight with a Nāga king Kāḷiya on the banks of the Jumna as the legend of this Yādava prince having destroyed the "black serpent" Kāḷiya clearly shows. Krishṇa overcame this dreadful non-Aryan chief, and the story is taken to symbolize the destruction of evil and the emanation of light and virtue in the world. Aryan intrusion and non-Aryan opposition is evident in the story of Agastya [44] and Vātāpi and Ilvala, two Asura chiefs whom Agastya is said to have reduced to ashes. Vātāpi and Ilvala were two Asura brothers living in the Daṇḍaka forest disturbing the ceremonies of the Aryan sages and destroying the *rishis* that had settled there for peaceful penance. They took the guise of learned Brāhmaṇs and invited the *rishi* Agastya to dinner at a *śrāddha* (annual obsequies). Vātāpi disguised himself as a ram which having been sacrificed was partaken of by the guests. After the feast was over, Ilvala called out for Vātāpi who would come out, being transformed into an Asura, ripping open the bowels of those that had eaten of him. This trick was futile on Agastya who was able by the force of his prayers to digest his food. Ilvala as usual called out for his brother, but the latter could not return to life. Ilvala sought to wreak his vengeance on Agastya, but was burnt by the fire that flashed from the powerful eye of that sage. This story is an example of a confused admixture of myth and fable, history and fact. If we disentangle what is legend and fairy tale in this story, we shall discover that it is intended to illustrate little more than the molestation that was caused by the non-Aryan Asura chiefs, and the effective way in which the Aryas overcame them.

XI

Alliances

But the evidence is strong of peaceful intercourse as well. The friendship of some of the non-Aryan chiefs with the Aryas is evidenced by Guha's kindness and Śabarī's offerings to Rāma. The Nishāda king Guha received Rāma, Sītā and Lakshmaṇa with cordial welcome, provided them with boats and rowed them across the ferry on the Ganges. Bharata in his journey to the forest in search of his brother received a similar reception at the hands of this non-Aryan chieftain. The story of Śabarī [45] is an epitome of a non-Aryan tribe that had been completely influenced by Aryan culture. Apparently, she belonged to the tribe of the Śabaras whose main occupation was hunting and bird-catching, and who are represented now by a tribe of the same name inhabiting the hills of Central India. She is styled a *śramaṇī*, led the pious and virtuous life of a nun and considered herself blessed by acquaintance with the prince of the Aryas. The Vānaras must have exhibited a ready disposition to welcome Aryan civilization since they entered into a league with Rāma and aided him in his expedition against Lanka. Rāma reinstated the Vānara king Sugrīva on the throne of Kishkindha and received his assistance against the " black tribes " further south. The Dānava chieftain Kabandha having been defeated in battle agrees to act as the intellectual guide of Rāma and Lakshmaṇa in their quest of Sītā. It was he that directed the brothers to Sugrīva. Every Hindu is well aware of the service which the faithful Hunumān rendered to Rāma in discovering Sītā who had been carried away and kept in captivity at Lanka by Rāvaṇa. Vibhīshaṇa strongly disapproved of Rāvaṇa's unwise and unlawful acts against Rāma. The words of Vibhīshaṇa [46] show how wholesome and reasonable the grounds were on which he wanted his brother to desist from undertaking the ruinous war with Rāma. His advice discloses a very high standard of equity and fairness which were incomprehensible to Rāvaṇa who was paving the way for his own fall, " like a man who, being seized by extreme thirst, attempts to quench it unconsciously with a cup of poison." His words of advice, as harsh to the ear as wholesome in effect, would never appeal to Rāvaṇa, who like an elephant bathed in fresh water would only throw mud on his own back. Vibhīshaṇa therefore deserted his brother and threw himself at the feet of the Aryan prince and became his confidant. Many non-Aryan chiefs allied themselves with either of the combatants and took part in the " Great War ".

XII

The Political Morality of the Age

The dealings in war and peace were marked by a standard of political morality and of moral duty in which the non-Aryas were not much behind their Aryan fellows.[47] The conditions regarding the agents of warfare in this period may be set forth in the following manner :—

(1) Everything in warfare should be fair and open.

(2) There should be some distinguishing badge or sign on both sides.

(3) The efficiency of the army depended on drilling, organiza-

tion and leadership. The king was the high commander and directly led the army to the battle-field in many cases. In others, the work was entrusted to able commanders.

(4) All should conform to the regulations of war.

In the Epics there is clear enunciation of the principles which were to guide the invaders. Here we have certain rules framed for the combatants corresponding to " military codes ". This is clear from the *Mahābhārata*,[48] where among the articles of agreement between the Pāṇḍavas and the Kauravas are :—

(1) We will make war on each other without stratagem or treachery.

(2) No man shall take up arms against another without giving him notice.

(3) When one is engaged with another, no third man shall interfere.

These regulations may be broadly classified as preventive and positive. Under the first head are included all the rules which may have been in observance even among primitive peoples, while the latter are a feature only in a society of an advanced character. The philosophy of war in ancient India is made up of both classes of rules. Not only the Aryas but the non-Aryas appear to have been guided by such noble ideas of international equity. In fact, Vāli's discourse with Rāma shows that the non-Aryas were no strangers to those rules of public morality, which, it was held, were observed or ought to be observed by the Aryas of the age. The ancient Indians had highly developed rules to ensure fairness in fighting. It was agreed that only warriors placed in similar circumstances should encounter each other in fair and open combat. A king should fight with a king, a car-warrior with one of his own class, a fighter on an elephant should have for his antagonist one of the same order, a cavalry officer should be met by a cavalry officer, and a foot soldier by a foot soldier.

XIII

The Ethics of Warfare

The treatment accorded to combatants on the enemy-side has differed in the different ages of the history of India. In the age of the *Rig-Veda*, when there were no advanced notions of intertribal morality, there was even wholesale destruction. In the wars that were fought between the Aryas and the Dasyus the opposing parties were actuated only by the desire to extirpate the foe, by means fair or foul. The idea then was that war was an engine invented by Indra to exterminate the Dasyus, and it was for being destroyed that they were born. In the Epic age it is found that the treatment accorded to inhabitants of occupied and conquered places was more humane.

The conversation between Vāli and Rāma [49] discloses to us that the hard blow that Rāma gave and that shot Vāli dead was an offence against international law even as known to the Vānara chief. Vāli asks:

> "What advantage hast thou obtained by stabbing me behind my back, O Rāma! I have given thee no offence, whether in thy capital or country. Thou oughtest to know, O King, that righteousness is among the badges of the true Kshatriya, who would never strike at one that is free from fault. Thy valour, alas! has been displayed against one who was hard beset by a fighting enemy, and who never cared to take up arms against thee."

Rāvaṇa's attempted seduction of Sītā was an act of war, and morally reprehensible, but a *casus belli* had been given him also in the mutilation of the members of his sister Śūrpanakhā.

XIV

Non-Aryan Ideas of Conduct

Even as regards those principles of equity which should govern the relations of nations in peaceful times, the non-Aryas appear to have possessed advanced ideas. It was accepted that to put to death an envoy was opposed to the general conduct of kings, and was condemnable by the whole world.[50] Rāvaṇa spared the life of Hanumān when it was pointed out to him that he was an envoy from Rāma, and that the person of an emissary was sacred and inviolable.[51] But there were certain recognized punishments that could be meted out to an offending envoy, such as causing mutilation of limbs, cropping of the hair, etc. Therefore Rāvaṇa gave the order for deforming Hanumān.[52]

A sense of moral duty among the non-Aryas of the age is proved by the desertion of Vibhīshaṇa and the wholesome advice of Kumbhakarṇa and Mārīcha to Rāvaṇa. Kumbhakarṇa gave a moral discourse on the wicked conduct of Rāvaṇa when he was awakened by the latter to fight against Rāma.[53] He admonished his brother that even at the outset he had done a thoughtless and wicked deed, elated by the pomp, power, and pride of Royalty, and unmindful of the inglorious consequences which he had then to take. Only that king, he said, could be called clever and calculating who would act in the present after having mastered the past and presaged the future. The reluctant Mārīcha had to be driven on pain of death to be instrumental in Rāvaṇa's lustful attempt at the abduction of Sītā. Mārīcha gave the timely advice, only to be rejected :—

> "Flatterers are plenty in this world, O King, but few are those that would give counsel, good and healthy, though bitter; and fewer still are those that pay heed to such willingly." [54]

A high feeling of political duty is shown in Kumbhakarṇa's adhering to Rāvaṇa. When the latter peremptorily said, "Let the dead past bury its dead; do what is best under the circumstances on hand," Kumbhakarṇa yielded and observed that what he said was well-intentioned and due to brotherly affection.

He waited only for his behest.[55] Is not a keen sense of chivalry evident in Rāvaṇa's refraining from the murder of Sītā when he found his overtures repeatedly rejected?

The Aryan bard may explain away the good points of his foes and the weaknesses of his own heroes; but he is really testifying to the advanced character of the non-Aryas when he says that they were really Aryas, but under the influence of a curse.[56] He is also conceding another large point when he describes the rule of the non-Aryan king as magnificent, the might of his arm as invincible, and the country of Lanka as prosperous and happy.

XV

Social Relations in the Age

The social relations of the non-Aryas and the Aryas had much improved since the Vedic period. Then we had only a few stray references to admixture of blood, but in the Epics there are several instances of such, leading perhaps to regular and permanent relationships. Śantanu, the king of Hastināpura, married Satyavatī, a fish-woman. Vyāsa is depicted as the son of Parāśara by a fish-girl, who was employed at a ferry on the Jumna.[57] Bhīma married Hiḍimbī, the sister of a powerful Rākshasa, on condition that she should not disclose her native ill-breeding, but behave like a woman of high birth and gentle breeding.[58] This is of special interest as conceding that non-Aryan women were capable of acquiring (or assuming) the noble and dignified bearing of the Arya, and becoming accomplished and refined like the latter. Arjuna married Ulūpī, a Nāga princess. He is likewise said to have gone to Maṇipur or Maṇalūr,[59] married the daughter of the *rāja* there, and begot Babhruvāhana by her. Abhimanyu, a son of Arjuna, was married to Uttarā, a daughter of the Matsya king Virāṭa.[60] Rāvaṇa was the son of Viśravas by Kaikasī, a Rākshasī.[61] More instances of the kind might be mentioned. It may be that some of these stories of marriages contain miraculous and mythical elements, but these could have found currency in India only at a time when the union of an Arya with a non-Aryan woman was not altogether foreign to the Aryan sentiment. It is possible that there was for a long time marriage-relationship between the royal line of the Kurus and that of the Matsya country, as is evidenced by Parāśara's marriage with a fish-woman, Śantanu's with Matsyagandhī, and Abhimanyu's with Uttarā, the daughter of Virāṭa, king of the Matsya country.[62]

XVI

Epic Colours and Complexions

The frequent unions of persons belonging to different classes and races are indicated, perhaps, in the different complexions of the characters in the Epic poems. Rāma, Krishṇa and Vyāsa were dark; Balarāma was white. Arjuna's colour is given variously as white and dark. Of heroines, Draupadī was dark, while Sītā's complexion was a golden yellow. A fairly good idea of the change that had taken place in the complexion and ethnic features of the Aryas of the age could be formed from the description given of the heroes and heroines in the *Mahābhārata*.[63] "Here is Yudhishṭhira, king of the Kurus, in complexion pure as gold, stalwart and strong in body like the undaunted lion, with a prominent nose and large, long and reddish eyes. Here is Bhīma (Vrikodara), whose gait is like that of an elephant in rut, fair as burnished gold, with broad and big shoulders, perfect in every limb, and with stout and long arms. By his side is the great archer Arjuna, young and dark in complexion, resembling the leader of an elephant-herd, with shoulders high like a lion, and eyes long like a lotus petal. Beside Kuntī, the two princes Nakula and Sahadeva, looking like Vishṇu and Indra, stand unequalled in the whole world for beauty, valour and virtue. Here is Draupadī, perfect in plan and noble in build, dark and graceful like the lily, with eyes like the lotus, very Lakshmī incarnate. Close by her is Subhadrā, the sister of Krishṇa, the wielder of the discus, whose body is of the hue of gold, and who is a phantom of delight even like the Moon. Here is the daughter of the Nāga king, a wife of Arjuna, who is as pure gold, and by her is Chitrāngadā whose complexion is like that of a fresh-plucked *madhūka* flower. Here is the chief wife of Bhīma, the daughter of the general who vied with Krishṇa in valour, with complexion like that of a lily full-blown. Here stands the wife of Sahadeva, the daughter of Jarāsandha of Magadha, graceful like the *champaka* flower. Beside her is the wife of Nakula, twined like a creeper to the former, beautiful like a blue lotus. Here is the daughter of the Virāṭa king, fair like molten gold, the widow of Abhimanyu, who laid down his life in the field of fighting. Besides, there are a hundred or more of white-robed ladies, the widows of the Kaurava princes slain in battle." [64]

In the *Brihadāraṇyaka Upanishad* [65] we have passages which show how the colour of the Aryas of the *Madhyadeśa* changed gradually owing to the mingling of castes and various other causes. " If the parents wish that they should have a son white in complexion, having knowledge only of one Veda, they should take boiled rice with milk and butter. If they wish to have a son reddish in complexion and with tawny eyes, but knowing two Vedas, boiled rice should be taken with curd and butter. If the desire be for a dark son, with red eyes, but having knowledge of three Vedas, the food advised is boiled rice mixed with water and curd. If the parents wish to have a learned son famous as a speaker, having the qualities of a Kshatriya, and possessing knowledge of all the Vedas, they are advised to add a little meat to the rice and butter. If the craving is for a learned and accomplished girl, sesame should be mixed with the rice and butter." These texts show that the offspring were of different complexions, white (*śukla*), reddish (*kapila*), and dark (*śyāma*). White complexion and full knowledge of the Veda, which were the peculiar features of the Aryas of the previous epoch, are not now seen necessarily to go together; nor do dark complexion and ignorance of the Veda, the peculiarities of the non-Aryan peoples of the Vedic period. A dark son with reddish eyes, as the passage shows, may have more knowledge of the Vedas than one with a white complexion. This is probably why in the *Kāṭhaka Saṃhitā* a Vaiśya is described as white, while the Rājanya or Kshatriya is of the smoke-colour. The gradual change in the complexion of the Aryas is illustrated in a passage in the *Mahābhārata* [66] where the colour of Vishṇu is said to change from age to age. In the Krita yuga it was white; in the Treta, yellow; in the Dvāpara, red; and in the Kali age it is black.

The influence of the food eaten on the nature, colour and the intellectual qualities and attainments of the offspring is also in evidence in the above passages. As Dr Hutton says of a belief among the Sema Nāgas, " the ill-consequences which are held to follow the use of certain animals and birds as food more often attend the offspring of the eaters than the eaters themselves." [67] This was among the various grounds on which interdining and the taking of forbidden food were so particularly interdicted in the social life of ancient India. It may also be pointed out that the long sojourn in the hot plains may have transformed the complexion of the white Aryas by covering it with the shadowed livery of the burnished sun.

XVII

Some New Criteria of Caste

The anxiety of Arjuna to preserve the purity of castes probably points to a tendency already existing towards a confusion of castes. " When impiety prevails, O Krishṇa, the women of the family become corrupt; women corrupted, there will be intermingling of castes, confusion of castes leads families to hell."[68] The intermixture of castes that was taking place is also hinted in a conversation between Yudhishṭhira and Nahusha (in the form of a serpent) when they met in a forest.[69] Nahusha asks the Pāṇḍava the definition of the word Brāhmaṇa, and he should release his brother Bhīma, who had been caught by him, only if a satisfactory answer was given. Yudhishṭhira replies: "Honesty, charity, integrity, patience and good conduct, forbearance and meditation, it is these that make a Brāhmaṇa." Nahusha asks, "If the four-fold classification is authentic, and is the basis of the society, what to say when these qualities are found in the Śūdras?" Yudhishṭhira says, finally, "A Brāhmaṇa may sometimes lack the good qualities found in a Śūdra. A Brāhmaṇa is not to be known as such merely by his name or from the accident of birth, nor is a Śūdra by his. Where virtue and righteous conduct is found, *there* is the Brāhmaṇa. A Śūdra is he who is without them." "It was impossible at the time to determine exactly the caste to which a person belonged by the fact of birth alone, owing to the admixture of castes that had taken place." We read elsewhere in the same Epic, "not birth, not sacrament, not learning make one *dvija* (twice-born), but righteous conduct alone makes it."[70] "Be he a Śūdra or a member of any other class, he that serves as a raft on a raftless current or helps to ford the unfordable, certainly deserves respect in every way."[71] It was getting to be slowly recognized that what really counts is righteous conduct and not credal faith. Śūdras worthy of respect were invited for the sacrifices performed by the Kshatriya princes of the age.[72] As these novel ideas and features appeared, a new criterion of caste came to be formed, viz. conduct and occupation. "The four orders have been created by me in accordance with the nature of men and their predisposition to duties," says the Lord in the *Gītā*.[73] That good character and worthy behaviour were the true tests of an Arya becomes clear in Manu's code where we have the following: "Behaviour unworthy of an Arya, harshness, cruelty, habitual neglect of the prescribed duties betray in this world a man of low and impure origin."[74] Caste became a question of conduct or character.

XVIII

Polyandry, Polygamy, and Monogamy

Monogamy was the rule in Aryan social life in the age of the Epics and the Brāhmaṇas; and we read that "a woman who is not loyal to her husband incurs the sin of killing an embryo, and certainly portends misery". It is also stated that "the same sin overtakes the man that is untrue to his wife who is devoted, chaste and pure".[75] But there are relics of polygamy even in the Vedic scriptures. In the *Aitareya Brāhmaṇa* we read, "One man may have more than one wife, but one woman has never more than one husband."[76]

It is possible that the polyandry of Draupadī was the relic of a custom borrowed from the non-Aryas. Polyandry was certainly an unknown thing in *Āryāvarta*, but was not uncommon outside the pale of Brāhmaṇic civilization, and was the prevalent custom among the Uttara-Kurus. The practice may have filtered into this region from the borderland of Tibet which has given the name to one distinct kind of polyandry.[77] We are told in the *Mahābhārata* that the Pāṇḍava brothers were given birth to in the Himālayan region, and they were brought by Brāhmaṇa sages to the court of Dhritarāshṭra and presented to Bhīshma.[78] Hence the Pāṇḍavas were always slighted by the Kauravas as people whose antecedents were not clearly traceable. It is probable that the practice of polyandry was got from the non-Aryan people on the Himālayas in the neighbourhood.[79] That this was a custom prevalent in the family of the Pāṇḍavas is indicated in a short conversation between Yudhishṭhira and Drupada, the king of Pāñchāla, when the former proposed that Draupadī that had been won by Arjuna's valour shall be the wife of all the five brothers.[80]

Drupada: One man may have many duly wedded wives, but it is nowhere stated that one woman may have more than one husband. Neither in scriptures nor in current practice is it accepted. O Kuntī's son, well-versed in the moral codes, wherefrom is this your sanction for a deed that is contrary to practice and precept?

YUDHISHṬHIRA : It is beyond our power to discover the origins of this practice. We only follow the old and righteous path taken by our ancestors. I do not tell an untruth, nor do I allow my mind to be led astray. What I say is the behest of my mother, and is therefore my earnest wish. I have heard of this custom as prevalent in our family, from the great sage Vyāsa himself. It has therefore to be accepted unquestioningly. Let no doubts haunt your mind on the point.

Apparently, it came as a surprise to the king of the Pāñchāla country, who was, however, persuaded to give his daughter in marriage to all the five.

The change from primitive marriage-forms to monogamy and settled family-life is apparently indicated in the following story in the *Mahābhārata*.[81] Formerly, women used to go about freely. They were not so secluded in their life as now, yet they were not regarded sinful, for that was the sanctioned custom of the times. That very custom is followed to-day by birds and beasts without any exhibition of jealousy, and is yet regarded with respect among the Uttara-Kurus. The present practice is attributed to Śvetaketu, the son of the great *rishi* Uddālaka. The son like the father was an ascetic of great merit. One day in the presence of Uddālaka, a Brāhmaṇa that had come to him held his wife by hand and told her, "Let us go." Beholding his mother seized by hand and led away, forcibly as it were, the son was moved by wrath. Seeing his son indignant, Uddālaka said, "Be not angry, my son, this is a practice sanctioned by antiquity." Śvetaketu disapproved of this custom and established in the world the present practice of family-life for men and women. This story does not show that before the age of the Great Epic the prevalent form of social life was matriarchal in India, and that the patriarchal form of family was established only now.[82] It is to be taken as reminiscent of the primitive practices that prevailed in distant antiquity in this country. It agrees well with the evolution of marriage-forms postulated by anthropologists of modern times.

XIX

The Status of Women

Women were held in great respect in family and social life in the age of the Mantras. The wife was the mistress of the household, and had full sway over her husband's father, mother, brothers and sisters.[83] Women moved out freely and witnessed sacrifices and ceremonies, and took part in social functions.[84] In the period of the Epics they had ceased to exercise such control over the members of their families as before, and a householder led by the words of a woman was despised.[85] It would appear that the seclusion of women had then become a recognized social custom, and they had not the freedom as their kind had in the previous period. Statements to the following effect are met with in Epic literature: "Women who could not be noticed even in their parlour by the Sun, are now seen by the men in the street, and Sītā, who was generally not visible even to the gods that measure the sky, was seen on foot in the royal road by the whole population of Ayodhyā." This practice of seclusion was, however, not insisted upon in emergencies and occasions of crises, such as the outbreak of a war, *svayamvara* (self-choice of the husband), sacrifices and marriages.[86] Though the reference in these passages is to the women of the royal household, it is reasonable to suppose that what applied to them should have been applicable to the general run of woman-kind.

The delineation by Vālmīki of the character of the heroines of his Epic is indicative of a change that had come in the ideas regarding the status of Indian women. A slight fall from the Vedic standard is noticeable in the *Śatapatha Brāhmaṇa* [87] and the *Maitrāyaṇi Saṃhitā*.[88] Perhaps the character of Kaikeyī prompted by Kubjā marks the transition to a stage when women came to be not held in such high esteem as before. Before the evil and venomous insinuations against Rāma and his mother, Kausalyā, were poured into her ears, Kaikeyī was a virtuous and graceful character. She always treated Rāma equally with her own son Bharata, and was at first overcome with joy when the happy tidings of Rāma's coronation was carried to her by Kubjā, her servant-woman. She gave her a valuable pearl-necklace for having heralded the news. Besides, she is seen to remark that it was highly becoming that the old king, following the good and wholesome rule of the Ikshvākus, should crown his eldest son as the heir-apparent. Kubjā found it very hard to drive venom into a pure and clean mind, to persuade the good queen that woe would betide her if Ayodhyā was left to be ruled by Rāma !

Daśaratha is made to exclaim, "Women are not at all bad as a class. I am speaking only of Kaikeyī." Kaikeyī alone is an exception to the general woman-kind who are good.[89] Later, women as a whole are described as attached to men in prosperity, but deserting in adversity, and Sītā, the ideal of Indian women, is an exception.[90] Later still, a few of the common foibles of women are seen attributed to Sītā. Lakshmaṇa is forced to exclaim, "Women are generally devoid of virtue, fickle and harsh by nature and disruptive in family," with reference to the rather harsh and cruel words Sītā used against him when he refused to go away, leaving her alone, fully knowing that Rāma could not have been defeated by Mārīcha, and that the call for help could not be his.[91] Of course, the attitude of Sītā is common and is easily explained. But it seems that the words were not worthy of that pure, noble and dignified character.

XX

The Gāndharva Form of Marriage

The Epics show that the *Gāndharva* form of marriage—the voluntary union in wedlock of a woman and her lover—was known to the Aryas of the time, e.g. that of Dushyanta and Śakuntaḷā. This form of marriage is seen in the *svayamvara* or choice by the woman herself of the husband, prevalent among the Kshatriyas. The *svayamvara* was of two kinds. In the one form, the bride selected her husband, having been already acquainted with the many qualities of his head, hand and heart, from among the suitors that were present at an assembly invoked for the purpose. In the second, a tournament was held to test the military ability of the candidates. Chivalry and valour were the test of a suitable Kshatriya, and he who won at the tournament had perforce to be accepted as the husband. The success at the tournament testified to the ability of the bridegroom chosen. This institution may have been borrowed from the Gandharvas, as the very term denoting the marriage indicates.[92]

XXI

Interdining

The Hindu society has laid down strict regulations in the matter of food. Social gatherings and convivial parties could not have existed in those distant times, and these were looked down upon. " Eating together " was generally prohibited, even among the members of the same class.[93] Mass-feeding was unknown except perhaps on occasions of sacrifices and marriage festivities.

The food that was taken was supposed to possess a powerful influence on the character and intellect of the person used to it. Man is what he eats. Taking forbidden food did certainly tend, according to the Indian notions, to lower one's psychic powers and intellectual qualities.

Hence, we find rules prohibiting food of certain kinds, in certain seasons and from certain hands. There are elaborate regulations regarding lawful and forbidden food for the various classes of the Hindu society in whatever status they be, *brahmachāri*, *grihastha* or *yogi*. The general feeling of repugnance to habits of interdining is illustrated in the question, "Where is the chance of supreme bliss for Brāhmans that partake of food from an outcaste?"[94] It is distinctly stated that Rāma, following the practice of the Kshatriya princes, refused to take the food offered him by Guha the Nishada chief.[95]

The general rule was that unclean and forbidden food must be avoided. But we have in the *Chchāndogya Upanishad* an instance of a Brāhmaṇa in dire necessity eating prohibited food. The story is thus narrated: When the Kuru country had been overrun by locusts, Ushasti Chākrāyaṇa took to begging alms with his wife at Ibhyagrāma from some unknown chieftain. The chief, who had already partaken of some of the beans he had with him, said, "I have no more beans than what remains after I have eaten." Ushasti said, "Give them to me," and he ate the beans that were offered. He was told then that there was something to drink, and if he pleased, he might quench his thirst. Ushasti replied, "If I drank of it, I should have drunk of what was left by another, and therefore unclean." The chief asked, "Were not those beans unclean for the same reason?" Ushasti's answer was, "No, for I should not have lived if I had not eaten the beans, but the drinking of water would be for mere pleasure." The inference is, as Śankara writes in his commentary,[96] that "the sin does not pollute the man in such straits". This and other instances such as those of Ajīgarta, Vāmadeva, Viśvāmitra, and Bharadvāja are explained by the general principle of *āpaddharma* by which "he who, when in danger of losing his life, accepts food from any person whatsoever is no more tainted by sin than the sky is by mud".[97]

XXII

Religious Beliefs and Practices

We may next glance at the mutual influence on religious beliefs and practices. We find that some of the non-Aryas had not only adopted the religious beliefs and observances of the Aryas but had attained great proficiency in the Vedas and the Brāhmanical sciences. All the sons of Viśravas are mentioned as having knowledge of the Vedas and as diligent in religious rites.[98] Vibhīshaṇa is represented by Śūrpanakhā in her interview with Râma and Lakshmaṇa as one who is virtuous and does not follow the practice of the Rākshasas.[99] Rāvaṇa approaches Sītā reciting the Vedas in order to inspire confidence in her. He is advised not to slaughter Sītā, having mastered the Vedas and being an eminent hero in religious rites.[100] He was so very proficient in the Vedic lore that a certain reclassification of the Yajur-Vedic texts has been attributed to him. He is said to have been buried with the ceremonies in vogue among the "twice-born", and learned Brāhmans officiated as priests at the ceremony.[101] Likewise the erudition of Kavasha Ailūsha is made much of in the *Aitareya Brāhmaṇa*.[102] The story about him runs as follows: He was the son of Ilūsha by a slave-girl. The *rishis* were performing a sacrifice on the banks of the river Sarasvatī. Ailūsha came there, but the priests would not admit him to their company as he was "low-born"! But he was so well versed in the Vedic lore and was such a great adept in the holy *śāstras* that by dint of his prayers he was able to divert the river from its original course to where he stood. The *rishis* saw the miracle, and realizing that Ailūsha was a man of extraordinary merit, took him into their company and permitted him to take part in the sacred rites.

We have in Vidura an instance of a man not belonging to any of the "twice-born" castes instructed in the Vedas and famous for his philosophy. In the *Pañchaviṁśa Brāhmaṇa*[103] there is the story of Vatsa who was accused of as being a Śūdra's son, and therefore unfit to take part in Vedic rituals. But he established his purity and manifested his greatness by walking unhurt through the flames of a fire-ordeal. Likewise, Jānaśruti Pautrāyana, a Śūdra king, was taught by the Brāhmaṇa priest Raikva "the deity that he worshipped".[104]

We may now consider how far the Aryas and the non-Aryas influenced each other in regard to the pantheon of the age. In the Epics we read for the first time of Kubera the god of Riches, the treasurer of the gods.[105] He is one of the Eight Guardians of the quarters—Indra, Agni, Yama, Nirriti, Varuṇa, Vāyu, Kubera, and Īśāna, and is assigned to the North filled in tradition by Soma (Moon).[106] He is represented as Vaiśravaṇa and as a brother of Rāvaṇa. The Brahmaṇaspati of the Veda now becomes transformed into Vināyaka or the Elephant-god, and is represented as the brother of Guruguha or Skanda and as a son of Rudra.[107] Vedic Rudra came to be identified with Bhairava, the terrible aspect of Śiva, and the favourite deity of Rāvaṇa, Bāṇa and Padma.[108]

XXIII

Rāvaṇa, the King of Lanka

Rāvaṇa was a non-Aryan chieftain who had enormous might of arm and of mind. He was both a physical and intellectual giant. Epic literature depicts him in some places as possessed of ten heads, and he is given the names Daśagrīva, Daśāsya, Daśānana, Daśamukha, Vimśadbhuja, etc. The usual names are Daśagrīva and Rāvaṇa. The fact that he had only one head, two eyes and two hands is clear from the description, given of Rāvaṇa by Hanumān, at first sight.[109] This is of great value, and has to be taken to be an authentic account of Rāvaṇa, for Hanumān has had no knowledge of Rāvaṇa before, and had no prepossessions at the time he saw the king of the Rākshasas.

Rāvaṇa is described as lying asleep, big like the Mandara mountain, and decked in precious ornaments. The breath that came out of his mouth resembled that of the infuriated serpent. He had stretched out his two stout and strong arms resembling the elephant's trunk, adorned with golden armlets, besmeared with the most fragrant sandals and scents and showing the scars of many a wound received in battle. He wore a golden crown set with pearls and precious stones, and his face beamed with the dazzling earrings that he wore. It is indeed difficult to explain why ten heads were assigned to this Rākshasa king. They may possibly be symbolical, mythical and *adhyātmic* in character. But the idea of giving a number of heads and hands to the images of gods and goddesses is quite common in India, and is peculiarly illustrative of the artistic taste, æsthetic talent and national temperament of the people of this country. The god Indra is said to possess a thousand eyes, and this feature is explained by Kauṭilya as being due to the fact that this chief of the gods was surrounded by a thousand ministers. They were his eyes, and "therefore Indra became in tradition the thousand-eyed though he had in reality only two eyes".[110]

XXIV

Cremation and Burial

One of the main features of Vedic civilization was the introduction of the worship of Fire by the Aryas into the lands that were colonized and inhabited by them. This is illustrated early in Indian tradition in the story of Purūravas, who is said to have taken fire from the region of the Gandharvas, and popularized it in its three well-known forms, *gārhapatya*, *āhavanīya* and *dākshiṇa*. It is not right to say, as some have done, with reference to this legend, that Purūravas was the originator of the worship of Agni among the Vedic Aryas. The first example of the use of the sacred fire is perhaps to be seen in the famous sacrifice performed by Daksha. Purūravas was the fifth in descent from Daksha as may be seen from the genealogical table given on p. 221. What Purūravas did was to popularize the fire-cult, and hence in the *Śukla Yajur-Veda* we read [111] that Fire, as the result of churning the firesticks, is spoken of as the offspring of Purūravas and Urvaśī. The same idea is brought out in this period by the account of Mādhava the Videha. As the geographical horizon of the Aryas increased, there was the increased spread of the worship of Agni.

The Aryas generally burnt their dead bodies, and burial was permitted only in exceptional circumstances. The non-Aryan practice was invariably, on the other hand, burial in one of the four forms found in the remains at Nal in Baluchistan and in those at Adicchnallur in South India.[112] These were (*a*) *Tholos* burial in kennel-like tombs ; (*b*) *Jar* burial, in a big jar in which were placed food and drink and garments in small pots along with some unburnt bone kept in another jar ; (*c*) *Larnax* burial in terra-cotta chests containing the whole body ; (*d*) *Urn* burial, in which ashes and burnt bones and certain implements of stone or bronze were kept in urns. In the Epic period there is evidence of the gradual introduction of the practice of cremation among the non-Aryan peoples of South India, with whom the prevalent form of disposing of the dead was burial. That was the practice among the Rākshasas as the following passage will show [113]: Virādha the Rākshasa asks Rāma to " cast away his body into the cave yonder and acquire merit thereby, for that is the age-long custom among the Rākshasas ". Jaṭāyu and Kabandha were cremated in the Aryan fashion, and the story of the latter is intended perhaps to indicate that this Dānava chief showed his willingness to prefer cremation to burial that was in vogue in their tribe. He asks Rāma to burn his body after death. Similarly, Vāli was cremated according to the custom of the Aryas; and Rāvaṇa's body was burnt and disposed of in the most elaborate and orthodox manner.

XXV

ARYAN *RISHIS* AND THEIR INFLUENCE

There was not only the unconscious blending in course of time of the religious practices of the two peoples. There were deliberate attempts made by Aryan *rishis* to Aryanize lands and peoples that were non-Aryan. Work of a missionary character was undertaken by some sages who introduced Aryan civilization and culture into the non-Aryan regions of South India. Agastya, Paraśurāma, and Uśanas Śukra are prominent examples of these.

Agastya was the first Brāhmaṇa bard to colonize the South.[114] He is spoken of as the conqueror of the South and appears as the friend and guide of Rāma on his way to the South. He dwelt in a hermitage on the Kunjara mountain and was the chief of the sages that had chosen the forests of the Dekhan for their penance. He was a very orthodox sage and is mentioned in the *Atharva-Veda* as an adept in sorcery and witchcraft.[115] He kept the Rākshasas under control and is said to have reduced to ashes the two Asuras Vātāpi and Ilvala. Rāma in his exile went to his abode, and the *rishi* received the brothers with great kindness and became their friend, adviser and protector. In early Tamil literature [116] we read that he went to Dvāraka in Gujarat, and taking with him eighteen families of local chieftains proceeded to the South, where the forests were cleared and cities and kingdoms founded. This story has been taken by some to refer to a migration to South India of the Dravidian tribes from the North. More properly this legend may be interpreted as indicating an advance guard of the Aryas from North India, who may have to some extent been responsible for the later growth of political and social institutions in South India, based on those pertaining to Aryan polity of early ages. Agastya is said to have had twelve disciples each one of whom was the author of a Tamil grammar, based on the *Agattiyam* (the grammar of Agastya). The most prominent of these was Tolkāppiyar.[117]

Paraśurāma, who cleared the earth of the Kshatriyas thrice seven times, made a gift of all his lands to Kāśyapa and retired to the Mahendra mountain in the South.[118] He appears deified as one of the incarnations of Vishṇu, is described in the *Rāmāyaṇa* as having met Rāma on his way to Ayodhyā after his marriage, and sustained a defeat at the hands of the latter.[119] He is in tradition the founder of the Malabar Coast which even now is known as Paraśurāma Kshetra. He is credited with having reclaimed the west coast of India, which was before his time submerged in the Arabian Sea. He peopled a portion of the country thus got, with the Brāhmans that he had taken with him. The tradition in Malabar is to the effect that these were the Nambūdiris, whose social and religious customs were, as is held among them, dictated by this *rishi*. It is also stated that Malabar owes to him the Bhagavatī cult, temples for the goddess numbering 108 built by Paraśurāma himself.

The third instance of a missionary sage, though he may not be considered to be quite as historical a character as the previous two, is Uśanas Śukra. He was perhaps the descendant of Uśanas Kāvya who figures as a *rishi* in the *Rig-Veda*.[120] He belonged to the Bhārgava line, and is referred to as the powerful priest of the non-Aryan peoples, Daitya, Dānava, and Asura. He is styled therefore as the *Daitya Guru*. This character becomes mythical because there is frequent allusion to his intimate connexion with the Asuras in their quarrels with the Devas.

XXVI

Maritime Activity

Whereas after a study of the previous period one may at the most be constrained to give the opinion that " it is not easy to refuse to recognize here the existence of larger vessels with many oars used for sea-voyages ",[121] there is evidence in the Epic age that the Aryas were fully acquainted with the use of ships on seas. In the *Pañchavimśa Brāhmaṇa*[122] we read that "those who go to sea without boat do not come out of that". "As men who desire to cross the sea get into boats full of provisions, the performers of *satra* (sacrifice) use the *trishṭup* formula."[123] These passages may show that navigation of the sea on boats was a practice prevalent in the age of the Brāhmaṇas. Instances of sea-voyage are not wanting in the *Mahābhārata*,[124] in which we come across "merchants" and "perturbed seas", boats "tossed about in the ocean", "merchants crossing the seas", etc. The Aryas had, besides, knowledge of some of the features pertaining to the sea, as the following observations in the *Rāmāyaṇa* go to show.[125] "The rivers empty themselves in the ocean which is the lord of waters." "The sea heaves in the full-moon night with roaring breakers." The Pāṇḍavas are said to have gone on a holy pilgrimage to the various shrines in India. It is possible that a portion of this itinerary was accomplished along the sea-coasts. At any rate, the description shows that they were fully acquainted with the sea. But the sea is referred to as the great friend of the Asuras, and perhaps sea-voyage was not undertaken by the orthodox, as it is stated that Brāhmans who go across the sea are reckoned as outcastes.[126]

It strikes one with surprise that the Aryas had cared little to develop their maritime activity. Confined to their cloister, immersed in intellectual and spiritual pursuits, with their thoughts directed towards the attainment of the Divine, the Aryas may not have naturally the inclination to think of the material gains that the sea would have afforded them. It did not appeal to the poet in his account of Rāma's expedition of Lanka, that a ship could be employed in getting to the island. Raghu, the ancestor of Rāma, while marching against the Persians, is made by Kāḷidāsa to prefer the round-about land-route to a passage across the ocean.[127] Perhaps these are accounted for by the fact that sea-voyage was considered sinful, being a profession forbidden to the orthodox Aryas. The Dharmaśāstras altogether forbid sea-voyages to the "twice-born" and prescribe very hard penances for the transgression of the rules. It was an art specialized by the non-Aryas famous in antiquity as the merchants who conducted the maritime trade between India and the sister-nations in Asia. Sea-voyages were also avoided because they were more tedious, risky, and expensive. As Kauṭilya says,[128] "Water-routes are liable to destruction, are impermanent, and are a source of imminent danger; whereas land-routes are of the reverse nature. Hence, the former are to be avoided though they may be productive of larger profits."

XXVII

Linguistic Changes

The language of the Vedas gradually changed into Sanskrit, which came to be the spoken language of the Aryas. The spoken language became subjected to great changes both in vocabulary and in literary form. The general changes that were brought on the Vedic language, its relation to the classical Sanskrit which was evolved later, and the differences between the two languages may thus be summarized[129]: "Its grammatical peculiarities run through all departments: euphonic rules, word-formation and composition, declension, conjugation and syntax. These peculiarities are partly such as characterise an older language, consisting in a greater originality of forms and the like, and partly such as characterise a language which is still in the bloom and vigour of life, its freedom untrammelled by other rules than those of common usage, and which, not like the classical Sanskrit, passed into oblivion as native spoken dialect, became merely a conventional medium of communication among the learned, being forced, as it were, into a mode of regularity by long and exhausting grammatical treatment. The dissimilarity existing between the two in respect of the stock of words of which each is made up is, to say the least, not less marked. Not single words alone but whole classes of derivations and roots, with the families that are formed from them, which the Veda exhibits in frequent and familiar use, are wholly wanting or have left but faint traces in the classical dialect, and this to such an extent as seems to demand, if the two be actually related to one another directly as mother and daughter, a longer interval between them than we should be inclined to assume, from the character and degree of the grammatical, and more especially the phonetic, differences."

These changes were partly due to the constant contact with non-Aryan dialects, and the Sanskrit language lost its ancient and natural character to become modern and artificial. The old language had been popularized and had led to the growth of a large number of Prākrit dialects. As Keith observes, the factor of race-mixture must have played an important part in the creation of the Prākrits, but he says not of course in the sense that these represent the treatment of the Vedic by the aborigines on whom it was forced by their masters, but as influencing the racial character and speech-capacity and habits of the Aryan tribes. It is not easy to determine when the Prākrits came to be formed, but they may be placed approximately to the close of the Epic period and the pre-Buddhist age. During the epoch of the Buddha Sanskrit had perhaps ceased to be ordinarily the spoken language, and was the language pre-eminently of the learned and the priestly class. Prākrits were the more popular language of the masses.

We have seen how in the Rig-Vedic age the non-Aryan language was unintelligible to the Aryas. In the Epic age, however, the two peoples are seen to understand each other. In the *Pañcha-viṁśa Brāhmaṇa* the *Vrātyas* are described as speaking *Dīkshita-vācham* (the language of the initiated), though they were un-initiated. Rāvaṇa spoke in language intelligible to Sītā. He is said to have approached her taking the guise of a hermit and reciting Vedic texts in order to inspire confidence in her. Asura chieftains Vātāpi and Ilvala spoke to Agastya in Sanskrit and even non-Aryan women are represented as conversing freely with the Aryan princes of the age. The non-Aryas who spoke Sanskrit may have committed mistakes in the pronunciation of Sanskrit words and in grammatical construction (*apaśabda*). "The necessities of intercourse compel the aborigines to use a broken 'pigeon' form of the language of a superior civilization." But it is said of Hanumān that his enunciation was clear. He did not mispronounce words and spoke like one well versed in grammar. "As generations pass, this mixed jargon of the non-Aryas more and more approximates to this model, and in process of time the old aboriginal language is forgotten and dies a natural death. It is only in the south of India, where aboriginal languages are associated with a high degree of culture, that they have held their own."

NOTES TO PART III

[1] *Śatapatha Brāhmaṇa*, i, 4, 1, 10, 13, 14, 17.

[2] *R.V.*, i, 18, 1 ; i, 126, 1 f.

Amandāntsomān prabhare manīshā Sindhāvadhi kshiyato Bhāvyasya | yo me sahasramamimītasavānatūrtorājāśrava ichchamānah | śatam rājñonādhamānasya nishkācchatam aśvān prayatāntsadya ādam | śatam Kakshīvām, asurasya gonām diviśravojaramātatāna || Upamāśyāvah Śvanayena dattā vadhūmanto daśaratha so' asthuh || See also *Śānkhāyana Śrauta Sūtra*, xvi, 4, 5.

[3] *Harivamśa*, chap. 94.

[4] *Bhīshma Parva*, 9.

Perum chōṟu payanta perunāḷirukkaippūm
panarpalanappuhār nagar vendan. (*Śilappadikāram.*)

Iraimpatinmarumporutukalattoḷiyapperuñ chōṟṟu mikupadam varaiyādu koḍuttōy. (*Puṟanānūṟu*, 2).

In the above passages a Chera king is praised as having supplied rations of rice to the contending parties in the Great Mahābhārata War.

[5] *A.V.*, v, 22, 5–14.

[6] *Rāmāyaṇa*, Kish. Kāṇḍ., 40–3.

[7] *Harsha Charita*, Tr. Cowell and Thomas, p. 230.

[8] *Mahābhārata* : Śānti, 58, 100–5.

[9] *Vishṇu Purāṇa*, i, 13. *Kākakrishṇotihṛsvāngī hṛsvabāhuh mahā hanuh | hrasvavān nimnanāsāgro raktākshah tāmramūrdhajah ||*

[10] *Bhāgavata Purāṇa*, iv, 14, 44.

[11] *Mahābhārata* : Śānti, op. cit. ; *Padma Purāṇa*, ii, 27, 42–3.

[12] *Vishṇu Purāṇa*, ii, 74. Khadru is mentioned as *Sarpamātā* in *Tait. Sam.*, i, 2.

[13] *ZDMG.*, for 1912, p. 72 n.

[14] The conversion of the Nāgas of Kashmir to Buddhism is thus narrated :—
Madhyantika, a disciple of the Buddha, wished to convert the Nāgas in the region. But the Nāgas put obstacles in his way and tried to cause injury to the *Sthavira* (Teacher) in various ways. They rained down arrows on the *Sthavira*, but, by the virtue and penance of the teacher, they became converted into soft and sweet-scented flowers. The Nāgas were surprised at this and said : "As one sees those summits of a glacier remain unchanged though struck by the rays of the sun, those summits of mountains on which all is harmless, so the drenching rain fell as a shower of various flowers, and the rain of arrows falling from the sky has become garlands of flowers." "The fire did not burn his body, nor did the weapons or poison harm it."

The Nāgas in great astonishment went to the *Sthavira* and inquired in all humility what he wanted, and the following is the conversation :—

STHAVIRA : Give me this place.

NĀGAS : A stone is not much of an offering.

STH.: The Blessed One has predicted that this place would be mine. This Kashmir country being a good country for meditation, henceforth, it is mine.

NĀG.: Did the Blessed One say so?

STH.: He did.

NĀG.: How much land shall be offered to you?

STH.: As much as I cover when seated cross-legged.

NĀG.: So be it, venerable one.

The *Sthavira* sat cross-legged and filled up the whole land as Trivikrama did in the case of Mahābali. (Rockhill, *Life of the Buddha*, pp. 165 f.)

[15] *Encyclopædia of Religion and Ethics*, citing Grunwedel, p. 208.

[16] *Maṇimekalai*, viii, 54, 60.

[17] *Jātaka*, vi, 150.

[18] Ibid., iv, 281.

[19] Nāgadwīpa is to the south-west of *Madhyadeśa*. (Alberuni, *India*, p. 296.)

[20] *Rāmāyaṇa*, Bāla Kāṇḍ., 5, 20; Āraṇya Kāṇḍ., 32, 13. Griffith's Tr., iv, 205. Ananta is mentioned as the chief of the Nāgas in the *Bhagavat Gītā*. Dharmendra is the best of the Nāgas in the *Jaina Sūtras*. Kārtavīryārjuna is said to have captured Māhishmatī from Kārkoṭaka the chief of the Nāgas, as we read in the *Mahābhārata* (iii, 66). Cf. *Kārkoṭakasya Nāgasya Damayantyāh Nalasya cha Rituparṇasya Rājarshch kīrtanam kalināśanam*, etc., where we find the relation of Naḷa and Nāgas.

[21] *Śilappadikāram*, i, 19, 20, 21–3. The Tangkhuls, a section of the northern Nāgas, were also skilful weavers of cloth. See Hodson, *Pr. Cult. of India*, p. 29. The extent of the Nāga country is thus given in the *Śilappadikāram*: *Nāga nannāḍu nanūṛi yōśanai viyanpātalattu vīḻntu keḍaitum* (The prosperous country of the Nāgas 400 *yojanas* in extent will perish sinking to the nether region). *Yojana* is eight miles. Their abode was on the hills, as we read in the *Śilappadikāram*: *Nakkaśāraṇar Nāgar vāḻmalai*.

[22] *Nīla nāgan nalkiya kalingam*.

[23] *Journal of Literature and Science*, xiii, pt. ii, art. 4.

[24] *Kalittokai*, iv, 1–5; xvi, 1–7.

[25] From *Ōḷa*, meaning wave of the sea.

[26] *Mahāvamśa*, 25, 30; 33, 42. The expulsion of the Kōḷs by the Nāgas should be assigned to pre-Buddhistic times, for according to early Buddhist traditions recorded by Yuan Chwang, Ceylon of the Buddha's time was peopled by the Nāgas "who set forth their precious commodities with labels of prices attached to them". Beal, *Life of Hiuen Tsiang*, 38, 101.

The Ōviyars were chivalrous and dashing warriors, furious like tigers in the battlefield.—*Śirupāṇāṛṛuppaḍai*, ii, 121–2.

The Paratavar, "well fed on fish and flesh and armed with the bow and arrow strike terror among the enemies by their rapid marches."—*Madurai Kāñji*, ll. 140 f.

[27] *Venriverkiḻḻikku Nāganāḍāḷ vonran magaḷ Pīlivaḷai tan payanta punirriḷankuḷavi*.—*Maṇimekalai*, xiv, 24.

[28] *Epigraphist's Reports for Southern Circle* for 1911.

[29] "Sea Power in Early South Indian History," by Professor S. V. Venkateswara, p. 8, in the *Journal of the Mythic Society*, Bangalore, for 1926.

[30] *Vāyu Purāṇa*, 62, 137–48.

[31] Kabandha, a Dānava chief, is also styled a Rākshasa.

[32] *Rāmāyaṇa*: Bāla Kāṇḍ., 11, 6; Āraṇ. Kāṇḍ., 39.

[33] *Mahābhārata*: Ādi, 67, 7. *Rākshasāścha Pulastyasya Vānarāh Kinnarāh tathā | Yakshāścha manujavyāghra putrāh tasya cha dhīmatah* ||

[34] Sund. Kāṇḍ., 51, 2 and 3. Hanumān tells Rāvaṇa: "*Rākshasendra Harīśah tvām bhrātā kuśalam abravīt*" | In Yud. Kāṇḍ., 20, 10, Rāvaṇa sends word to Sugrīva: "*Tathā hi me bhrātrsamo Harīśa.*"

[35] Rice, *Gazetteer of Mysore*, i, 277. The words *Vānara* and *Rākshasa* are thus derived in the *Jaina Padma Purāṇa* and in the *Pampa Rāmāyaṇa* :—

Tathā Vānarachinhena cchatrā divi niveśinā
Vidyādharāh gatāh khyātim Vānarā iti vishṭapè (vi, 215)
Rākshasastanayo jāto manovegāngadhāriṇah
Rākshaso nāma yasyāyam nāmnā vamśah prakīrtyate (v, 378).

[36] Udyoga, 29, 30 and 31.

[37] Havell, *Hist. of Aryan Rule in India*, p. 42.

[38] The Forest was chosen for its seclusion, inspiration, and a calm communion with Nature and Nature's Gods.

[39] *Rāmāyaṇa*, Bāla Kāṇḍ., 21, 18.

[40] *Rāmāyaṇa*, Ayod. Kāṇḍ., 116, 11 and 13.

[41] *Mahābhārata*, Aśvamedha, 84, 7 ff.

[42] Ibid., Vana Parva, 268 and 269. [43] *Rāmāyaṇa*, Kish. Kāṇḍ., 16 ff.

[44] Ibid., Āraṇ. Kāṇḍ., 11, 55 ff. [45] Ibid., 74.

[46] Ibid., Yud. Kāṇḍ., 16 and 17.

[47] See Viswanatha, *International Law in Ancient India*, chap. 8.

[48] Bhīshma Parva : Jambūkhaṇḍanirmāṇa, 1.

[49] *Rāmāyaṇa*, Kish. Kāṇḍ., 15, 17, 18, 23, 24, 44.

Parāngmukham vadham kritvā ko nu prāptastvayā guṇah |
Vishaye vā pure vā te yadā nāpakaromyaham ||
Damaśśamah kshamā dharmo dhritih satyam parākramah |
Pārthivānām guṇā rājan daṇḍaśchāpyaparādhishu ||
Māmihāpratiyudhyantam anyena cha samāgatam |
Udāsīneshu yosmāsu vikramaste prakāśitah ||

[50] *Rāmāyaṇa*, Sund. Kāṇḍ., 52, 5 and 6.

Rājadharmaviruddham cha lokavritteścha garhitam |

[51] Ibid., 52, 5 and 21.

Vadham na kurvanti parāvarajñā | *Dūtasya santo vasudhātipendrāh* || *Sādhurvā yadi vāsādhuh paraiesha samarpitah* | *Bruvan parārtham paravān na dūto vadham arhati* ||

[52] Ibid., 52, 15. *Vairūpyamangeshu keśābhighāto mauṇḍyam tathā lakshaṇasannipātah* | *Etān hi dūte pravadanti daṇḍān vadham hi dūtasya na nah śrutopi* || For rules of international conduct relating to Diplomatic Agents, the reader may be referred to the author's *International Law in Ancient India*, chaps. on Diplomacy and Agents, Instruments and Methods of Warfare.

[53] *Rāmāyaṇa*, Yud. Kāṇḍ., 63, 4 and 13.

Pradhamam vai mahārāja krityam etadachintitam |
Kevalam vīradarpeṇa nānubandho vichāritah ||
Hitānubandham ālochya kāryākāryam ihātmanah |
Rājā sahārthatatvajñah sachivaih sa hi jīvati ||

[54] *Rāmāyaṇa*, Āraṇ. Kāṇḍ., 37, 2.

Sulabhāh purushāh rājan satatam priyavādinah |
Apriyasya tu pathyasya vaktā śrotā cha durlabhah ||

Rāvaṇa says in reply (40, 2): *Na chet karoshi Mārīcha hanmi tvām ahamadya vai* |

[55] Rāvaṇa: *Asmin kāle tu yadyuktam tadidānīm vidhīyatām* | *Gatam tu nānuśochanti gatam tu gatameva hi* ||

Kumbhakarṇa: *Bandhubhāvādabhihitam bhrātrsnehāccha pārthiva* | *sadrśam yattu kālesmin kartum snigdhena bandhunā* ||

[56] Examples are: Tāḍaka and Mārīcha in Bāla Kāṇḍa, Virādha and Kabandha in Āraṇya Kāṇḍa, and Rāvaṇa and his brothers.

[57] Ādi Parva, Amśāvataraṇa, 63.

[58] Ibid., 168, 17. *Viśeshato matsakāśe mā prakāśaya nīchatām | Uttamastrī-guṇopetā bhajedhā varavarṇinī* ||

[59] Maṇalūr is in Tinnevelly District. There are two different readings, Maṇalūr and Maṇipura (Ādi, 63).

[60] *Mahābhārata* : Virāṭa Parva, 77, 15.

[61] *Rāmāyaṇa*, Uttara Kāṇḍa, 9, 6, 7, and 28. The account varies in the *Mahābhārata* where Rāvaṇa is the son by Pushpotkaṭā (Vana, 276).

[62] Virāṭa is Matsya country. Perhaps the kingdom had the fish-banner.

[63] *Mahābhārata* : Āśramavāsika, 27.

[64] This is perhaps the earliest passage where we have reference to the wearing of white garment by widows, a practice that continues to this day.

[65] *Br. Up*., vi, 4, 14–18.

[66] Vana, 192, 31. *Śvetah krtayuge varṇah pītastretāyuge mama rakto dvāparamāsādya krshṇah kaliyuge tathā* |

[67] *Sema Nāgas*, p. 95.

[68] *Bhagavat Gītā*, i, 40 and 41. *Adharmābhibhavāt Krishṇa pradushyanti kulastriyah | Strīshu dushṭ... Vārshṇeya jāyate varṇasankarah | Sankaro narakāyaiva etc* ||

[69] *Mahābhārata* : Vana, 182, 21, 31, and 32.

[70] Ibid., 314, 10.

[71] Ibid., Śānti, 78, 38. *Apāre yo bhavet pāram apḷave yo bhavet pḷavah | Śūdro vāpyadi vāpyanyah sarvadhā mānamarhati* ||

[72] Ibid., Sabhā, 36, 41 ; *Rāmāyaṇa* : Bāla Kāṇḍa, 12, 16.

[73] *Bhagavat Gītā*, iv, 13. *Chāturvarṇyam mayā srishṭam guṇakarma vibhāgaśah* |

[74] *Anāryatā nishṭhuratā krūratā nishkr...yātmatā* |
Purusham vyanjayantīha loke kalushayonijam ||

[75] *Vyuncharantyāh patim nāryā adyaprabhriti pātakam* |
Bhrūṇahatyā samam ghoram bhavishyatyasukhāvaham ||
Pativratām etadeva bhavitā pātakam bhuvi |

[76] *Ait. Br*., iii, 23. *Vedepyevam śrūyate ekasya bahvyo jāyā naikasyā eva bahavah santi* | See *Mahābhārata*, Ādi, 210, 27, cited *infra*.

[77] Polyandry is of two kinds : (*a*) " Tibetan," where a woman has all the brothers for her husbands ; (*b*) " Malabar " form, in which the husbands need not be brothers, as in the first case. The latter is apparently more primitive than the former.

[78] *Mahābhārata*, Ādi, 135.

[79] As Hunter writes, " It is likely that the Scythic, Nāga, and the non-Aryan races with their indifference to human suffering, their polyandric households, and the worship of the terrific aspects of the divine, have left their mark deep in the terrorizing of Hindu religion and in the degradation of women."—*Indian Empire*, p. 238.

[80] Ādi, 210, 27–31.

[81] *Mahābhārata*, Ādi, 128.

[82] See section 1 of Chapter II.

[83] *R.V*., x, 85, 26, and 46.

[84] Ibid., x, 86, 10.

[85] Daśaratha is despised as *Striyā vākya vaśam gatah* in Ayod. Kāṇḍ., 21, 2.

Adrshṭapūrvā yā nāryah Bhāskareṇāpi veśmasu |
Dadrśuh tā mahārāja janā yātāh pure prati ||
Mahābhārata, Śalya, 29, 74.

Yā na śakyā purā drishṭum bhūtairākāśagairapi |
Tāmadya Sītām paśyanti rājamārgagatā janāh ||
Rāmāyaṇa, Ayod. Kāṇḍ., 33, 8.

[86] *Vyasaneshu cha krichchreshu no yuddhe na svayaṁvare* |
Na kratau na vivāhe cha darśanam dushyate striyah ||
Rāmāyaṇa, Yud. Kāṇḍ., 116, 28.

[87] *Śat. Br.*, i, 3, 1, 9, 12, 13.

[88] *Mait. Sam.*, iii, 6, 3. They are classified as "evil beings". "The Brāhmaṇas clearly indicate a gradual decline in their position." *Vedic Index*, i, 486.

[89] *Rāmāyaṇa*, Ayod. Kāṇḍ, 12, 102.
Dhigastu yoshitā nāma śaḍhāh svārthaparāh sadā |
Na bravīmi striyah sarvāh Bharatasyaiva mātaram ||

[90] Ibid., Āraṇ. Kāṇḍ., 13, 5. *Samastham anurañjanti vishamastham tyajanti hi* | Cf. *Milinda Praśna*, iv, 16, where women are classified as unstable, fickle and mean.

[91] Ibid., Āraṇ. Kāṇḍ., 45, 30. *Vimuktadharmāh chapalāh tīkshṇā bhedakarā striyah* |

[92] There is perhaps an example of the Gāndharva form of marriage in *R.V.*, i, 112, 19, where Vimada carries off Purumitrā with her consent but against the will of her father.

[93] *Ait. Ār.*, v, 3, 3. These exceptions are seen in *sagdhi* (common dinner) and *sapīti* (common drink).

[94] *Rāmāyaṇa*, Bāla Kāṇḍa, 59, 14. [95] Ibid., Ayod. Kāṇḍa, 87, 15.

[96] *Ataśchaitām avasthām prāptasya . . . etadapi karma kurvatah nāghasparśa ityabhiprāyah* | Com. on *Ch. Up.*, i, 10.

[97] *Manusmriti*, x, 104 f.

[98] *Mahābhārata*, Vana, 276, 13. *Sarve vedavidah śūrāh sarve sucharitavratāh* |

[99] *Rāmāyaṇa*, Āran. Kāṇḍa, 17, 24.
Vibhīshaṇastu dharmātmā na tu Rākshasacheshṭitah |

[100] Ibid., Yud. Kāṇḍa, 109, 23. [101] Ibid.

[102] *Ait. Br.*, ii, 3, 19. The story of Jābāla Satyakāma of the *Chchāndogya Upanishad*, who is said to be of "unknown parentage", will be dealt with *infra* next chapter. Its real significance has been misunderstood.

[103] *Pan. Br.*, xiv, 6, 6. [104] *Chchāndogya Upanishad*, iv, 2.

[105] *Rāmāyaṇa*, Sund. Kāṇḍ., 9, 12; *Mahābhārata*, Vana, 275, 15, where he has *amaratva* and *dhaneśatva*.

[106] The guardians of the "Four Quarters" in the *Atharva-Veda* (v, 27) are Agni (east), Indra (south), Varuṇa (west), and Soma (north).

[107] *Ait. Br.*, i, 21; *R.V.*, ii, 23, 1. The hymn is *Gaṇānām tvā Ganapatim' havāmahe kavim kavīnām upavaśravastamam jyeshṭha rājam Brahmaṇām Brahmaṇaspatih ānaśrṇvan ūtibhissīdasādhanam* |

[108] It is possible, as Hunter holds, "that the later aspects of the worship of Śiva combined the Brāhmanical doctrine of a personal god with non-Aryan bloody rites." *Ind. Emp.*, 238.

Rudra in Sanskrit is synonymous with red. The Dravidian word for red is *śiva*, identical with *rudra*. The following lines by Māṇikkvāśagar intended to be used for the play with balls (*ammānai*) which South Indian girls indulge in is interesting in this connexion :—

"With bracelets tinkling sound, while earrings wave, while jetty locks
Dishevelled fall, while honey flows and beetles hum,
The Ruddy One who wears the ashes white, whose home
None reach or know, who dwells in every place, to loving ones
The true, the Sage whom hearts untrue still deem untrue,
Who in Ai Āṛu dwells, sing and praise, *Ammānai* see."

Pope's Tr. *Māṇikkavāśagar.*

Though the above fact may not lend much weight to a plausible theory that the worship of Śiva in its later forms may have been borrowed by the Aryas from the Dravidians, the evidence is clear enough of the influence of the one cult on the other so far as the worship of this deity is concerned.

Śiva seems to have held the first place among the Gods before the period of the *Rāmāyaṇa*, e.g. Kausalyā says: *Mayārchitā devagaṇā Śivādayah* (Ayod. Kāṇḍ., 25, 45). The transference of the chieftaincy from Śiva to Vishṇu is perhaps indicated in a story which says that in a quarrel that took place between Śiva and Vishṇu as to their comparative strength it was the latter that triumphed (Bāla Kāṇḍa).

[109] *Rāmāyaṇa*, Sund. Kāṇḍ., 10.

[110] *Arthaśāstra*, p. 29. Cf. *chārachakshur mahīpatih*. In the *Atharva-Veda* we have (iv, 6, 1), *Brāhmaṇo jajñe prathamo daśaśirsho daśāsyah*, explaining the origin of the Brāhmaṇa. The ten heads assigned to the Brāhmaṇa in the *mantra* is interesting, and it may give us a clue to one of the various explanations of the word *Daśagrīva*. In the *Arthaśāstra* we read, *Indrasya hi mantriparishad rishīṇām sahasram | tat chakshuḥ | tasmādiyam dvyaksham sahasrākshamāhuh ||* The Jaina *Pampa Rāmāyaṇa* accounts for the ten faces of Rāvaṇa by describing that in the room in which he was born there was a mirror with ten facets, and the head of Rāvaṇa was reflected in all these, and therefore it was said that he had ten heads though in reality he had only one head.

[111] *Śuk. yaj. Ved.*, v, 2.

[112] In the *Maṇimekalai*, we have the following forms of disposing of the dead: cremation, exposure, burial, cave-burial in natural pits, and jar-burial.

[113] *Rāmāyaṇa*, Āraṇ. Kāṇḍ., 4, 20.

> *Avaṭe chāpi mām Rāma prakshipya kuśalī vraja |*
> *Rakshasām gatasatvānām esha dharmah sanātanah ||*

[114] *Rāmāyaṇa*, Āraṇ. Kāṇḍ., 11, 83.

> *Dakshiṇā dikkritā yena śaraṇyā puṇyakarmaṇā |*

[115] *A.V.*, ii, 32–3. Agastya appears as *Māna* (measured) in *R.V.*, vii, 33, 13. This word is perhaps the same as the word used for "measure" in the Veda. For this reason, possibly, Agastya is even to-day in the Hindu imagination a very short *rishi*.

[116] Nacchinārkiniyar on *Tolkāppiyam*, by Araśan Shaṇmukanar, p. 106.

[117] The names of the twelve disciples of Agastya are mentioned as: Tolkāppiyar, Ādan Kōṭṭaśan, Duralingam, Śemputchey, Vaiyāpikan, Vāyppiyan, Panamparān, Kālaramban, Avinayan, Kākkapadiniyan, Natrattan, and Vāmanan.

[118] *Mahābhārata*, Śānti, 48, 64 f.

> *Trissapta krtvah prithvīm krtvā nikshatriyām prabhuh |*
> *Dakshiṇām aśvamedhānte Kāśyapāyādadattatah ||*

[119] *Rāmāyaṇa*, Bāla Kāṇḍ.

[120] *R.V.*, viii, 14.

[121] *Vedic Index*, i, 461. In the *Rāmāyaṇa* contrivances of various kinds are mentioned for crossing the waters: *plava, nau, duroṇa*, and *sanghāṭa* (Ayod. Kāṇḍ., ii, 55).

[122] *Pan. Br.*, xiv, 5, 17. *Yo vā apḷavah samudram prasnāti na sa tata udeti |*

[123] *Ait. Br.*, vi, 21. *Tadyathā sairāvalīm nāvam pārakāmāh samāroheyuh evamevaitā trshṭubhah samārohanti |*

[124] e.g. *Vaṇikjanānām kshubhito yathārṇavah* (Droṇa, 26, 66).
Vibhrashṭā naurivārṇave . . . (ibid., 45, 8).
Tīrtvā samudram vaṇijah samrddhā (*Saup.*, 10, 23).

[125] *Rāmāyaṇa*, Bāla Kāṇḍ, 17 ; Ayod. Kāṇḍa, 5.

[126] *Surārinil:yah śaśvat sāgarah saritām patih.* (*Mahābhārata*, Śānti, 76, 13.) See profession forbidden for the Brāhmans *infra*, Part IV.

[127] *Raghuvamśa*, iv, 50. *Pārasīkān tato jetum pratasthe sthalavartmanā* |

[128] *Arthaśāstra*, p. 300.
Samudragatih asārvakālikah prakrshṭabhayayonih | *nishpratikāraścha vāripathah* |

[129] *Journal of American Oriental Society*, iii, 296.

PART IV

THE EPOCH OF MODERN HINDUISM

THE EPOCH OF MODERN HINDUISM

I

KINGDOMS—ARYAN AND NON-ARYAN

In the Buddhist age we find mention of non-Aryan kingdoms not much inferior to those of the Aryas in splendour and prosperity. Of the sixteen great kingdoms (*mahājanapadāh*) mentioned in Buddhist literature[1] some are distinctly non-Aryan. These were Anga, Magadha, Kāśi, Kosala, Vajji, Malla, Cheḍi, Vamśa, Kuru, Pāñchāla, Maccha, Śūrasena, Aśśaka, Avanti, Gandhāra and Kambhoja. The earliest dynasty known in Indian historical period—the Śaiśunāga—was non-Aryan. The Purāṇas say in regard to this line of Kings that its founder would make an end of the Kshatriyas.[2] We also read that the kings of the earth after Mahāpadma will be Śūdra in origin; and the Nandas were Śūdras and perhaps of a servile class. The king of Kosala, Pasenadi, was evidently not a Kshatriya, but he is styled a rāja and was not inferior to his Aryan fellow-kings. The Mauryas were certainly of very low extraction and, if we may believe the story in the *Divyāvadāna*,[3] Aśoka was the son of Bindusāra by a barber-woman. The Buddhist period discloses also the existence of some states with republican institutions, if all of them may not really be republics,[4] such as the Śākiyas of Kapilavāstu, Bhaggas of Sumśumāra hill, Būḷis of Allakappa, Kalamas of Kisaputta, Koḷiyas of Rāmagāma, Mallas of Kuśinara, and of Pava, Moriyas of Pippaḷāvana, Videhas of Mithila, and Licchavis of Veśāli. Some of these were non-Aryan republics as their names signify. Further, the inscriptions of Aśoka disclose the names of the Dravidian kingdoms of the Dekhan which were looked on by the Maurya emperor as outside the sphere of his authority, being independent border kingdoms.[5] In the same period there was the establishment in the north-west frontier, of the semi-Indian provinces of the Indo-Bactrian and Indo-Parthian princes; the firm rule of the Kushāṇas in Hindustan; the settlement of the Kshatrapas in the west; and the invasions of the wandering tribes from outside, such as the Śakas, Yuechis, and the Huns. Thus, all our authorities show that non-Aryan kingdoms were advanced in the period under survey, and India was subjecting herself to foreign influences. Though these may not have left any permanent or far-reaching marks on the cultural institutions of India, they certainly gave a new mould to her political life, and fashioned the social structure by introducing into it new blood and new ideas, which has made Indian society more complex and her social institutions more complicated.

II

The Influence of Buddhism and Jainism

The new religions of the Buddha and Mahāvīra promised a good and easy substitute for the old ceremonial religion of the Vedas. They seemed to many to open the door to a new era, not only of hope, but of promise. Though in their original form they were only a modification of Brāhmanism, they soon grew to be separate systems of easy devotion. The Buddha's message of love, renunciation and peace attracted numerous recruits from among those who got frightened by the difficulties of Brāhmanical science. The Śākyas were an Aryan clan, and the founder of Buddhism was an Aryan Kshatriya prince of the solar race. But these had mingled themselves with the non-Aryan folk and accepted many of their habits and ways of living They were, therefore, not allowed to intermarry with other Aryan clans and seem to have developed the un-Aryan system of endogamy.[5a] Thus, the clan to which Gautama Buddha belonged was itself liberal and tolerant, and it is therefore no wonder that a scion of the Śākya clan should have founded a new religion in which the non-Aryan population possessed a tower of strength. The aspect of Buddhism which appealed most to the non-Aryas was the reduction of the caste distinctions to a dull level, and they should have welcomed the creed of a reformer who held that " whosoever are in bondage to the notions of birth or of lineage, or to the pride of social position or connexion by marriage, they are far from the best wisdom and righteousness ".[6] Hence, there is hardly room for doubting that the ranks of the Buddha were mostly recruited from the lower castes and classes of the Indian society. Buddhism was essentially a religion of the proletariat.

The authority of the Vedas was itself questioned, and people were taught to place their reliance on reason, not revelation, and to realize that efficacy lay in brotherly feeling and universal love rather than in inhuman sacrifices or costly rituals. An attempt was made to overthrow the very fundamental concepts of the Vedic Hindus, as is clear from the new definition of the four Vedas, which, Yuan Chwang says,[7] was current in the Buddhist India of his time. The four Vedas are described as the science of health, architecture for worship and religious ceremonies, war and medicine. These *Upa-Vedas* which were relegated to a subordinate position are seen now to take the first rank, and supersede the traditional classification. As Fergusson writes,[8] it may be said that no Aryan race in the pure form would have been converted to Buddhism or made to accept its main doctrines, for the leading features of that faith, atheism and absence of caste, are essentially non-Aryan. The chief scriptures of Buddhism are not in Sanskrit but in Pāḷi and Māgadhi, the language of the masses. The pillars of the new faith were not the ancient Aryan dynasties of the Indo-Gangetic plain, but the low-born dynasty of Magadha and, later, the Dravidians of Ceylon. The supremacy of Buddhism under Aśoka and the tendency for that religion to become a political religion led naturally to a Brāhmanical reaction the influence of which resulted in a revolt against the " inquisitorial tyranny of Aśoka's system ".[9]

III

The Effect of the Philosophical Systems

There were certain internal tendencies appearing in the Hindu society itself which disclose the innate aptitude of the Arya for accepting the liberal principles of toleration and religious freedom. The non-Aryan and lower classes were given relief with the rapid rise of rationalistic thought and philosophy that characterized the sixth and fifth centuries B.C. The Aryas took the lead [10] in this movement for exemption from the round of ceremonies and for vouchsafing all an approach to the godhead, in whatever station of life one might be, or to whatever class or creed one might belong in the Hindu social classification. The highest spiritual attainment was made possible for every one as a Hindu. Thus, factors external and internal were working for the simplification of the complicated ceremonial system of the previous periods. The orthodox philosophy of the Sãnkhya, Yoga and Vedãnta which enunciate the principle "the same am I to all beings and I am spread out evenly before all", emphasized the importance of *Jñãna* (knowledge divine) over *Karma* (duties). It has been interpreted that the *Bhagavat Gĩtã* [11] gives a secondary place to Vedic lore, because the latter attaches much importance to *vishaya* (subjects) characterized by the "three *guṇas*"—*satva*, *rajas* and *tamas*. Krishṇa advises Arjuna to get rid of these shackles, for "the external forms do not make the monk, it is only an attitude of non-attachment that makes one". The sage and law-giver Yãjñavalkya expresses the same idea in other words. "A man is virtuous not for his abode in the forest; it is only righteous conduct that makes one a hermit." The masses must have profited by the philosophical reaction, for, though the Vedas were prohibited to them, the Darśanas were not, and these latter were not claimed as the monopoly of any particular order in the society. It is true that the Śũdras were not to be allowed, according to the Smritis,[12] to hear the recitation of the Vedic texts, to repeat them, or retain them; and that the priest was, in general, prevented from explaining to them the holy law. But it was recognized that he was free to perform such ceremonies as required only the use of the *mantras* in the Purāṇas,[13] which were found in practice to be as efficacious from the spiritual point of view as those in the Vedic scriptures.

The tendency to question the validity of the Vedic sanction finds ample and emphatic illustration in the following words of the Buddha: "Do not be guided by rumours, by that which is recorded in sacred books, by reasons or deductions which appear to be reasonable or logical simply because of their external appearance of the possible; do not believe because it is the ascetic or teacher that speaks; but when by your personal conviction you recognize that such and such things are bad and to be rejected, that they are blameworthy and that they are fit to be discarded, that they lead to evil and to suffering, you must reject them." [14]

IV

Daiva and Āsura

The old distinction between Deva and Asura which applied at first to the Indian Aryas *versus* the Assyrians, and later to the gods and the demons, does not appear to have held rigorously in this period. The gradual fusion of the two cults, and the influence of the new philosophical systems, added to the force of the rationalistic teachings of the Buddha, led to a broad classification of all practices and observances into *daiva* and *āsura* irrespective of the doers of the deeds. Such practices belonged to the first class as were good and righteous, while the latter included all unwholesome and unrighteous actions. We read in the *Bhagavat Gītā*: "There are only two classes of beings in God's creation—*daiva* and *āsura*." [15]

V

The Doctrine of Transmigration

Both the Sãnkhya and the Vedãnta as well as the Buddhist and Jaina works teach that the soul never dies, but passes through an endless series of lives. It is said to " throw off the old and worn-out clothing, and wear new robes ".[16] This doctrine is known as transmigration. This is held by many scholars as not consonant with the teaching of the Veda and as an innovation in the Aryan religion. It may be observed that, as the Vedas contain the germs of the later philosophical treatises in India, they contain the rudimentary ideas of a doctrine in which the soul of the deceased, instead of being destroyed, appears again enshrouded in a new physical frame. Ancient Indian scriptures contain such a bewildering compound of mysticism, symbolism, magic and religion that it is likely that those that work in the field are apt to lose sight of such features and facts as could not be easily comprehended under their own rules of interpretation and reasoning, as being outside the vision of the Vedic seers and singers of distant antiquity. It is desirable that we take the note of caution sounded by Max Müller,[17] not to adopt " that laziest of all expedients, that of ascribing all that seems barbarous in Indian religion to the influences of the aboriginal inhabitants of the country of whom we know next to nothing ". There is a tendency with scholars to attribute all ideas in Hinduism that seem unaccountable according to accepted notions and theories, to the influence of the non-Aryan peoples.

Bloomfield [18] is of the opinion that the doctrine of transmigration is likely to have been borrowed by Brãhmanical Hinduism from some of the aboriginal non-Aryan tribes of India. We read in the *Cambridge History of India*,[19] "We have no reason to doubt that such ideas were prevalent among the aboriginal tribes with which the Aryans mixed. But these vague ideas are totally inadequate to account for the belief in transmigration, and the theory must, it would seem, have been a discovery of the school of seekers after the nature of truth, who arrived at it on the one side from the popular beliefs of the peoples among whom they lived, and on the other from the conception of the Brāhamaṇas that death could be repeated in the next world." Keith writes that this doctrine "is not an early one in Indian philosophy. Most authorities are agreed that it can be found only in the Upanishads, that is to say, very little before 600 B.C., if indeed at all before. Nor can we safely say that the doctrine as an articulate theory existed long before it appears in the literature. We must not exaggerate the fact that the Buddha accepted the doctrine into a view that it was then a universal philosophical belief".[20]

Let us examine whether there are in the Vedic scriptures any evidences of the doctrine of transmigration. The theory of the soul being enshrouded in a new body is hinted in a funeral hymn of the *Yajur-Veda* and of the *Atharva-Veda*[21] which is addressed to the dead body, and which reads thus: "This garment has now come first to thee; remove that one that thou didst wear here before; knowing, do thou follow along with what is offered and bestowed, where it is given thee variously among men of various connexion." After this prayer, a new cloth is thrown over the body. In the above passage is suggested the simile of the soul wearing a new body, as the man is made to wear a new cloth. After death the man was supposed to be split up into three parts, one going to the earth, one to the region of the sun and wind, and the third being *aja* (unborn).[22] This suggests the idea of rebirth for the soul. The dead body is thus addressed in two passages of the *Pig-Veda*[23]: "Go according to thy merit (*dharma*) to earth or heaven." This may probably indicate that the Aryas had knowledge of the principle that was developed later, that the nature of the rebirth depended on the quality of the deeds done or virtue attained in the previous birth.

"Leaving sin and evil, (the soul of) the dead man seeks anew his dwelling, and bright with glory wears another body." [24] "Varuṇa, O my Lord, have mercy on me; may I not enter again this house of clay." [25] In these passages there is reference to the soul taking a new body which is described as the earthy tenement. Ushas, the goddess of dawn, is addressed in two passages of the Veda as "the one that is born again". It cannot be doubted that *punarjāyamāna* and *punarbhu* as applied to this deity have some reference to a belief in a "new birth", besides being the natural observation of a daily phenomenon. These texts show that the Vedic Aryas were acquainted with some of the elementary ideas of metempsychosis. Out of such hazy ideas arose the fully developed doctrine of transmigration. The evolution of this principle may have received an impetus from the view current among the animists that the souls on the death of men can pass into new forms, animal or vegetable.[26] In the light of the evidence adduced above, it will not be right to suppose that the doctrine of transmigration was borrowed by the Aryas from the non-Aryan or aboriginal peoples of India. It may be a heritage of both the Aryan and non-Aryan peoples, and is the cornerstone of the religion of the Hindus as well as the Buddhists.

VI

Social Classification

The social grades among the people of this period show some more complexity than in the previous epoch. The Jātakas show that besides the usual four castes there were certain low tribes (*hīnajātiyo*) and low trades (*hinaśippāni*), and lastly, the Chaṇḍāḷas, Pulkaśas and slaves.[27] Towards the close of the period we find foreigners who had settled permanently on the Indian soil, such as Śakas, Pahlavas, etc. There was apparently a tendency to bring all classes of people into the social system. But Rhys Davids [28] goes a little too far when he says, "poor men could become nobles and both could become

Brāhmans," that "the fact of intermarriage is undoubted", and that "the greatest chasm between the proudest Kshatriya on the one hand and the lowest Chaṇḍāḷa on the other was bridged over by a number of imperceptible stages". Such quotations as he could give from the Jātakas show, no doubt, that changes of occupation were not uncommon and that there were irregular unions, the offspring of such unions sometimes styling themselves as Kshatriyas and Brāhmans.

It is clear that some confusion had risen in society about the caste system. The following conversation in the *Ambaṭṭha Sutta of the Dīgha Nikāya* [29] is interesting in this connexion :—

BUDDHA : What think you, Ambaṭṭha ? Suppose a young Kshatriya should have connexion with a Brāhmaṇa maiden and from their intercourse a son should be born. Now would the son thus born to the Brāhmaṇa maiden of the Kshatriya youth receive a seat and water from the Brāhmans ?

AMBAṬṬHA : Yes, he would, Gotama.

BUD. : But would the Brāhmans allow him to partake of the feast offered to the dead or of the rice boiled in milk or of the offerings to the gods or of the food sent as a present ?

AMB. : Yes, they would, Gotama.

BUD. : But would the Brāhmans teach him their scriptures or not ?

AMB. : They would, Gotama.

BUD. : But would he be shut off or not from their women ?

AMB. : He would not be shut off.

BUD. : But would the Kshatriyas allow him to receive the consecration ceremony of one of their kind ?

AMB. : Certainly not, Gotama.

BUD. : Why not that ?

AMB. : Because he is not of pure descent on the mother's side.

The Buddha concludes the conversation with the remarks, "Then, Ambaṭṭha, whether one compares women with women, or men with men, the Kshatriyas are superior and the Brāhmans inferior."

There is clearly an attempt made by the lower orders in the society to decry the merits of the Brāhmaṇa caste and to extol the Kshatriyas, probably, because they formed the royal caste. The Kshatriyas are described in the *Anguttara Nikāya* [30] as "fair in colour, fine in presence and stately to behold". In the Jātakas, Brāhmans are spoken of as "low-born" when compared with the Kshatriyas.[31] The same spirit is in evidence in the Upanishads [32] where we have instances of Kshatriyas possessing more religious wisdom than the Brāhmans. Pravāhaṇa Jaivali, a kshatriya sage, asked Śvetaketu Āruṇeya five questions which puzzled the latter. Śvetaketu went to his father Gautama and said, "That fellow of a Rājanya asked me five questions, and I could not answer any of them." Gautama being himself perplexed went to the king, who replied, "This knowledge did not go to any Brāhmaṇa before you and the teaching belonged in all the world to the Kshatriya class alone." The famous Ajātaśatru king of Kāśi is also said to have instructed a proud Brāhmaṇa in the *Ātmavidyā*. The same fact is illustrated in the story of King Aśvapati solving the difficult questions on theology which could not be answered by a Brāhmaṇa priest.[33]

It is probable that the story of Nahusha contains the question, why the members of the priestly caste should not be made to render menial service or engage themselves in low occupations. In Nahusha's own language the story runs thus [34]: "I was a king called Nahusha, known as the son of Ayus, and fifth in descent from Soma. By my sacrifices, austere fervour, sacred study, self-restraint and valour, I acquired the undisturbed sovereignty of the three worlds. When I had attained that dominion, pride took possession of my soul: a thousand Brāhmans bore my vehicle. Becoming elated by the pomp of my royalty, and contemning the Brāhmans, I was reduced to this condition by Agastya." "Formerly, as I moved through the sky on a celestial car, intoxicated with self-conceit, I regarded no one but myself. All the inhabitants of the three worlds, Brāhmanical *rishis*, Gods, Gandharvas, Yakshas, Rākshasas, Pannagas, paid me tribute. Such was the power of my gaze that on what creature soever I fixed my eyes, I straightway robbed him of his energy. A thousand of the great sages bore my vehicle. That misconduct it was, O king, which hurled me from my high estate. For I then touched with my foot the sage Agastya who was carrying me. Agastya in his wrath called out to me, 'Fall thou, a serpent.' Hurled therefore from my magnificent car, and fallen from my prosperity, as I descended headlong I felt that I had become a serpent. I entreated the Brāhmaṇa (Agastya) that my curse may be terminated. 'Thou, O reverend *rishi*, should forgive one who has been deluded through inconsiderateness,' and Yuddhishṭhira, the king of righteousness, freed me from his curse." The failure of Nahusha shows also the power of Brāhmanical penance.

That some endeavours were made by the Buddhists and the Jainas to defy the old and prevailing classification is in evidence in the definition of the word Brāhmaṇa given in the *Uttarādhyayana Sūtra*.[35] "He who does not injure living beings in any of the three ways, thought, word and deed, is a Brāhmaṇa ; the Brāhmaṇa does not speak an untruth from anger or for fun ; by one's actions one becomes a Brāhmaṇa or Kshatriya or Vaiśya or Śūdra."

> "Not matted hair nor heritage of birth
> Can prove the Brahman ; nay, but sterling worth
> And truthfulness and inward purity.
> What boots your sack-cloth and your tonseled hair?
> On outward things, poor fools, ye lavish care !
> Ye who are rotting, rotting inwardly."[36]

Patañjali,[37] the great grammarian and philosopher, seems to make a distinction between Brāhmans by birth only and those with the additional qualifications penance (*tapas*) and knowledge (*jñāna*).[38] By neglecting the Veda the Brāhmaṇa becomes degraded into a Śūdra.[39] As an elephant made of wood, as an antelope made of leather, such is a Brāhmaṇa without Vedic learning, these three having nothing but the name.[40]

VII

Novel Marriage Systems

In the Dharmaśāstras we meet with marriage of eight kinds.[41] They are *Brāhma*, *Daiva*, *Ārsha*, *Prājāpatya*, *Āsura*, *Gāndharva*, *Rākshasa*, and *Paiśācha*. These forms had come to be accepted in the period of the Smritis, and are thus described: The free gift of his daughter by the father to a man learned in the Veda and of good conduct is the Brāhma form. When she is given away to the bridegroom fully decked with ornaments with the advice, "This is thy wife, may both of you perform together your lawful duties," the marriage rite is known as Prājāpatya. The marriage where the bride's father takes from the bridegroom one or two pairs of bulls and cows is known as Ārsha. When she is given to an officiating priest within the religious enclosure, while a sacrifice is being performed, we have the Daiva kind of marriage. That voluntary union in wedlock of a woman and her lover resulting from a union of hearts is called Gāndharva. In the Āsura type the bridegroom is said to give as much wealth as he can afford to the bride's father. When the maiden is wedded after being forcibly captured from her parent's home, there is the Rākshasa variety. When a man by stealth seduces a girl while sleeping or when she has lost her senses and afterwards weds her, the marriage rite is termed Paiśācha.

Of these forms of marriage some appear to be distinctly due to non-Aryan influences. Brāhma, Daiva, Prājāpatya and Ārsha are the only strictly Aryan forms, for these alone were lawful for a Brāhmaṇa. The Gāndharva is permitted for the Kshatriyas and some would even recommend it to all the castes, because it is based on mutual affection of the contracting parties.[42] Though Gāndharva, Āsura, Rākshasa and Paiśācha have also received recognition in the law-codes, they ought to belong, as the names signify, only to the non-Aryan peoples indicated by them. The Āsura form was prevalent in the period of the Epics in the Kekaya country and among the Uttara Mādras; and it is stated that both Daśaratha and Dhritarāshṭra got their wives Kaikeyī and Gāndhārī from the respective countries paying their kings huge presents of money. Similarly, the seizure of Subhadrā by Arjuna, like the attempts to carry away Sītā and Draupadī by Rāvaṇa and Jayadratha, may be cited as instances of the infiltration of the Rākshasa form into the social system of the same period of Indian history.

Modern marriage customs among some of the primitive peoples of South India agree with these practices. For example, the practice is prevalent among the Todas of the Nilgiri district of the gift of buffaloes at the marriage, by the bridegroom to the bride's party. It may be that buffaloes were given because these animals were the totem of this tribe, and therefore held sacred and presented at the ceremony of marriage. But the practice of giving buffaloes seems also reminiscent of a possible acceptance by this tribe of what was prevalent as the Ārsha among the more advanced tribes. The Rākshasa form of marriage obtains among the Kaḷḷars and the Maravars of the Tinnevelly district of the Madras Presidency, and more clearly among the Khonds of Central India and among the Yenadis of Nellore district. This form is known as "marriage by capture", and may be described thus: On the day fixed for the marriage the bride duly decked and covered with a blanket is carried by the uncle accompanied by the village-girls to the husband's house. On the road the procession is met by the bridegroom and his party with their faces and bodies covered, and armed with bamboo sticks. The bridesmaids begin an attack on the bridegroom-party with stones and sticks, and the people that accompany the bridegroom resist the attacks with their bamboo posts. This mock-fight goes on when the uncle of the bridegroom snatches the bride and carries her off to the proposed husband's house. This form contains two interesting elements: seizure of the girl and the apparent claim that the uncle had to have the girl for his own son. The latter is indicative of the prevalence of the system of "marriage of cousins" among the Dravidian tribes. Among the Nāyāḍis of Malabar there is a strange ceremony in connexion with marriage. The bride is kept alone inside a hut with a pole on hand which she stretches out now on one side now on another to be seized by him who can. All round, stand young men eagerly attempting to snatch the stick. The game goes on like this for a while and he that forcibly wrests the stick from off the maiden's hand is declared the bridegroom. Here is a primitive method of testing the bridegroom's strength on which depended his eligibility to have the girl for wife. This reminds us of that form of Gāndharva marriage in which the bridegroom's valour was tested among the Kshatriyas at a tournament, and he that won got the girl.

VIII

Viśvāmitra and Vasishṭha

We find that as a result of the miscegenation that was going on in the society of the Hindus, various mixed and sub-castes were formed.[43] Gradual passage from one caste to another seemed possible, and is indicated in the literature of the period. The change of castes in the higher ranks is denoted by the legend of Viśvāmitra becoming a Brāhmaṇa.[44] There should have existed more than one Viśvāmitra in Indian history and tradition. But the lives of all the Viśvāmitras taken together would lead us to the conclusion that the story was one of gradual evolution of a Kshatriya prince from his original status to that of a *Brahmarshi* (Brāhmaṇa sage). His ambition was that he should be placed on the same level with Vasishṭha, who stands in Indian tradition for the perfect and orthodox Brāhmaṇa ideal. As we have already narrated, Viśvāmitra appeared as the bard of the ten kings of non-Aryan and mixed tribes against Vasishṭha who was the priest of the pure Aryan race of the Tritsus under their king Sudās. In this battle Viśvāmitra and party were defeated, and Vasishṭha got the triumph over his rival. This struggle that appears between the two sages is continued to the later ages. The two are seen again in the *Rāmāyaṇa* to enter into a quarrel over a cow Śabalā, the yielder of all that was desired. Viśvāmitra the *Rājarshi* goes to the hermitage of Vasishṭha, and is accorded a hearty reception that befitted a king. He is surprised that in the wilderness so much was possible for Vasishṭha, and knew that it was all due to the divine cow that the Brāhmaṇa sage had with him. He must have it at any cost. Arguments were of no avail with Vasishṭha, and a serious quarrel ensued. Viśvāmitra had to retreat discomfited and disgraced. The cow Śabalā over which the engagement took place between the two may be interpreted as nothing less than the *Brahmavarchas* (effulgent Brāhmanical wisdom) that Vasishṭha had possessed to an eminent degree. This divine knowledge represented in the cow would not leave the Brāhmaṇa sage and could not be acquired now by this Kshatriya saint (*Rājarshi*). After this defeat, the spirit of emulation is roused in the latter, and he is prepared for self-restraint, mortification and abstinence. He learns that what cannot be achieved by force may be attained by peace, love, and goodwill that are the result of penance. He betakes himself to the lonely forests, having realized the charms of solitude, to issue to humanity his lasting and momentous message from there. He performs the most severe penances, but meets with formidable obstacles on his path of progress, which seemed to put his mettle to the test. The difficulties he had to encounter were many and varied in nature. The path to heaven was lined with thorns. The impediments appear in the shape of Śunahśepa, Menakā, Triśanku and Hariśchandra.[45]

The legend of Śunahśepa is thus narrated in the *Rāmāyaṇa* Ambarīsha, the king of Ayodhyā, was performing an elaborate sacrifice, when Indra, the chief of the gods, becoming jealous of the powers of the king, carried off the animal that was intended as the sacrificial victim. The priests gave the verdict that the loss could be made up only by substituting a human victim. After trying in vain to find out the lost animal, the king found a *rishi* by name Richīka who had three sons one of whom he was prepared to part with. The father was attached to the eldest and the mother to the youngest. Śunahśepa, the middle one, finding that his parents were in a dilemma, offered himself to be sacrificed. He was sold for a crore of nishkas (gold pieces), a hundred thousand cows and large quantities of jewellery. Śunahśepa was being taken along, and he met on the way his uncle, Viśvāmitra, to whom the story was told. Viśvāmitra contrived a way out of the difficulty, to vouchsafe his nephew long life, and to keep the promise. He taught Śunahśepa two divine verses which were to be repeated when he was about to be sacrificed. According to the account given in the *Aitareya Brāhmaṇa*,[46] the verses were: "Which god now, of all the immortal Beings, shall we invoke? Who shall give us back to the great Aditi, that I may behold my father and mother? Let us invoke the graceful name of Agni, the first of the Gods. He shall give us back to the great Aditi, and at the same time enable us to behold our father and mother." When these verses were repeated, as he was about to be immolated, the gods being pleased bestowed long life on Śunahśepa, who thereafter became the adopted son of Viśvāmitra, with the name Devarāta. In this story Viśvāmitra shows that by the magic of his *mantras* he was able to endow a mortal with immortality. But before he could reach this acme of his penance, he had to overcome various bonds that seemed to tie him down, and make the horizon farther and farther from his reach.

The story of Menakā is intended to show that to get rid of desires and to be detached like the globule of water on a lotus leaf are among the essential conditions for the realization of spiritual salvation. It has given the occasion for the famous stanza in Sanskrit: "Even sages like Viśvāmitra and Parāśara given up to very hard penance, subsisting on Nature's gifts like wind, water and leaves, even they have yielded to passion and become enamoured of the charms of women. What then needs be said of ordinary folk accustomed to rich, delicious and substantial food?" He realizes that after the birth of a daughter, Śakuntaḷā, as the Buddha realized in later times after the birth of Rāhula. He therefore continues his penance.

Yet another difficulty presented itself, and that was in Triśanku. Triśanku was a good and pious king of the solar race. He was ambitious to be translated to heaven with his physical body, and would perform such sacrifice as would yield him the desired result. Vasishṭha, his family priest, declared it impossible. Vasishṭha's sons, who were then approached, cursed him to become a Chaṇḍāḷa. He appealed to Viśvāmitra, who gave him the promise to lift him up to heaven, as he had wanted. A sacrifice was performed and as a result Triśanku ascended to heaven. But his way was obstructed by Indra and the other gods. The proud sage in his wrathful egoism retorted that Indra would be displaced from his high pedestal. As a compromise, the prince was given a place midway between heaven and earth, and is supposed to have taken his place among the stars in the sky. Viśvāmitra did not feel satisfied, and the fate of his protege—he was cursed to hang head downwards—taught him a new lesson.

The story of Hariśchandra is one of the most pathetic in Indian literature, the king having been reduced to the worst straits by Viśvāmitra. The story of this king is given in a very elaborate form in the *Mārkaṇḍeya Purāṇa.* He was a *Rājarshi* renowned for his justice, piety and charity. On one occasion while the king was hunting, he heard the sound of some female lamentations which apparently came from the Sciences which were being mastered by Viśvāmitra in a way unknown before, and which cried out in alarm at the superiority achieved by the sage.[47] Hariśchandra as the defender of the weak and the oppressed among his subjects ran to the rescue of these, thereby provoking the wrath of Viśvāmitra. The Sciences were instantly cursed by the sage to perish. The king felt helpless and said that he had merely done the duty of a Kshatriya, which lay in the bestowal of gifts on the poor and the needy, protection of his subjects and war against enemies. Viśvāmitra demanded a gift of Hariśchandra, and the good king promised anything of the former's choice, gold, his own son, his body, wife, life, kingdom and good fortune. Little by little the sage stripped the king of all his belongings, leaving him nothing but his wife and son, barely clothed. The king was driven to flee with his queen Śaibya and son Rohitāśva. He went to Benares, there to meet the ubiquitous and unsatiated sage, who demanded his wife and child. The king that never swerved from the truth, parted with his wife and child in great grief to satisfy the relentless Viśvāmitra. He was now alone and helpless; the last rag had been taken from him. He offered to sell himself when more was demanded. He sought service under a Chaṇḍāḷa. But this Chaṇḍāḷa was the god Dharma himself. Hariśchandra was now put to guard a cemetery. Meantime his wife and son were in service with a Brāhmaṇa, and one day the boy was bitten by a snake to death. So the mother took the dead body of the child to be cremated at the burning ghat. The king and queen recognized each other after some time and broke out into lamentations. At last they both agreed that, having lost the only solace of their life, this life was not worth keeping, and resolved to lay their frame at the very pyre which was to consume the child. At this critical juncture appeared on the scene Viśvāmitra, Dharma and all the gods, who proclaimed that "he, his wife and son had conquered heaven by their works". Viśvāmitra takes to much harder penance to reach perfection.

In this way the great sage got rid of the various shackles such as lust, anger, desire, pride and jealousy which acted as drags on his onward march. He got gradual recognition from being a *Mahārāja*, first as a *Rājarshi*, then as a *Maharshi*, and lastly as *Brahmarshi*. He was not satisfied until Vasishṭha would claim him as equal to himself. The merit of Viśvāmitra lies in the fact that he was a wonderful example of one who worked his way to the highest bliss by dint of his own personal efforts, in spite of natural predisposition to passion of every kind.

The story of Viśvāmitra only illustrates how it was not easy even for one endowed with such large strength, wisdom and power to get elevated from the status of a Kshatriya to that of a Brāhmaṇa. It was only as a result of very severe processes of self-discipline and interiorization that even a Kshatriya could achieve the spirituality of a Brāhmaṇa. When by a simple wave of the magic wand (*Brahmadaṇḍa*) Vasishṭha was able to destroy the immense hosts that had accompanied Viśvāmitra, the latter exclaims, "Fie upon the valour of the Kshatriya; verily the valour is of the Brāhmaṇa!" [48]

IX

Elevation and Degradation of Castes

Thus, the passage of a person of a lower caste to the higher was not a fact very easily accomplished. But the possibilities are shown for an offspring to become gradually elevated in successive births, as a result of caste-mixture. "By the power of austerities and of high birth these races obtain here among men more exalted or lower rank in successive births." [49] Seven generations are declared necessary for elevation in the case of *anuloma* marriages, i.e. "if the daughter of a Brāhmaṇa and a Śūdra female and her descendants all marry Brāhmans, the offspring of the sixth female descendant of the original couple will attain the qualities of a Brāhmaṇa, and eventually Brāhmanical status." [50] Similarly, for degradation, "if the son of a Brāhmaṇa and of a Śūdra female and his descendants all marry Śūdra wives, the seventh descendant will sink to the level of a Śūdra." Complications cropped up in the social structure, and the question that the Indian law-givers had to solve was two-fold. First, what was the status of the offspring of these inter-caste unions, and secondly, were they to follow the caste of the father or of the mother? Elaborate regulations had to be framed for determining exactly the caste to which a particular child should belong. The problem was somewhat similar to the modern one of "war-babies", though brought about by different circumstances.

X

Rules regarding Marriage and Inheritance

The general rule in regard to marriage was that no one should be allowed to marry out of his or her own caste. Intermarriage among castes, whether *anuloma* or *pratiloma*, was considered inadvisable and undesirable.[51] *Anuloma* implied the marriage of a man of a higher caste with a woman of a lower one, and *pratiloma* meant the reverse—that of a woman of a higher caste to a man of lower grade. At first, even the former was prohibited on principle. We read, "Children of a Brāhmaṇa by women of the three lower castes, of a Kshatriya by wives of the two lower to him, and of the Vaiśya by a woman of the Śūdra caste, are all called *apasada* (base-born)." [52] We find evidence of this ideal in the Buddhist texts. There is a story in the *Divyāvadāna*,[53] where a Chaṇḍāḷa chief Triśanku requested for his son the hand of the daughter of a Brāhmaṇa. Triśanku says, "Give your daughter Prakritī to my son Śārdūlakarṇa as wife; I shall pay you as much money as *kulaśulka* (present due to your family) as you deem fit." The Brāhmaṇa Pushkarasāra got offended and told Triśanku, "No one, be he a Brāhmaṇa, Kshatriya, Vaiśya or Śūdra, Chaṇḍāḷa or Pukkaśa can marry out of his own caste." However, it eventuated that a man of the higher castes could take a wife from any of the lower castes or from all, but not *vice versa*.[54] This is why in our works, secular and religious, the marriage of a Brāhmaṇa with women from all the four castes is legalized.[55] As regards the right of inheritance, with some small variations we find that the son by a Brāhmaṇa woman was entitled to four shares of the property; that by a Kshatriya to three; the one by a Vaiśya woman to two; and that by a Śūdra woman had one share. That is,

The son by a	Brāhmaṇa woman	got	4/10.
,, ,,	Kshatriya	,,	3/10
,, ,,	Vaiśya	,,	2/10
,, ,,	Śūdra	,,	1/10

Similarly, "if there are three sons of a Brāhmaṇa (by wives of different castes), but no one by a Śūdra among them, they shall divide the estate into nine parts." That is,

The son by a	Brāhmaṇa woman	got	4/9
,, ,,	Kshatriya	,,	3/9
,, ,,	Vaiśya	,,	2/9

"If there are three sons by wives of different castes, but no Vaiśya among them, they shall divide the estate into eight parts." That is,

The son by a	Brāhmaṇa woman	got	4/8
,, ,,	Kshatriya	,,	3/8
,, ,,	Śūdra	,,	1/8

"If there are three sons but no Kshatriya among them, they shall divide into seven parts." That is,

The son by a Brāhmaṇa woman got 4/7
,, ,, Vaiśya ,, 2/7
,, ,, Śūdra ,, 1/7

"If there is no Brāhmaṇa wife among them, the sons shall divide the property into six parts." That is,

The son by a Kshatriya woman got 3/6
,, ,, Vaiśya ,, 2/6
,, ,, Śūdra ,, 1/6

Next, "If there are sons of a Kshatriya by a Kshatriya, a Vaiśya and a Śūdra wife, the mode of division shall be the same." That is,

Tne son by the Kshatriya woman got 3/6
,, ,, Vaiśya ,, 2/6
,, ,, Śūdra ,, 1/6

"If there are two sons of a Brāhmaṇa, the one by a Brāhmaṇa woman, and the other by a Kshatriya woman, they shall divide the estate into seven parts." That is,

The son by the Brāhmaṇa woman got 4/7
,, ,, Kshatriya ,, 3/7

"If there are two sons for a Brāhmaṇa by a Brāhmaṇa and a Vaiśya wife, the estate was to be divided into six parts." That is,

The son by the Brāhmaṇa woman got 4/6
,, ,, Vaiśya ,, 2/6

"If a Brāhmaṇa had two sons, one by a Brāhmaṇa wife and the other by a Śūdra, the estate was divided into five parts." That is,

The son by the Brāhmaṇa woman got 4/5
,, ,, Śūdra ,, 1/5

"If a Brāhmaṇa has only one son, he shall own the whole estate, whether he be by a Brāhmaṇa, Kshatriya or Vaiśya wife."

"If a Kshatriya has only one son, either by a Kshatriya or a Vaiśya wife, the rule shall be the same."

"If a Vaiśya has only one son, born of a Vaiśya wife, the rule is the same."

"The only son of a Śūdra by a Śūdra wife shall be the heir to the whole property."

"A Śūdra, who is the only son of a father belonging to the 'twice-born' caste, shall inherit only one half of the property."

"Sons who are equal in caste to their father shall receive equal shares."

"If there are two sons by a Brāhmaṇa wife, and one son by a Śūdra wife, the estate shall be divided into nine parts; and of these, the two sons by the Brāhmaṇa wife shall take four parts each, and the son of the Śūdra wife shall have a single part."

"If there are two sons by a Śūdra, and one son by a Brāhmaṇa wife, the estate was to be divided into six parts. The son of the Brāhmaṇa wife was to have four parts, while each of the two sons by the Śūdra wife was to have one part."

XI

Anuloma and Pratiloma

Intermarriage among castes having become a current practice,[56] the problem that the law-givers had to solve was, which form of marriage may be tolerated, *anuloma* or *pratiloma*, being the less of the two evils? We know, on eugenic grounds, that the vitality of that race will be imperilled in which marriages are frequent of women of the higher castes with men of the lower ones. In these cases the efficiency of the species diminishes quickly. That this principle was clearly known to the Hindu law-givers is evident from the following: "The marriage of a Śūdra with a Brāhmaṇa woman entitles the issue to be classified as a Chaṇḍāḷa, the most miserable of human beings."[57] To prevent degradation by *pratiloma*, the *Manusmriti* lays down that "the person that is begotten by an Aryan on a non-Aryan female will have the qualities of an Arya, while he whom an Aryan mother bears to a non-Aryan father remains unlike an Arya." "Men who are outcastes, who approach females of higher rank, beget races still more worthy to be excluded."[58] The idea is that *pratiloma* leads to degradation. Legal safeguards also appear to have been provided against *pratiloma* connexions, for, whereas a man of the first three castes who has illicit connexion with a Śūdra woman is merely to be punished, a Śūdra who commits the offence with a woman of the higher castes is to suffer capital punishment.[59] The ancient Indians that framed the rules had known that society had gone off the rails and may have had in their minds the spiritual and moral vigour of the Hindu race as the most important consideration. The rules disclose the instinct of race-preservation. If, as it has been shown, the Brāhmaṇa stood for a high standard of intellect, morality, and good conduct, it is no wonder that the higher classes should have been jealous to perpetuate the qualities of the Brāhmaṇa, keeping in mind the sound eugenic principles of heredity.[60] As the Greek philosopher and poet, Theognis of Megara, put it, when the good mingles with the base, the stock of our folk becomes tarnished.

XII

Kshetra and Bīja Nyāya

The following general rules found in the *Vishṇu Smriti*[61] will furnish at the same time the general principles which the Brāhmanical law-givers laid down as regards intermarriage between castes :

"Sons begotten on women equal in caste to their husbands are equal in caste to their father."

"Sons begotten on women of lower castes become of the caste of their mothers."

"Sons begotten on women of higher castes are despised by the 'twice-born'."

Thus, whereas the first was normal, and the second, though leading to degradation, may have been tolerated, the last was condemned altogether. The bases on which these rules were framed were the *kshetra* and *bīja nyāya*. The latter was taken to be the more important criterion, as having perhaps larger influence on the intellectual and moral qualities of the offspring. As we read in the code of Manu,[62] " of the two, *kshetra* and *bīja*, some praise the first, some second, some both. The proper decision is that the seed is more important, even though good seed in bad soil becomes degenerate." So far as the purity of the race was concerned, the mother was more important a factor than the father. We find in the *Vasishṭha Smriti*,[63] " the *Āchārya* is ten times more venerable than an *Upādhyāya* ; the father a hundred times more than the *Āchārya* ; and the mother a thousand times more than the father." The *Bhagavat-Gītā* deals clearly with the necessity for safeguarding the purity of the women in the family and society, on the important ground, viz. " if women become wicked and corrupted, there will be impurity of castes." [64] On these grounds *pratiloma* marriages were absolutely prohibited, whereas *anuloma* connexions being less detrimental to the progress of the race were left less condemned. Absolute prohibition was out of the question now, and could not be enforced. In this way an attempt was made to minimize the evil effects of the forces working against the purity of castes by preserving as far as was practicable the purity of women of the higher classes.

XIII

Regulations regarding Occupations

The law-givers seem to have realized that the intermixture of castes was brought about not only by the admixture of blood (*yoni*), but by the pursuit of forbidden occupations (*āchāra*), for, " in the absence of any distinctive function or profession, Aryas and *anāryas* are equal 'in status'."[65] The confusion of occupations is illustrated clearly in Jātaka literature. We have examples of a Brāhmaṇa physician, a weaver as an archer, a Kshatriya prince as an archer, a trader, a labourer, and an idol-maker, a Seṭṭhi as a trader and as a potter, Brāhmaṇa traders, and Brāhmaṇa hunters and trappers. Kuśa, a prince, becomes an apprentice by turn under a potter, a basket-maker, florist and cook.[66] Therefore as a preventive measure, it was ruled that the occupations of the higher castes should not be adopted by the lower classes, and that the former should not degrade themselves by engaging in occupations intended for the latter.[67] It was enjoined as a state-duty to regulate the occupations pertaining to the various classes in the society. The king is advised to pay attention to the laws of various localities, families, and different classes of people, and make the four classes fulfil their respective duties.[68] In the Nasik cave inscription Gautamīputra Bālaśrī is proud of "having stopped the contamination of the four *varṇas* (castes)". A man of low caste who through covetousness lives by the occupations of a higher one, shall be deprived of his property and banished from the realm.[69] In the Buddhist scriptures we read that the usual way in which outcasting was done was by shaving the man and cutting him dead by pouring ashes over him, thus banishing him from the land and the township.[70] Similarly, various punishments were prescribed for members of the higher castes who took to the occupations of the lower ones. But in dire necessity those who are unable to live by their own lawful occupation may adopt that of the caste just below theirs.[71] As we read in the Tāḷaguṇḍa pillar inscription,[72] a Brāhmaṇa in extreme emergency exchanged the *kuśa* grass and fuel (*samit*) which were the emblems of his caste, to the bow and arrow that were the insignia of the Kshatriya. A teacher at Kāñchīpuram was forced to do so at the time of a war that was waged between the Pallavas and the Kshatrapas. Ordinarily, as we find even in the *Arthaśāstra* of Kauṭilya, a man was prevented from changing his own profession or trade for another. As new sub-castes had been formed as a result of the various crossings in the social grades, the occupations of the various castes and sub-castes were fixed so that there may not be in future interchange of occupations resulting in turn in other serious consequences. The occupations were fixed in the following manner [73]: Chaṇḍāḷa, executor; Māgadha, poet; Āyogava, artist (carpenter in the *Manusmriti*); Vaidehaka, trader in dancing girls; Pukkaśa, hunter; Sūta, horseman and charioteer; Ambashṭtha, physician; Nishada, fisher; Kshattri, Ugra and Pulkaśa, those who catch and kill animals that live in lairs; Dhīgvana, leather-worker; Vena, drummer. Besides, as Yuan Chwang says of his time, different classes and castes seem to have been distinguished from each other by a distinguishing sign, and perhaps given distinct quarters in the city. "Butchers, fishers, public performers, executioners and scavengers have their habitations marked by a distinguishing sign." In town-planning in ancient times this principle was insisted on.[74]

XIV

Regulations regarding Food and Touching

Next, it was found necessary to make the regulations about food and touching very rigorous. An Arya is advised not to take what remains after a Śūdra had eaten.[75] The food touched by him is unfit for eating. If an Arya is touched while eating his food by a Śūdra, it should be abandoned.[76] Even in the Jātakas we read that a Brāhmaṇa would be deprived of his status for taking a drink mixed with the rice-water an outcaste had used.[77] We read, however, though the rules were generally so strict, that at a pinch a Śūdra could prepare the food to be taken by his "twice-born" master, if he was a servant of the family from birth, and therefore well known, or if he was under the supervision of men of the three higher castes.[78] The idea implied in this was that if the Śūdra had been brought up in the household of the twice-born even from childhood, he would have acquired the clean and gentle habits of his masters, and therefore, in virtue of his qualities, he ceased to be a Śūdra. It is clear that significance was attached not only to the accident of birth, but to the general upbringing of the child, to whatever caste it might belong. The mental and intellectual attainments of the child depend both on nature and nurture. The environments in which the child is placed, and the atmosphere the child is made to breathe must determine his character and inclinations, as they must modify his tastes and temperament. Brāhmanical virtues would be naturally imbibed by one in Brāhmanical surroundings. It needs no saying that one of the most serious causes for the degradation of the Brāhmaṇa is his bringing up in unwholesome environment, resulting in the acquisition of qualities untidy, unclean and immoral. Thus, the "twice-born" tend to be Śūdraized, as the Śūdras become Brāhmanized. On the same principle, the food of a Śūdra disciple was permitted for the teacher, if the former had for a long time been residing with him, intent on the acquisition of spiritual knowledge, and was of good conduct and approved religious merit. According to Āpastamba, a *Brahmachāri* (student) that has been discharged by his teacher may take food from a Brāhmaṇa on account of the giver's character and qualities, and not because he happens to be a Brāhmaṇa by birth.[79] This also indicates that insistence was placed on Brāhmanical qualities. In a later work, the *Śukranīti*,[80] we read that in regard to marriage-alliances and dinner-parties considerations of caste ought compulsorily to weigh, but efficiency was to be the only criterion in the matter of appointment to political offices in the state. These show the great eagerness that the higher castes had evinced for effecting a compromise, as far as was practicable, in the social life of the period. The stanza cited from the *Śukranīti* will be seen to denote a period of great improvement and concession to the lower classes, for in the period previous to its age, the ministers and other high officials were drafted from the higher castes alone, as we find in the *Arthaśāstra* of Kauṭilya.

XV

General Remarks on the Rules

These resulting regulations appear to have been actuated by motives of a varied nature. The following principles may be said to emerge out of them. Eugenic considerations should have resulted in the desire to preserve the purity of castes which by slow processes of admixture were getting degraded, to prevent the social and family evils and abuses that sprang from the intermixture of castes and occupations. Caste laws were laws of spiritual eugenics intended to foster and promote the evolution of a superior race.

As it has already been shown, the tendency of the age was to shake the foundations of Brāhmanical religion. Hence, it would be nothing out of the way if the higher classes in the Hindu society should have taken precautionary steps, somewhat hard as they were, to protect themselves and the main features of their religious and social fabric, at least on the principle of self-preservation and the preservation of the species.

We cannot fail to notice in these rules of restrictions the result of a powerful reaction with a view to counteract the heretical doctrines of the Buddha and Mahāvīra. The supremacy of Buddhism under Aśoka and Kanishka apparently led to a reaction, and the law-codes disclose only the opposition to the retrograde tendency fostered by the Buddhist influences of which one may find clear expression in the Jātakas and other Buddhist works.

General principles, hygienic, physiological and sometimes

sentimental in character, may have induced the law-givers to frame such rules in regard to interdining and touching. The injunction was not merely that food should not be taken from a Śūdra. Penances were prescribed even for such cases as are cited below.[31]

"If a Brāhmaṇa eats what has been left as remnant by a Brāhmaṇa, he should live only on milk for one day."

"If he eats what has been left by a Kshatriya, he must subsist only on milk for three days."

"If he eats what was left over by a Vaiśya, the penance is only milk-diet for five days."

"If he eats what was left as remnant by a Śūdra, he must live only on milk for seven days."

Similar rules are found for the other "twice-born" castes also. As a general rule, food in large company was prohibited, as well as from unknown people, and on certain occasions and places. The regulations about food were particularly severe, because of the influence exercised for good or for evil by the food taken, on the nature and character of the person taking it. It was on this ground that foodstuffs were classified under three heads, *rājasa*, *sātvika* and *tāmasa*.

The food that is conducive to longevity, strength, health, and equanimity, that is sweet and pleasing to the taste and agreeable comes under the class *sātvika*. That which is exceedingly sour, pungent, saltish, and causing a sense of thirst comes under the *rājasa* category. It only brings on misery and grief to the taker. Food that is old, rotten, insipid and foul-smelling, that is remnant from another's table, is classified as bad and unwholesome (*tāmasa*).

The first brightens up the intellect and the spirit, the second makes the recipient restless and fiery, and the last makes one dull and indolent.[32]

These rules may also have originated from the unclean and filthy habits of the lower classes. People that took non-vegetarian food and drank liquor were considered the filthiest and most polluting, for the higher classes looked with abhorrence at these and similar practices. Though the eating of flesh of different kinds and the drinking of the *soma* were permitted to the Aryas in the early ages, and that too only on occasions of sacrifices, these practices came to be interdicted in later times, for obviously substantial reasons. Those who ate beef and took intoxicating liquor were looked upon as the worst sinners. The learned say that the word for flesh (*māmsa*) is derived thus: "Me he (*mām sa*) will eat in the next world, whose flesh I am tasting here."[83] Besides, if meat was eaten, it was only after having been offered in sacrifice to the gods. "The sin of him who kills deer for the sake of gain, is not so great as the sin of him who eats meat that has not been offered to the gods."[84] Drink was worse than meat-eating, according to the testimony of all our scriptures,[85] and as Strabo has observed, "the Brāhmans never touched any intoxicant drink except at sacrifices." The abstinence from these gave the higher classes a superior position in social life which is even now kept by them to some extent.[86] The ideal is expressed in the following passage of the code of Vishṇu: "These two, he who performs a horse-sacrifice annually for a hundred years and he who does not eat meat, shall both obtain the same recompense for their virtue."[87]

Beef-eating was considered the worst of sins, and we need not seek far for the reasons for such a view. The cow has been from the age of the *Rig-Veda* onwards a favourite totem with the Aryas, and though the *Rig-Veda* is not without instances of cow-killing (*goghna*), the animal had become sacred and worthy of worship, as is shown by a passage in the *Atharva-Veda*.[88] It is no wonder that the animal that gives in plenty the essentials of existence for man in daily life, and particularly the articles for his religious ceremonies, such as ghee and milk, should have been sanctified by the Aryas, and held by them as sacred and fit to be worshipped. Of all the animals, the cow has the largest power of converting what is fodder for cattle into articles of food for man. The sacredness of the cow may also be due to the fact that the animal was the favourite of Gopāla Krishṇa, and should have received increased importance with the rise of the worship of Vāsudeva who could not be separated from his cows. It may also be that beef was given up because of its costliness, as we are led to conclude from the *Mahābhārata* [89]: "The rich eat food in which flesh predominates; the middling take milk and its products; while the poor partake generally of oil preparations." What applied to meat-eating in general applied in particular to beef. Lastly, the doctrine of *ahimsa* which came to be adopted with redoubled strength after the lesson from the Buddhists and the Jainas, should have gone a great way to put a stop to the practice of meat-eating. It cannot be said that *ahimsa* was a doctrine borrowed by the Hindus from the Buddhists and the Jainas. It finds clear enunciation for the first time in the *Chchāndogya Upanishad* [90] where five ethical qualities, *tapa*, *dāna*, *ārjava*, *ahimsa*, and *satya*, are said to be the fees given in a sacrifice of which the whole life of man is an epitome. The castes that shunned these bad habits and accepted and followed Brāhmanical customs and practices were, of course, considered to cause less pollution.

In a still later period, the admittance of descendants of foreigners within the Aryan pale must have made the caste-rules more strict. The Śakas, Huṇas and the Kushans in the course of their occupation of India intermarried with the warlike Kshatriya clans of the North, and their descendants took rank with the Kshatriyas. To prevent the recurrence of such miscegenation was one of the most serious objects of concern with the givers of the sacred laws.

XVI

Toleration—Social and Religious

The tendency of Buddhism and Jainism was of course to level the caste distinctions, and it is strongly expressed in the following way in the *Dīgha Nikāya* (90a): "It is mere empty words to give it out among the people that the Brāhmans are the best caste and every other caste is inferior, that the Brāhmans are the white caste, every other caste is black, that only the Brāhmans are pure, not the non-Brāhmans, that the Brāhmans are the legitimate sons of Brahma." Gautama is said to have taken a Chaṇḍāḷa maiden as his disciple. The story is thus narrated in the *Divyāvadāna* (90b): Ānanda, the disciple of the Buddha, addresses the Chaṇḍāḷa maiden Prakritī, and the following conversation ensues:

Ānanda: Sister, give me water to drink.

Prakritī: O venerable Ānanda, I am the daughter of a Chaṇḍāḷa.

Ānanda: O sister, I do not ask thee to name thy family or caste. If thou hast water to spare, please give it me. I shall take it.

Prakritī offered the water to Ānanda, who took it. Later, the maiden falls in love with the Buddhist monk and wishes that he should marry her. She is taken to the Buddha, who receives her into his *sangha* after a brief conversation.

Prakritī: I want the venerable Ānanda as my husband.

Buddha: Have you been permitted by your parents to marry Ānanda?

Prakritī: I have been permitted, O Bhagavān; I have been permitted, O Sugata.

Buddha: Then let them signify their consent in my presence.

The parents having given their assent, Prakritī was taken as a *Bhikshuṇī* (nun) and married Ānanda.

Toleration in religion was a main creed of some of the most

remarkable of the Buddhist kings. In Rock Inscription XII of Aśoka we read (90c):

"His Sacred and Gracious Majesty the king does reverence to men of all sects, whether ascetics or householders, by gifts and various forms of reverence. His Sacred Majesty, however, cares not so much for gifts or external forms as that there should be a growth of the essence of the matter in all sects. The growth of the essence of the matter assumes various forms, but the root of it is restraint of speech, to wit, a man must not do reverence to his own sect or disparage that of another without reason. Depreciation should be for specific reasons only, because the sects of other people all deserve reverence for one reason or another. By thus acting, a man exalts his own sect and at the same time does service to the sects of other people. By acting contrariwise, a man hurts his own sect and does disservice to the sects of other people. For he who does reverence to his own sect while disparaging the sects of others, wholly from attachment to his own, with intent to enhance the splendour of his own sect, in reality by such conduct inflicts the severest injury on his own sect."

Kanishka even while he adhered to the Buddhist faith continued to honour both the old and the new gods.

This spirit of toleration was in evidence among the Brāhmanical kings as well. The Guptas who were Brāhmanical Hindus devoted to the worship of Vishṇu "followed the usual practice of ancient India in looking with a favourable eye on all varieties of Indian religion". The most tolerant of the early monarchs was perhaps Harsha. His father was particularly a devotee of the Sun, while he worshipped both the Hindu gods and the Buddha. "This religious ecclecticism was the reflection of and result of the state of popular religion at the time." [91] To adapt the words of the poet Swift, there was enough religion in this country to love one another, but not enough to hate one another.

This spirit of toleration in religion paved the way later for the introduction of even *vrātya* outsiders into the higher classes. We have perhaps indication of this tendency in the legend of the migration of a "twice-born" tribe from Śaka *dwīpa* to Jambu *dwīpa*. The story of this advent is thus given[92]: "Sāmba, the son of Krishṇa by Jāmbavatī, constructed a temple for the Sun on the banks of the river Chandrabhāgā (Chenab), but no local Brāhmaṇa would accept the office of the priest in the temple. He thereupon asked Gauramukha, the priest of Ugrasena, who in turn asked him to get the Magas, who were special Sun-worshippers from Śaka *dwīpa*. Sujihva, a Brāhmaṇa of the Sun clan (*Mihira gotra*), had a daughter by name Nikshubhā, with whom the Sun fell in love. The son of these was known as Jarasabda or Jarasasta (Zarathushtra) and from him sprang all Magas. Thus is given the account of the Magi. They wore a girdle round their waist which was given the name *Ayyanga*. Then Sāmba went on Garuḍa's back to Śaka *dwīpa*, brought some Magas from it and installed them into the office of priests of the temple that he had constructed."

We have also examples of degraded Brāhmans and Kshatriyas, e.g. Paulastya Brāhmans are reckoned as degraded Brāhmans, and Manu considers[93] that some tribes like the Draviḍas, Kambhojas, etc., were outcaste Kshatriyas. These had styled themselves as Kshatriyas, but were apparently not looked upon by the law-givers as such, and were placed on a separate footing. The *Harivamśa* and the Purāṇas[94] relate that the kings of South India, Pāṇḍya, Chōḷa, and Keraḷa were the descendants of Yayāti, the Aryan king of the North. We read that Daṇḍaka[95] was a son of Ikshvāku, and from him was derived the forest of Daṇḍaka. As the Greek historian observes,[96] "the kingdom of Pāṇḍion, which is situated in the southern extremity of the peninsula, was founded by an Aryan race whose ancestors had occupied the regions watered by the Jumna. This may be inferred both from the name of the king and that of his capital which was called Mathura after the celebrated city which adorned of old, as it does still, the great tributary of the Ganges." Though this statement may have been based on hearsay evidence and on the similarity of names, it is clear that the names of the city of Madura in South India, and the Pāṇḍya kingdom of which it was the capital, should have been borrowed from the ancient names in North India, Mathura and Pāṇḍava. In the Tamil works[97] we read that the Pāṇḍyas and Chōḷas claimed their ancestry from the Aryan kings of the North. The Pāṇḍyas style themselves as *Pañchavans*, as having descended from the "five brothers", and the Chōḷas are supposed to have sprung from Śibi, and hence were known as *Śeppiyar* or *Śembiyar*. But there is little evidence to warrant the view that is held by Dr D. R. Bhandarkar[98] that "Tribes of the names of Keraḷa (Chera) and Satiya were originally staying in North India from which they migrated to the South and established colonies which in the early period at any rate were known not as Keraḷas and Satiyas but as Keraḷaputra and Satiyaputra". Anyhow, it is clear that in this period Aryan ancestry came to be invented for non-Aryan kings and kingdoms.[99]

XVII

The Spread of Caste System in North and South India

The Tamil kings were elevated to the rank of Kshatriyas in spite of their connexions with the ancient Veḷir or Veḷḷāḷa tribes. These latter were on that account called *Iḷangōkkaḷ* or crown princes. The Brāhmans prepared at their request genealogies which traced their ancestry to either the Solar or the Lunar line of the Aryas of the North. This left the exact status of the Veḷḷāḷas in an unsettled state. They had to be included in the same category with the less civilized mountain tribes like the Nāgas and the Kurumbas. But this division would wound the feelings of the Veḷir nobility. Hence a new scheme of classification was devised, which depended on the regions which these tribes happened to occupy.[100] Thus, in South India, geographical division came to be a new criterion of caste along with birth and occupation. In later times, this principle of division was accepted by the higher classes of the Aryas also, and the result has been the division of the major castes among the Hindus into a motley of endogamous sub-divisions each hailing from a particular district or geographical division.

Similarly, the introduction of castes into the outlying regions of North India is thus indicated in the Purāṇas.[101] Bali, who belonged to the line of Yayāti, is said to have had five sons—Anga, Vanga, Sumha, Puṇḍra, and Kalinga, who are known as Bāleya Kshatriyas. There were also Bāleya Brāhmans who were Bali's descendants. The *Vāyu Purāṇa* says, "Bali gave birth to sons that formed the four castes."

XVIII

Religious Assimilation

The Aryas in the previous epochs were not unfamiliar with the black arts of magic and witchcraft, for these, by the way, formed the essential elements of all primitive religion. In the *Rig-Veda*,[102] enchantment, sorcery, wily and godless arts of magic and witch-craft are mentioned as peculiar to the Dasyus. It will not be wrong to suppose that the non-Aryas practised these arts to perfection, and their rites and observances when they gradually got filtered into the Aryan religion were given a prominent place in the fourth Veda, the Atharvan. Though some of the hymns of the *Atharva-Veda* may be as old as, if not older than those of the *Rig-Veda*, it is probable that the compilation of the Atharva *mantras* into a collection (*samhitā*) may have taken place later than that of the hymns of the *Rig-Veda*. The Atharvan is not ordinarily mentioned among the Vedas. The early records[103] speak only of *Trayī Vidyā*. It is not mentioned in the *Chchāndogya Upanishad*. The Brāhmaṇa texts mention only the three Vedas. It appears as a *Chchandas* in the *Purusha sūkta* hymn. The Jātakas make mention only of three, and this may go to show that the Atharvan as a Veda had not been recognized in the earlier days of Buddhism. Manu speaks of the *Trayam Brahma Sanātanam*, but alludes to the Atharvan in the passage, "Let him use without hesitation the sacred texts revealed by Atharvan and Angiras." The *Arthaśāstra* has *Trayī Vidyā*, but contains a large number of spells and magical practices in the last chapters. In the last-named work the Atharva is classified with *Itihāsa*, and these two are also styled as Vedas. Perhaps the citations from Manu and Kauṭilya show the transition period when the practices of the Atharvan came to be largely used, but when they had not been fully canonized as a Veda, for among the qualifications of the high priest in the *Arthaśāstra*[104] was the power of "performing such expiatory rites as pertain to the Atharva". The importance attached to these non-Aryan practices is thus dwelt on in certain parts of the *Mahābhārata*[105]: "In early works the *Āchārya* who taught gratis all the Vedas is declared to be worth ten *Upādhyāyas*. This *Upādhyāya* is the direct etymological ancestor of the modern ojha—wizard. In ancient times he was a sub-teacher who taught for a livelihood one part of the Veda and the Vedānga and he is identified in the *Purohita*. This ancient ratio is inverted in the *Mahābhārata* and the *Upādhyāya* made worth ten *Āchāryas*." According to the testimony of I'tsing,[106] the *Āchārya* was very important, being a teacher of discipline, while the *Upādhyāya* is relegated to a subordinate position, for he conveyed only oral instruction. Thus non-Aryan forms of worship and observances came to be incorporated into the Vedic system of the Aryas, and their canonical character was slowly recognized.

XIX

The Evolution of Mahāyāna

Buddhism and Jainism were pre-eminently the religions of the non-Aryas, and we find that in course of time these were profoundly influenced by the religion of the Aryas. The Vedic Aryan gods Varuṇa, Agni, Vāyu, Īśāna, and Parjanya were adopted by the Buddhists, and they occupy a subordinate place in the Buddhist pantheon. The Buddhist Śakka was an adaptation of the Aryan Indra, and he is joint ruler of the gods with Prajāpati and Brahma in the Buddhist works. "The development of the Mahāyāna school of Buddhism which became permanent and fashionable from the time of Kanishka was in itself a testimony to the varying power of Brāhmanical Hinduism. The newer form of Buddhism had much in common with the older form of Hinduism, and the relation is so close that even an expert often feels the difficulty in deciding to which system a particular image should be assigned."[107] The Mahāyāna or the "Great Vehicle" was a product of Brāhmanical influences.

The Mahāyāna form of Buddhism appears in two branches, the "Paradise Mahāyāna", the main tenet of which was that a great Buddha known as *Amitābha* (of immeasurable light) was in charge of a paradise called *Sukhāvatī*. Whoever by dint of good and righteous deeds, and by constant and faithful prayer to *Amitābha*, aspires and strives to reach the land of bliss in the West, will be born to live in bliss there for ever.[108] The second branch is known as the "Full Mahāyāna". The Mahāyānists of this school believe that there are a good number of Buddhas and Boddhisatvas. These are held as worthy objects of devotion, and are believed to respond with grace to the worship offered to them. The *Saddharma Puṇḍarīka*, a very important text of the Mahāyānists, speaks of the incarnations of the Buddha and his descent upon the earth from time to time to protect the weak and the oppressed, and to destroy the wicked and the sinful. "The Mahāyānists created a showy worship, with processions, music and incense; and a rich liturgy was prepared for each Buddha. The monks took charge of the cult; so that the old *chaitya* became a temple and the monk a priest."[109] The goddess Śirima Devatā of the Buddhist scriptures appearing in company with the Sun, the Moon and Earth, who finds no mention as a goddess in the Vedas, receives great importance in modern Hinduism. Other deities whose worship may have been borrowed by the Aryas from the non-Aryas, or that received a new impetus from the latter, are the spirits of the mountains, the guardians of the quarters, the Garuḍas, trees and serpents.[110] The Buddhist influence on the Brāhmanical religion and the contempt of the Brāhmans for the Buddhists are thus shown in the *Mahābhārata*: "They will revere Eḍūkas, they will neglect the gods. The earth shall be piled with Eḍūkas and not adorned with god-houses."

XX

Aryan and non-Aryan Gods and Goddesses

In South India also we have remarkable evidence of the influence of the non-Aryas on the Aryan religious systems and practices. The Dravidian deity *Śāsta* or *Ayyanār* receives recognition of the Aryan villagers of South India. *Ayyanār* or Harihara in Sanskrit is supposed to be the offspring of Śiva and Vishṇu in the guise of Mohinī. "It is more probable that he represents a primitive Dravidian deity, recognized and more or less adopted by the incoming Aryans, and provided with orthodox parentage."[111] The non-Aryan god Muruga or Vela is Aryanized into Guruguha Skanda or Subrahmaṇya, and is a popular god with the Aryas.[112] The most powerful goddess in Tamil land, Koṟṟavai of the *Śangam* literature, becomes identified with Durgā, Umā, or Kāḷī, the spouse of Śiva.[113] Aryan

Nāgnajitī, a consort of Krishṇa, is adapted in the Dravidian Veda of the Vaishṇavas, the *Nāḷāyira prabandham*, to become Nappiṇṇai.

In North India a favourite goddess is Tārā. The worship of this deity seems to have been borrowed from that of the Mahāyāna Buddhist Tārā—Ugra Tārā, Ekajātā or Nīlā. This deity is thus described [114]: "She has from four to twenty-four arms and is generally standing, and stepping to the right on corpses. She has the third eye, is laughing horribly, her teeth are prominent, and her protruding tongue, according to the *Sādhana*, is forked. Her eyes are red and round. Her hips are covered by a tiger-skin, and she wears a long garland of heads. She is dwarfed and corpulent, and her ornaments are snakes." The story of the introduction of the worship of Tārā will show that that goddess was at first worshipped only among the non-Aryas, but was later included into the Hindu pantheon. "The great sage Vasishṭha practised the hardest penance for a long time concentrating on a *mantra* that had been taught him by his father. Vasishṭha discovered that there was no good of the practices of self-denial and torture which were demanded in the Yoga as paths to self-discipline. So Vasishṭha repaired to his father to request that he may be taught another *mantra*. He was now advised to pursue his yoga with the same *mantra*, in the worship of the Devī Buddhesvarī according to the *śākha* of the *Atharva-Veda*. Vasishṭha then went to the Kāmakhya hills (Assam) and once again applied himself to the strict observance of the orthodox methods of the yoga. The goddess at last condescended to appear before him, and said that he had adopted an altogether wrong path. Her worship, said the Devī, was unknown to the Vedas; it was known only in the country of Mahāchīna (China), a country of Buddhistic practices, and Vasishṭha would gain his object if he received instructions from Vishṇu, now residing there in his incarnation as the Buddha. So Vasishṭha went to Mahāchīna. But he was amazed to find that the Buddha was drinking wine in the company of women. His doubts were soon dispelled by the Buddha, who ultimately initiated him into the mysteries of the worship."[115]

XXI

Religious Rites

It is natural that against the heretical influences that were forcing their way into the Aryan religion the "twice-born" classes should make their position doubly strong by elaborating rituals and ceremonials, the details of which could not so easily be grasped by the lower orders in the society. If the Hinduism of the present day has become a dreary round of ceremonies, and noted for its external forms, it is the direct outcome of the reaction of the higher classes against the tendencies that went to shake the very foundations of their religious and social system. The Brāhmans have been considered, rather unfairly, to have been solely responsible for the multiplication of rites and ceremonies, and to have fortified themselves by creating a barrier incomprehensible to the lower classes.

We note, however, that the Kshatriya kings of ancient India were to a great extent instrumental in creating this complicated system of ceremonies and sacrifices. The kind of sacrifice which a king was able to perform was taken to be indicative of the title which he deserved. By performing the *Rājasūya* one became a *Rāja*, and by the Vājapeya, *Samrāṭ*; and the latter was superior to the former.[116] He who had performed a horse-sacrifice was a *Sārvabhauma*.[117] The kings were naturally jealous of each other's rise to power and greatness, and did not tolerate one that performed sacrifices not in keeping with his title. The performance of sacrifices was thus a criterion by which was decided the grade to which a king was entitled. Thus, the priests had to satisfy the whims of monarchs who vied with each other to show off their prowess and splendour, and who fostered and financed public sacrificial performances (*śrauta*) more tedious and more costly than the old domestic (*grihya*) sacrifices of the Aryas. These elaborate sacrifices could not be undertaken by any save the wealthy men of the tribe and especially the king; "and we must therefore picture to ourselves the priests as maintained by the rich men the *Maghavans*, bountiful ones of the *Rig-Veda*."[118] Brāhmanism appears, therefore, to have owed much of its progress to the munificence of the Kshatriya princes of ancient India.

Even in these ceremonies, we note that there was a division of labour by which the members of the various castes were assigned duties which go to show the interrelation of the various parts of the social organism. Though none but trained experts in the Vedic lore were permitted actually to partake in these sacrificial rites, we read of instances where even enslaved men and women of the Śūdra caste appear to have been allowed to take some part in the solemn sacrifices of the Aryas. Milking the cows was a function that had to be entrusted to Śūdras, and the culmination of the *Gavāmayana* sacrifice was marked by the dancing of Śūdra women.[119] In another ancient ritual the Śūdras were introduced as the sellers of *soma* juice.[120] The performer of the Viśvajit sacrifice is ordained to spend three days, we know not for what purpose exactly, in the midst of Nishādas.[121] The point is that the Śūdras, though inferior in social and spiritual status, were assigned definite functions in the most sacred religious ceremonies of the Aryas, and served a definite purpose, however subsidiary that may have been.

XXII

Evolution of Ideas regarding Sacrifices

Ideas about the efficacy of sacrifices and costly rituals were themselves undergoing gradual changes. It was beginning to be accepted that pompous and tedious sacrifices like the *Aśvamedha* were not so productive of virtue, as they happened to be in earlier times. The philosophy of sacrifices was that a small act of sin may be pardoned, if by that, large and beneficial results could be achieved. Thus, one sacrifice performed by the famous *rishi* Rishyaśringa made the whole country of Lomapāda, which had been visited by a famine, get plentiful showers of rain, and scattered plenty over a desert land. Another sacrifice performed under his auspices is said to have given the world a superman in Rāma. "Sacrifices cause the whole universe to prosper; therefore is the slaughter of beasts for a sacrifice no slaughter."[122] The following story from the *Mahābhārata*[123] illustrates that sacrifices which entail slaughter of living beings were not so efficacious as that high and supreme sacrifice, viz. of the self. The Pāṇḍava brothers performed an *Aśvamedha* on a very elaborate scale. In the midst of the assembly of princes, potentates and priests, a mongoose which had a portion of its body rendered golden, made its appearance and began to decry the ceremony for which all had congregated there. The princes were surprised at this, and asked what led the animal to give such a bad verdict as he had given. The tale that follows is then put into the mouth of the mongoose. In Kurukshetra there lived a Brāhmaṇa with his wife, son and daughter-in-law. They were eking out their livelihood by alms. One day when the family that had been starving for a long time had just got enough of corn-flour for its members, an old man, an unknown guest weary with hunger, put in his presence begging of them food to eat. As was the usual custom in Hindu households, the guest had first to be satisfied. The man gave him his portion of the corn-flour, but the appetite was not appeased of the old man. The mother gave hers. With every handful offered he, like Oliver Twist, asked for more. His hunger seemed to be on the increase. The son and daughter gave then their due. When all had been given, the old man seemed satisfied. The gods showered their blessings on the noble family for the glorious act of self-denial and sacrifice, and they were all raised to the heaven. Meantime the mongoose got out of its lair and having caught the scent of the corn-flour rushed into the cottage and as it rolled about the place where lay strewn a little of the flour, its body got the hue of gold. So much was the power of the sacrifice that had been made. "O king, this *Aśvamedha* is certainly of no merit when compared with the sacrifice made by the Brāhmaṇa family of Kurukshetra." Once this principle was accepted, salvation and redemption from this world depended not on costly material sacrifices, but on the larger spiritual sacrifice of the self. The latter was equally open to all Hindus irrespective of caste, wealth or social position. The influence of Buddhism and Jainism may have hastened the acceptance of this philosophy of sacrifices. Sacrifices were condemned in the Buddhist texts.[124]

> "The sacrifices called the Horse, the Man,
> The peg-thrown site, the drink of victory,
> The bolts withdrawn, and all the mighty fuss :—
> These are not rites that bring a rich result.
> Where diverse goats and sheep and kine are slain,
> Never to such a rite as that repair,
> The noble seers who walk the perfect way.
> But rites where no slaughter, nor no fuss
> Are offerings meet, bequests perpetual,
> Where never goats and sheep and kine are slain,
> To such a sacrifice as this repair,
> The noble seers who walk the perfect way.
> These are the rites entailing great results,
> These to the celebrants are blessed, not cursed,
> The oblation runneth over ; the gods are pleased."

Two more stories may be narrated which show the unsettled state of the feeling the people of India had towards animal-sacrifices. "Indra was once performing a sacrifice. When the time came for the killing of the beasts that were ordained for the sacrifice, the great sages seeing the piteous looks of the victims were moved with compassion and said to Indra, 'This is not a righteous sacrifice, for slaughter is against righteousness.' But Indra for infatuation did not consent, and there was a great dispute between him and the *rishis* as to whether one should sacrifice with animate or inanimate offerings. By common consent they referred the dispute to Vasu, king of the Cheḍis, whose decision was that one should sacrifice with whatever could be obtained. The king of the Cheḍis went, however, to the lowest depth of the earth for having thus carelessly decided the question." [125]

Following the principle of *ahimsa* laid down in the above narrative, Agastya began a sacrifice lasting for twelve years, avoiding the slaughter of animals. The gods were at first dissatisfied with it and ceased to function properly. There was a famine in the land and the *rishis* implored Agastya in vain not to incur the displeasure of the gods by introducing sacrifices of a new kind. Agastya would not yield. Rather, by his miraculous powers he brought down rain from the heavens, and there was plenty in the land. The gods were full of joy at what Agastya had achieved. But the *rishis* had yet their misgivings, and they approached the sage once more with a request that animal-sacrifices may be sanctioned, for they would please the gods more than others. At the end, we are told, that, due to the great pressure brought on him, Agastya was pleased to declare that the slaughter of animals for sacrifices alone may be permitted, and this has continued to be the practice among the orthodox down to this day.[126] We have therefore the following rules in the law-codes: [127]

"A Brāhmaṇa must never eat the flesh of animals unhallowed by *mantras*; but, obedient to the primeval law, he may eat it, consecrated with Vedic texts."

"As many hairs as the slain animal has, so often will he, who killed it without holy sanction, suffer a violent death in future births."

"There is no greater sinner than that man who, though not worshipping the gods and the manes, seeks to increase the bulk of his own flesh by the flesh of other beings."

As sacrifices could not be performed or undertaken except by the aristocratic section of the community, a substitute was suggested for the generality of the Hindu population, and that was holy pilgrimage. As pilgrimages were made for worship in temples and places where, it was accepted, there was the manifestation of the Divine, they implied intense devotion, and hence *tīrthayātrā* and *bhakti* were closely connected to each other.[128]

XXIII

Some New Practices in Hinduism

Some habits and customs which were not recognized by Brāhmanic authority are found to be prevalent among the Aryas of the period. The age had advanced so far in tolerance that though the standard rule of conduct was what prevailed in *Āryāvarta*,[129] certain new practices were considered permissible for the orthodox Brāhmans. These should have been due either to Dravidian or Buddhistic influences. Sir J. G. Frazer is of the opinion that the social system under which the community was divided into endogamous groups with exogamous sections, peculiar to the Indian Aryas, may have been borrowed from the Dravidians, "for this is found among no other member of the Aryan stock."[130]

XXIV

Exogamy—Gotra

Exogamy appears among the Hindus in the form of marriage outside one's *gotra*. It is accepted, and held rigorously among the Hindus, that in a marriage the first essential condition is that the contracting parties should belong to distinct and different *gotras* or clans. The word *gotra* occurs in the *Rig-Veda*[131] either in the sense of a " cowstall " or " cowherd ". But even in the Vedic period we find that there were four primary clans of *rishis*—Angiras, Atharvan, Bhrigu, and Vasishṭha. We read in the *Mahābhārata*[132] that originally there were only four *gotras*—those of Angiras, Kaśyapa, Vasishṭha, and Bhrigu. But the word seems to have been used to denote definitely a clan or family in the *Chchāndogya Upanishad* and the *Āśvalāyana Grihya Sūtra*.[133] Later, the *gotras* may have been connected with the names of the *Saptarshis*—the seven prominent Aryan sages. The personnel of the seven has changed a little in the evolution of Indian religion and society. In the *Āśvalāyana Śrauta Sūtra* the seven names found are those of Viśvāmitra, Jamadagni or Bhrigu, Bharadvāja, Gautama, Atri, Vasishṭha, and Kāśyapa. Hence, according to all our law-givers *gotra* denotes a descendant of one of the seven *rishis*, with an eighth added, viz. that of Agastya.[134] Thus, all the prevalent *gotras* among the "twice-born" are supposed to have been derived from the names of the *rishis* mentioned above, all taken together, viz. ten. *Gotra* is defined in the *Pravaramañjari* as including " the sons, grandsons, and previous and succeeding generations of a *rishi*. A *rishi* is a *mantradrashṭā* ".[135]

Prohibition of marriages within the same *gotra* appears from the Sūtra period.[136] Ordinarily the *gotra* of a boy was that of his father. But there were cases where a new *gotra* was acquired by a person whose *gotra* was unknown or who was of another.[137] The change of *gotra* is illustrated in the story of Śunaśchepa who gets the Viśvāmitra *gotra* because that *rishi* was his protector and preceptor. When the relations and antecedents of a certain person are unknown, he will adopt the *gotra* and *pravara* of the *Āchārya*. The story of Satyakāma Jābāla in the *Chchāndogya Upanishad* seems to illustrate the case in point. It has generally been taken to denote the passage of a non-Brāhmaṇa from his status to that of a Brāhmaṇa. It is understood from this story that Satyakāma attained to the position of a Brāhmaṇa, in virtue of his Brāhmaṇa qualities, though he was of low and unknown parentage. The story is thus narrated in the *Chchāndogya Upanishad*: Satyakāma addressed his mother Jabālā thus: "I wish to become a Brahmachārin; of what *gotra* am I?" She said: "I do not know of what *gotra* thou art. When I had to move about much as a domestic servant, I got thee in my youth. I am Jabālā by name. Say that thou art Satyakāma Jābāla." Satyakāma went to Hāridrumata Gautama and said, "I wish to become a *Brahmachārin*, sir, under you. May I come?" Having been questioned as to his family-antecedents, Satyakāma spoke the truth, as he was instructed by his mother. Gautama replied, "No one but a Brāhmaṇa would thus speak out. Go and fetch fuel, friend, I shall initiate you. You have not swerved from the truth." Really, Satyakāma may have been a Brāhmaṇa lad who did not know his *gotra* or had not been definitely assigned to any, because he had not been "initiated". But the mention of the *gotra* and prostration before the *Guru* were the essential conditions of initiation (*Brahmacharya*). The boy could not satisfy this condition. The *Guru* knew that he possessed Brāhmanical virtues and admitted him to the studentship. He got therefore the *gotra* of his *Guru*. The principle that is indicated here is that a boy whose *gotra* was unknown will get that of his *Āchārya*, at the time of his initiation. But in later times the definition of the word *Āchārya* became more comprehensive. The term included[138] the father, the initiator, the teacher, and the priest. The lad is led normally to *Brahmacharya* by his father, but where this is not possible for some reason or other, he gets the *gotra* of the *Āchārya*.

The practice of marrying outside one's *gotra* dates from the period of Sūtra literature. Marriage within the *gotra* was apparently not looked upon as a reprehensible habit before the Sūtra period, as a study and examination of the genealogical tables relating to the heroes and heroines of the Epics tends to show.[139] It is therefore probable that the practice of exogamy may have received an impulse from, if it is not directly due to, the contact with the non-Aryan races.

XXV

Other Influences

The doctrine of *ahimsa* which appears half-accepted by the model Epic heroes was quickened by Buddhist and Jaina influences. As we read in the *Manusmriti*,[140] "to eat flesh and to drink wine are the natural inclinations of the human mind. To abstain from them is beneficial." The hero who was accustomed to eat meat is found to say in the *Mahābhārata*, "they say that meat is a pleasant and strengthening food, but it is also stated that they who indulge in it go to hell; my mind is befuddled on the point." [141] These disclose an era of transition when the doctrine of *ahimsa* was accepted as a righteous principle, but when meat-eating was not altogether rejected in practice as being unwholesome. This idea becomes clear also from the views held in regard to the efficacy of animal sacrifices, which have been examined.

Certain forbidden practices which had no sanction in the holy texts are seen permitted for the Brāhmans in the period under survey. Manu allows magic for them,[142] and Gautama holds that a Brāhmaṇa may use arms if life be threatened. The Tāḷagunḍa pillar inscription of Kākutstha Varman shows how in dire necessity a Brāhmaṇa was forced to take up arms, leaving his old and legitimate duties. Kauṭilya [143] is of the opinion that Brāhmans could not become adepts in military sciences, and that an army made of Brāhmans did inefficient fighting in the battle-field. They were unaccustomed to bear arms by their very nature; that was a profession disallowed to them. But the Brāhmaṇa sage Droṇa is seen to excel all others in his time in the military arts and sciences, and students from various parts of India came to him, and sought him as their preceptor.[144] The Brāhmans of the North sold wool and went on sea-voyages—both of them forbidden practices.[145] The southern *Sūtrakāras* permit certain customs not allowed by others, such as eating with one's wife and marrying the daughter of the maternal uncle or paternal aunt.[146] These are apparently customs borrowed from the Dravidians of South India. It has also been held [147] that the regulation of marriage by totemic names and the prevalence of the practice of levirate (*niyoga*) in the period of the law-codes were both of them due to non-Aryan influences. But the latter finds some warrant even in the *Rig-Veda*, and should not be supposed to have been entirely a borrowing by the Aryas from the non-Aryan peoples of India.[148]

The practice of *Satī* was prevalent in the *Śangam* period in South India, and the Brāhmans of the South are described as attempting to dissuade the widows from self-immolation. In the *Puṛanāṉūṛu*, the following passage appears, and it shows that the Tamil dame was determined to dedicate her body to the same flames that consumed the body of her beloved lord, against the sage counsel of the Brāhmaṇa priest. She addresses as follows :—

" O ye of wisdom full, O ye of wisdom full,
Ye bid us not go forth to death ; ye would restrain,
O ye of wisdom full, but evil is your counsel here ;
We are not of those content to live forlorn,
And feed on bitter herbs, where once they feasted royally.
We lie not on rough stones, who slept erstwhile on sumptuous couch.
The pyre's black logs heaped up in the burning ground
To you seem indeed terrible ; to us,
Since our mighty spouse is dead,
The waters of the pleasant lake where blooms
The lotus flower, and the fierce fires are one."

Elsewhere a woman seeks to be buried with her lord, and is found to say, "O, Potter, Shaper of the urn,—make the funeral urn large enough for me too." The Brāhmans of South India may have been responsible for the abolition of this inhuman practice which was apparently prevalent in the *Śangam* age.

XXVI

Changes in Language and Style

Of all the sources of our study comparative philology has perhaps yielded the least satisfactory results. As ethnologists themselves admit, language is no certain test of racial affinities, and in spite of the efforts of eminent scholars in the field, it has not been possible to adjudge properly the contribution of the two cults in the evolution of the Indian vernaculars or the various changes that came over Sanskrit and the Prākrits as a result of the racial admixture.

Prākrits were evolved from Vedic Sanskrit, and these became the everyday-language of the masses. Sanskrit as a spoken language had perhaps ceased to exist in many parts of India by the third century B.C., and in the so-called "Renaissance period" of Sanskrit literature works in Sanskrit seem to have been written for a learned and cultured public and not for the people at large. Pāḷi and Māgadhī especially received a literary impulse from Buddhism. Aśoka's inscriptions are mostly in Māgadhī, and the Jaina *Sthaviras* appear to have used Paiśāchī for their scriptures.[149] The Buddhist scriptures of Ceylon were written in Pāḷi. But as time went on, the Brāhmanical revival resulted in the diffusion and extension of Sanskrit which was preferred by the ruling classes to the more popular dialects, as the inscriptions of the Gupta kings evidently show. The Aśokan inscriptions were written in language easily to be understood by the man in the street, for some form of Prākrit appealed more directly and easily than Sanskrit to the comprehension of the generality of his subjects. But the inscriptions of Rudradāman, the Kshatrapa of Ujjain, were written in elaborate Sanskrit. These, it is held, are exceptional, and scholars are also of the opinion that Sanskrit as a spoken language had ceased to exist by the second century A.D. But the Ghosūṇḍi inscription found in Udaipur District and assigned by Bühler to the third century B.C. must set at rest any doubt that Sanskrit had ceased to be a spoken language after the time of Aśoka. This inscription is now taken to be the earliest which uses classical Sanskrit.[150] It records the setting up of a stone for worship at the Nārāyaṇa-vāṭa for the Bhagavāns Sankarshaṇa and Vāsudeva as well as the construction of a hall of worship for these deities.[151] The following conclusion seems to be irresistible: Sanskrit was not only the language of the learned and cultured folk, but was also the spoken and written language at least in West India, comprising Rajputana, Malwa and Kathiawar, used by princes to adumbrate their glorious deeds in the period from 300 B.C. to 200 A.D. The result of the influence of non-Aryan on Aryan language and *vice versa* is thus dwelt on by Sten Konow:[152] "We have before us a series of languages and speeches, which to all appearance are purely Aryan, but of which the grammatical system in many respects shows that the foreign non-Aryan element has been assimilated and has exercised its influence on the internal structure of the language."

The style of composition of the sacred works of literature was changed to remove or at least to simplify the difficulties of Brāhmanical teaching. A novel style is adopted in the Sūtras, and the object of these "could be no other than to offer practical manuals to those who were discouraged by too elaborate treatises and who had found a shorter way to salvation opened to them by the heretical teaching of Buddha". The same period witnessed also the compilation of Purāṇic literature which with its simple stories and moral anecdotes written in an easy style offered itself as readable history and as a substitute for the more difficult treatises already extant.

XXVII

Sanskrit and Tamil

As Max Müller says,[153] "all the living languages of India, both Aryan and Dravidian, draw their very life and soul from Sanskrit." It is, however, to be noted that the structure of the Tamil language shows that it has grown and developed on independent lines. While Tamil literature and culture owe a great deal to Aryan literature and culture, it has to be granted that the Tamil language is practically free from outside influences. Whereas in North India the Aryan language was charged with some non-Aryan elements, the influence of Sanskrit still predominant, in the South we find that the reverse is true—we have Dravidian dialects charged with Sanskrit elements, the former not losing their individuality. If we examine works of Sanskrit literature, we note that in the Sanskrit of the South, words of Dravidian origin have made their appearance undisguised save by formal Sanskritization, and a cerebral *l* is common. Non Aryan borrowings may be seen also in the language of the North, whether taken from the local tribes or borrowed from the South.[154] But in one important respect Tamil has been affected by contact with Sanskrit. The vocabulary of the latter has got widened, apparently due to the influence of Sanskrit and other languages, e.g. there are 62 synonyms for the word earth; 60 for mountain; 50 for water; and 34 for wind.

The academies of the Tamils that met at Madura, known as the *Śangam*, popularized Sanskrit literature in South India. Some of the early Tamil authors were Brāhmans—Agastya, Gautama, and Kapila. The first is famous in Tamil literature as the author of the first Tamil grammar and as the teacher of twelve grammarians of the Tamil language. The main works of the *Śangam* have borrowed or adapted their themes from the works of early Sanskrit literature ; and there are indications of direct borrowings in methods of composition, the framing of the plot, and in the narration of moral anecdotes and illustrative stories. For example, the divisions of the *Kuṛal*, which is like "an apple of gold in pictures of silver", correspond to those of the *Kāmandaka-nītisāra*, which in turn is based on the *Arthaśāstra* of Kauṭilya. Many of the ideas and expressions found in the work show direct borrowings from the *Mahābhārata*, *Manusmriti*, and the *Artha-śāstra* of Kauṭilya. The *Brihat Kathā* of Gunāḍhya has given the central plot for many a writer of the *Śangam* and the post-*Śangam* period. An example of Tamil romance, which is a borrowing from this Sanskrit theme, is the *Udayanan kādai*.[155]

XXVIII

India and Abroad

A study of the monuments belonging to this period shows that a few of the details of art and architecture were borrowed from Persia and Chaldaea. In fact, no art was ever absolutely indigenous to any country. The pillar was the only lithic form of architecture that Persia had to lend. The borrowings in sculpture are perhaps more numerous. The decoration of the later *vihāra* caves of Nālandā and of the *sanghārāmas* of Gandhāra may have been the result of western influences. A direct influence of Babylonia on Indian art may be traced in the Buddhist *vihāra* caves of western India. The four or five-storey *vihāras* which we hear of afterwards undoubtedly recall the impression of a Babylonian temple of God. The sculpture of the *stūpas* of Barahut and Sānchi combines many "non-Aryan elements with the Aryan ideas which dominate it".[156] The idea of issuing ethical exhortations was perhaps borrowed by Aśoka from the practice of Darius whose Nakshi Rustam inscription "is preceptive, not historical".[157] It is very likely that these influences from outside India were brought on Aryan thought and styles of art by the Dravidians who had intercourse with the western peoples from times immemorial. Thus, Indian culture shows itself not merely as a composite culture, the result of the blend of the various streams in India, but as capable of adapting what was regarded as remarkable in the culture of foreign peoples, and make it part and parcel of its own.

As India was ready to receive from foreign countries ideals of art and architecture, so her culture spread to distant lands. In this way was laid the foundation of a greater India beyond the seas. The influence of her culture spread over Serindia and distant Java and the Spice Islands in the east. "From the Brahmaputra and Maṇipūr to the Tonkin gulf we can trace a continuous string of petty states ruled by those scions of the Kshatriya race, using the Sanskrit or the Pāḷi language in official documents and inscriptions, building temples and other monuments after the Hindu style, and employing Brāhman priests for the propitiatory ceremonies connected with the court and state." There is ample evidence that Indian colonists from the Dekhan had from a very early time colonized important places in the region of the Iravadi and Indo-China.[158] The Indian colonization of Java, besides going to show the extraordinary developments that should have taken place in the maritime adventure of the Hindus of the period, clearly indicates the onward march of Indian culture to dominate over new lands, and make itself more comprehensive than before. According to Javanese tradition the migration of Indian culture to Java is thus narrated :—

There was a Hindu king Śakapratīva who went to Java in 78 A.D. to preach the tenets of Buddhism to its people. Probably, he may have been sent there by the Kushāṇa Emperor Kanishka. Śakapratīva is said to have taken with him two servants and a knife for writing the doctrines of the Buddha. In Central Java he met with the cannibal king whom he was able to defeat. The kingship of the island was then offered to Śakapratīva. He ruled the country for forty days, gave the people laws and taught them the alphabet. The Buddhist scriptures were written for the benefit of the Javanese who became thereafter converted to Buddhism. Besides, Śakapratīva is also said to have introduced the era which went by his name as the Śaka era in the island.

The introduction and progress of Buddhism in Chāvakam (Java) is thus indicated in the *Maṇimekalai*: The heroine Maṇimekalai is said to have proceeded to the shrine of Champāpati and later to Java, which had its capital at Nāgapuram. The king of the place was Puṇyarāja, son of Bhūmichandra. From the time of the birth of this prince the rains had never failed, harvests had been plentiful, and famine and pestilence had never visited the land. On questioning who the lady was, Puṇyarāja was told that "there was none equal to this maid in all Jambudvīpa. She was a nun of great piety and virtue that had come from Kāverippaṭṭaṇam, and possessed marvellous and miraculous powers". The king, who was now endowed with a new vision of his previous birth, knew that he was only the adopted son of Bhūmichandra. He therefore resolved on giving up the throne and becoming a recluse. He betook himself to Maṇipallavam, and became acquainted with the Buddhist doctrines. After having mastered the tenets of the new faith, he left back to his own kingdom and there ruled over the land in peace.

XXIX

North and South Indian Styles of Architecture

According to Havell,[159] the architectural record of the South goes to prove that Dravidian civilization derived its main impulse from the gradual extension southward of Indo-Aryan culture, for the so-called Dravidian style of architecture is only Indo-Aryan design suited to the symbolism of the Śaiva cult, and shows little direct inspiration of Dravidian ideas. Fergusson says,[160] "the feature in Dravidian architecture which presents the greatest resemblance to the northern styles is the reverse slope of the eaves above the verandah; I am not aware of its existence anywhere else south of Nepal (than in Malabar), and it is much more likely to have been copied than reinvented." It is interesting to note in the Tamil work *Maṇimekalai*[161] that in Kāveripaṭṭaṇam, the Chōḷa capital, Magadhan artisaṇs, mechanics from Maharāshṭra, smiths from Avanti, and Yavana carpenters were employed in the construction of the royal house.

XXX

Non-Aryas the Carriers of Indian Commerce

India continued her commercial relations with foreign lands, and we have clear evidence that the non-Aryas were the carriers of Indian trade. As Mommsen says,[162] "In the Flavian period . . . the whole west coast of India was opened up to the Roman merchants as far down as the coast of Malabar, the home of the highly esteemed and dear-priced pepper for the sake of which they visited the ports of Musiris and Nelkynda." For a thousand years from 500 B.C. to 500 A.D., Ceylon was the chief emporium of the trade of India with the east coast of Africa, Yemen and Malabar, and the ultra-Gangetic peninsula extending to China.[163]

Indian trade with the West was mainly carried on in the three parts of India—Barbaricum, Barygaza and the Malabar coast.[164] The merchants of Barygaza and the neighbouring country went to Arabia for the trade in gums and incense, to Africa for gold, and to Malabar and Ceylon for the much valued pepper and cinnamon.[165] Thus they had the carrying trade of the whole of the Indian Ocean. Yet, the port of Barygaza and the land about Barbaricum were not quite convenient for trading purposes. The passage to Broach (Barygaza), says the *Periplus*, was difficult and dangerous. Barbaricum, which has been identified with Lower Sindh, was far away from the interior, and therefore cut off from communications with the centres of trade. In the time of Ptolemy it had ceased to be a trading centre of any importance.[166] The most important and the safest destination for ships bound to India was the Malabar coast, and it has continued to be such down to this day. The Malabar coast was the emporium of the trade with the West. As Pliny writes, "Below the white island commences the kingdom of Koprobatas (Keraḷaputra), styled Limurike, the first mart of which is Nasora, then Tundis, a large village close to the shore, and next to these Mooziris, a flourishing place frequented both by native vessels from Ariake and by the Greeks from Egypt."

That the Dravidians of the west coast of India were the carriers of commerce between India and the western world is further clear from the account in the *Periplus* to the effect that from there were exported great quantities of fine pearls, ivory, silk-cloth, spikenard from the Ganges, maḷabothrum from the places in the interior, transparent stones of all kinds, diamonds and sapphires, tortoise-shells and muslins of the finest sort called the "Gangetic". Thus commodities produced near the Ganges and the interior were taken to the Malabar coast for export thence. In the period of the *Śangam*, the west coast of South India, the country of the Chera, was renowned for its maritime activity, not only commercial, but warlike, as the passage in the *Puṛanāṉūṛu* seems clearly to indicate. "We (other vessels) are little barks that sail not on the western main, where Cheran's warlike fleets are seen." The Malabar coast was the centre of the trade with the Greeks as is borne out by the description of the town of Musiris, "where the beautiful large ships of the Yavanas (Greeks), bringing gold, come splashing the white foam on the waters of the Periyār river, which belongs to the Chera, and return laden with huge quantities of valuable pepper." The Chera king Śenguṭṭuvan is praised as presenting to the trading visitors the rare products of the seas and mountains that were within his domain. This is also clear from the Tamil poem *Pattuppāṭṭu*,[167] where we read that the people of the South traded in the following commodities: the gems and gold of the Northern Mountain, the sandal and cedar of the Western Ghats, the pearls of the South Sea, the corals of the Eastern Sea, the products of the Gangetic Regions, and of the Cauvery Delta, edible stuff from Ceylon and spices from Kāḻakam (?). Commerce with Babylon and Greece was flourishing in this period, as is evident from the Jātaka,[168] and other literature. The names of the commodities imported into Greece from India were mostly Dravidian, e.g. oryza (*ariśi*-rice), injivera (*inji*-ginger), karpion (*karuvu*-cinnamon). The *Baveru Jātaka* has been taken to indicate the account of a trading voyage to Babylon, and if this identification be right, it is evidence of the trade between India and Babylonia flourishing in this period, a trade that had plied from times immemorial.

Trade with China and the East was busy about the period, as the Greek travellers speak of the importation of Chinese silk to India.[169] The silk from China is also mentioned in the *Arthaśāstra*[170] of Kauṭilya. One of the Jātakas describes the voyage of certain merchants of Barukaccha for the "golden land" (Suvaṇṇabhumi), which has been variously identified.[171] It is highly probable that the Buddhist and Hindu antiquities in Java as well as the vestiges of Hindu beliefs and practices in the island were also taken over the sea by the Dravidians of South and East India.

XXXI

Internal Trade

The Greek records show that there was a brisk internal trade between the Aryas and the aboriginal population of India. The Kynocephali sold to the civilized Indians dried fruits, a red dye-stuff and a gum exuding from the siptaghora tree, and obtained in exchange, bread, oatmeal, cotton-cloth and weapons.[172] This trade in India flowed through the large routes of traffic connecting North India with the Dekhan. Of the two main routes, the northern and the southern, the latter is spoken of favourably by Kauṭilya[173] against the opinion of his "teacher", on the ground that it leads to regions where conch-shells, diamonds, precious stones, pearls and gold are available in plenty. In the time of Megasthenes[174] enormous developments had taken place in the means of communication connecting one part of India with another. He mentions a grand trunk road which connected the various parts of the empire of Chandragupta. The course of the road and the towns it touched are described by him. This road was constructed in eight stages and passed through the following places: Pushkalāvati, Taxila, the regions of the Jhelam, Bias, Sutlej, Jumna, and the Ganges, Hastināpura, Rhodopha, Kalimpaxa, Prayāg and Pāṭalīputra. Kauṭilya speaks of communication by land and by water, and is partial to the former method of transport.[175] The means of communication made it easy for the people of one part of India to come into frequent contact with those of the other parts, as they helped to remove existing barriers between caste and caste, and district and district.

XXXII

Sea-voyage and Shipping

Even in this period sea-voyage was considered undesirable for the Aryas. The Smritis enjoin "that one who has gone on sea-voyages should not be invited for *śrāddhas* (annual ceremonies for the manes).[176] But, apparently, the opinion was gaining ground that sea-voyage was not altogether forbidden for the Aryas, as we read that the Brāhmans of the North did not consider it sinful. Under the Mauryas on the other hand, ship-building must have been a flourishing industry.[177] Among the various superintendents in the *Arthaśāstra* there is one in charge of ships, and there are very elaborate rules guiding the conduct of ships that visited the coasts of a state.[178] The following are some of them: The superintendent of ships had to observe the regulations prevalent in trading towns as well as the orders of the superintendent of port towns. All ships that passed along the coasts and alighted at harbours were to pay tolls. Pirate ships were to be seized and destroyed. The same treatment was to be meted out to ships that were destined to a hostile country and to those that violated the rules in sea-port towns. Persons known to convey a secret mission or carry weapons or explosives should be arrested by the port-officers. The cargo of merchantmen that did not put on their characteristic ensign or flag was to be seized, but ships that were spoilt by water were to be allowed some concession in customs and duties. They were to be permitted to set sail when the season was favourable for their departure. Vessels that were drifted ashore by storms on the sea were to be treated by the superintendent with paternal care and affection. These regulations will show that rapid strides had been taken by the industries of shipping and ship-building in the Mauryan polity. They had developed so far as to require such elaborate treatment as has been given them in the *Arthaśāstra*. The mention by Megasthenes of a Board of Admiralty among the Six Committees which made up the War-Office of Chandragupta Maurya goes to prove the same point, besides indicating that in the Maurya period ships were used for trade as well as in warfare. Ship-building must have received an impetus from the commercial enterprise of the non-Aryas who were the prime carriers of the sea-commerce of those ages. Ship-building and maritime activity was a speciality with the Andhras. This is proved by the remarkable find of their coins[179] on the east coast, bearing the design of ships. In the South Indian Buddhist Antiquities we have illustration and description of three of these ship-coins belonging to the Andhras of the first and the second centuries A.D. In the Jātaka literature ships are mentioned which carried from 200 to 700 passengers, and we are told that in his occupation of Ceylon, Vijaya's ships carried 700 men.[180]

XXXIII

Dravidian Ship-building

The literature of the *Śangam* epoch discloses the fact that the Dravidians of South India were good ship-builders and were experts in the navigation of the seas. The Tamil work *Maṇimekalai* has a story of a shipwreck, and adventures on the sea are not uncommonly met with in works of *Śangam* literature. The arts of seamanship were developed in South India independently of outside influences.[181] The words for sail and mast, *pāy* and *pāymaram*, are clearly Dravidian. The oar was the *harigōlu* or *kōl*, " a stick used to propel a float across a current," and later the term meant the coracle itself. The native words for boats are varied and many, e.g. *ōḍa* or *ōṭe* (made of reed), *dōṇi* (dug-out), *teppam* (float), *kalam*, *marakalam* and *kappal*. As we read in the *Periplus*, there were " ships of the country coasting along the shore as far as Damarica (Tamiḷakam), and other very large vessels made of single logs bound together called *sangāra* (*chengāḍam*, Malayāḷam; *sanghāṭa*, Sanskrit), but those which make the voyage to Chryse and the Ganges are called *colandia* and are very large ".[182]

It is possible that the Dravidians influenced Aryan ideas of navigation. Some of the nautical terms occurring in Sanskrit literature appear to be based on Tamil. The word *aritra* (oar) of the Vedic texts is perhaps derivable from *harigōla* or *harivagōla*, the stick that propels a boat. The *veṇu* and *veṇuka* of the *Arthaśāstra* correspond to the Dravidian *ōḍam*. The terms *uḍupa* and *kōl* are perhaps adaptations of the Tamil and Kanarese words *ōḍa* and *harigōla*.

XXXIV

The Final Division of Functions

The non-Aryas were not simply the media of communication between India and the outside world. They had become an essential factor in the economic life of India. The details of agricultural operations in the lands of lords, Aryan and non-Aryan, became in course of time a monopoly of the non-Aryas. Agriculture came to be a despised occupation with the three higher classes in the Hindu society. In the ancient Aryan scheme of social classification, *vārtā*, which comprised agriculture, cattle-rearing, trade and money-lending, was the occupation of the Vaiśya class. Now it came to be confined to the last class, the Śūdra. Besides the restrictions in regard to forbidden occupations enforced by the sacred laws of the Aryas, the principle of *ahimsa*, in its extreme and rather curious form, seems also to have led to agriculture becoming a prohibited calling. The following is found in the code of Manu [183]: "People think that agriculture is good as an occupation. It is, however, looked down upon by the virtuous, for the iron-tip of the plough furrows the earth as well as destroys the creatures that live in it." Having settled for a long time in villages where the main occupations were agriculture and pasture, the Aryas specialized in philosophical and intellectual studies, and had very little inclination for manual professions.[184] Hence the industries and handicrafts remained entirely in the hands of non-Aryas, as also the fine arts of sculpture and painting. The result was, as Fergusson says,[185] that all the literature of India was Aryan, all her architecture non-Aryan.

Even in the *Rāmāyaṇa* we have allusions to the art of portrait-painting practised by the non-Aryas. Indrajit deceived Hanumān by killing an image of Sītā which could hardly be distinguished from the original; and a model of Rāma's head produced before Sītā looked such an exact reproduction of him as to cause intense grief in her. The Aryas explained away all this as being *māyā* (illusion).[186] The non-Aryan tribes were clever in the art of metamorphosis. They were adepts in the black arts, and could transform themselves into any animal-form. This practice is even now current among some of the Dravidian tribes of South India. They profess to have the mystic power of changing their human to animal forms because of their devotion to certain "black gods" comprised under the general category *kuṭṭic-chāttān*. Even in the *Rig-Veda* [187] the Rākshasas are described as capable of assuming animal forms at will; in the *Rāmāyaṇa* the non-Aryan tribes are spoken of as *kāmarūpiṇah*; Mārīcha becomes a golden deer and Hanumān assumes various shapes.

The non-Aryan talent for fine and beautiful works of sculpture finds ample illustration in the description by the poet of the funeral car that was got ready by the Vānaras for taking the dead body of Vāli.[188] Allowing for poetic fancies and imagination, it has to be accepted that the description shows that the non-Aryan tribes should have been, no doubt, adepts in the fine arts of painting and sculpture. These are among the professions forbidden for the "twice-born".[189] The Aryas disdained manual labour, and this accounts for the degradation of Indian arts and the importation of Greek models as in the Gandhāra sculptures. To this day, the *śulva sūtras* and the *śilpi śāstras* are in the hands of the lower classes known in South India as the *kammāḷar*. The artisan class was very comprehensive in the time of Kauṭilya,[190] and included not only handicraftsmen but retail dealers, medical practitioners, washmen, dramatists and musicians. It includes now all those engaged in the sixty-four *kalās*.

The fundamental principles of Indian Dramaturgy are no doubt of Aryan origin, being based on the *Bharata Śāstra*, but it is interesting to find that the art of dancing and dramatic representation in its most scientific form is practised in South India, especially in Malabar, where we have various forms of the drama—

Kathakaḷi, Krishṇāṭṭam kaḷi, Chākkiyār kūttu, Pāvakkūttu, Ōṭṭamtuḷḷal, etc.[191] The sculptures of the ninety-three dancing postures found in a gateway of the Naṭarāja temple at Chidambaram are illustrative [192] of the marvellous development that the art of dancing had reached among the people of South India, pre-eminently the land of the Dravidians. As Dr Ray observes, "The intellectual portion of the community being thus withdrawn from active participation in the arts, the spirit of inquiry gradually died out among a nation naturally prone to speculation and metaphysical subtleties, and India for once bade adieu to experimental and inductive sciences."[193]

NOTES TO PART IV

[1] e.g. *Vinaya*, ii, 46 (S.B.E.); Anguttara, i, 213.

[2] *Vishṇu Purāṇa*, iv, 24. [3] No. 26; (*Pāmsupradāna*).

[4] *Jātaka*, Nos. 150 and 531. Camb. Tr. i, 242, and v, 141.

[5] Rock Edicts, ii and xiii. [5a] Bühler in *Athenaeum* of March, 1897

[6] *Dialogues*, i, 120. [7] Watters, *Yuan Chwang*, p. 159.

[8] *Tree and Serpent Worship*, pp. 57 and 58. It will be shown that metempsychosis, which also Fergusson holds as un-Aryan, has got some basis in the early Vedic texts.

[9] Smith, *Early History of India*, p. 194.

[10] In a later age, the Lingāyet sect was founded by a Brāhmaṇa, Basava, though the main tenets of the Lingāyets were opposed to Brāhmanism. They reverence the Vedas, but disregard the later commentaries on which the Brāhmaṇas rely. They profess to be free from all caste distinctions. They are puritanical in the matter of food and drink. No true Lingāyet will taste meat or smell liquor. They say that by birth all are equal, and men are not superior to women. Marriage in childhood is wrong, the contracting parties should have the voice, and widows should be allowed to remarry. *s.v.* Lingāyet in Thurston's *Castes and Tribes of South India*.

[11] *Traiguṇya vishayā Vedāh nistraiguṇyo bhavārjuna* |

[12] e.g. *Manusmriti*, iv, 80, 81; *Vasishṭha*, xviii, 14 and 15.

[13] *Śukranīti*, iv, 4, 32 (Oppert's Ed.).

Śūdro varṇaśchaturtho'pi varṇatvātdharmamarhati |
Veda mantra svadhā svāhā vashaḍkārādibhirvinā |
Purāṇādyuktamantraiścha namo'ntaih karma kevalam ||

[14] *Anguttara Nikāya, Tika Nipāta*, 65, p. 7.

[15] *Bhagavat Gītā*, xvi, 6. The evolution of the word *Asura* may be briefly noticed here. Originally, the word seems to have been used to denote a powerful celestial being, whether bright or dark, good or bad. Both the Devas and the Asuras are said to have sprung from Prajāpati. (*Śat. Br.*, xiii, 8, 1, 5.) Next, it was an appellation to "demons" who opposed and fought with the "gods". Asura was an "*Adeva*". Thirdly, the word was used to denote a race of non-Aryas of ferocious activity and of great energy. As we read in the *Śat. Br.*, their speech was indistinct and incorrect. Lastly, the word included all "ungodly and unrighteous practices".

[16] *Bhag. Gītā*, ii, 22.

Vāsāmsi jīrṇāni yathā vihāya navāni gṛṇhāti naroparāṇi |
Tathā śarīrāṇi vihāya jīrṇāni anyāni samyāti navāni dehi ||

[17] Max Müller, *Contribution to the Science of Mythology*, ii, 598.

[18] *The Religion of the Veda*, p. 254.

[19] Vol. i, 144. [20] *JRAS.* for 1909, p. 574.

[21] *A.V.*, xviii, 2, 57. [22] *A.V.*, xviii, 2, 48.

[23] *R.V.*, x, 16, 3. *Sūryam chakshuh gacchatu vātamātmā* | *dyām cha gaccha prithivīm cha "dharmaṇā"* ||

[24] *R.V.*, x, 14, 8. *Hitvā yāvad yaṁ punarastamehi saṅgacchasva tanvā suvarchāh* |

[25] *Mūshu Varuṇa mṛṇmayīm imam rājannaham gamam mṛḷā sukshatra mṛḷaya* | In *R.V.*, i, 92, 10, Ushas is addressed as *Punarjāyamānah*. He is *Punarbhū* in *R.V.*, i, 133, 2.

The doctrine of transmigration had become well established in the Upanishadic period. We have in the *Cch. Up.*, *Tadya iha ramaṇīyacharaṇābhyāso ha yatte ramaṇīyam yonim āpadyeran* | *Iha kapūya charaṇā abhyāso ha yatte kapūyām yonimāpadyeran* || Similarly in the *Kaṭhopanishad* we find *yonimanye prapadyante śarīratvāya dehinah* | *Sthāṇumanyenusamyānti yathā karma yathā śrutam* ||

[26] *Camb. Hist. of Ind.*, op. cit.

[27] *Jātaka*, 474. Tr., iv, 217 ; *Anguttara*, i, 162.

[28] *Buddhist India*, pp. 55, 56, and 60.

[29] *Sacred Books of the Buddhists*, ii, pp. 65–95.

[30] *Anguttara*, i, 148.

[31] *Jātaka*, v, 257.

[32] e.g., *Cch. Up.*, v, 3, 1, 7.

[33] *Cch. Up.*, v, 11.

[34] *Mahābhārata*, Vana Parva.

[35] *Uttarādhyayana Sūtra*, xxv, 24, 23.

[36] *Dhammapada*, 393–4. Saunders' tr. in " Heritage of India " Series.

Tam aham brūmi Brāhmaṇam yam hi saccham cha dhammo cha, so sukhī so cha Brāhmaṇo |

[37] *Mahābhāshya* on Pāṇini, v, 1, 115.

[38] *Tapaśśrutam cha yoniścha etat Brāhmaṇakāraṇam* | *Tapaśśrutābhyām yo hīnah jātibrāhmaṇa eva sah* || *Mahābhāshya* on v, 1, 115.

[39] e.g., *Vasishṭha*, x, 4.

[40] Ibid., i, 1, 1, 10.

[41] *Manu*, iii, 21–34 ; *Yājñavalkya*, i, 58–51 ; *Gautama*, iv, 6–15 ; *Āpastamba*, ii, 11, 17–21 ; *Vasishṭha* has only six kinds, i, 29 ff. ; *Baudhāyana*, i, 11, 20.

[42] *Baudhāyana*, i, 11, 20, 16.

[43] e.g., *Manusmriti*, x, 8, 56.

[44] For biographical details of *Viśvāmitra* see *Rāmāyaṇa*, Bāla Kāṇḍa.

[45] *Lobha*, *krodha*, *mada*, and *mātsarya* are illustrated in the story of the fight with Vasishṭha over Śabalā. *Kāma* and *moha* in the story of Menakā. *Mada* and *mātsarya* in the stories of Śunahśepa and Triśanku. *Krodha* and *mātsarya* in Hariśchandra's story.

[46] *Ait. Br.*, ii, 460 f.

[47] It is perhaps for this reason that among the important *rishis* of this country, Viśvāmitra is taken to represent the ear (*śrotra*), which denotes learning. Similarly, Vasishṭha is seen to stand for the mind (*mana*), Gautama for speech (*vāk*), Kasyapa for the eye (*chakshu*), and Atri, Angiras, or Bhrigu for breath (*prāṇa*).

[48] *Na balam Kshatriyasyāhuh Brāhmaṇāh balavattarāh* |
Dhik balam Kshatriya balam Brahmatejobalam balam ||
Rāmāyaṇa, Bāla Kāṇḍa, 57, 22.

[49] *Manu*, x, 42 and 65 ; *Vasishṭha*, ii, 23.

Tapobījaprabhāvaistu te gacchanti yuge yuge
Utkarsham chāpakarsham cha manushyeshviha janmatah |
Śūdro Brāhmaṇatāmeti Brāhmaṇaśchaiva Śūdratām ||

[50] *Manusmriti*, x, 64. See *S.B.E.*, xxv, p. 416 and note.

[51] *Manu*, iii, 15, 17, 18, and 19 ; *Vasishṭha*, xiv, 11 ; *Vishṇu*, xvi ; *Āpastamba*, ii, 13, 4 and 5 ; *Yājñavalkya*, i, 57.

[52] *Manusmriti*, x, 10.

[53] *Divyāvadāna*, pp. 623–5.

[54] *Manu*, iii, 13 ; *Yājñavalkya*, i, 57 ; *Vasishṭha*, i, 24 and 25 ; *Vishṇu*, xviii.

[55] *Vishṇu*, xviii. See also *Baudhāyana*, ii, 2, 3, 2–10 ; *Gautama*, xxviii, 35–40. The distribution of property varies a little from the others in the *Vasishṭha Smriti*. Here the son by a Brāhmaṇa woman got three shares ; that by

the Kshatriya, two; Vaiśya and Śūdra, each one share. See also Kauṭilya, *Arthaśāstra*, p. 163.

[56] Instances of intermarriage in the *Jātaka* are seen in i, 421, 422; ii, 319 f.; iii, 9–11; vi, 422.

[57] *Manusmriti*, x, 12. [58] Ibid., x, 67 and 31.

[59] *Āpastamba*, ii, 10, 27, 8 and 9.

[60] The very high moral ideal implied in the word Brāhmaṇa may be seen in:—

"The moon with all the stars may fall to earth;
This earth, its hills and forests may reach the sky;
The waters of the mighty deep may all dry up;
But by no chance can the mighty *rishi* tell a lie."

See Rockhill, *Life of the Buddha*, p. 67.

[61] *Vishṇu*, xvi, 1 and 2. [62] *Manusmriti*, x, 70 f. [63] *Vasishṭha*, iii, 48.

[64] *Bhag. Gītā*: *Strīshu dushṭāsu Vārshṇeya jāyate varṇasankarah* |

[65] *Rāmāyaṇa*, Bāla Kāṇḍa, 6, 17; *Gautama*, x. Manu says (x, 24): "Mixed castes are formed as a result of adultery between castes, marriages not recognized by the law, and by the neglect of occupation prescribed for each caste." In the *Maṇimekalai* Chitrapatī, the grandmother of Maṇimekalai, the heroine requests the prince Udayakumāran to restore her grand-daughter to her rightful occupation from being a Buddhist nun which she had become.

[66] *Jātaka*, iv, 361; i, 356, 357; ii, 87; iv, 84; iv, 169; iv, 531; vi, 372; iv, 15; v, 22; ii, 200; vi, 170; v, 290–3 respectively.

[67] *Manusmriti*, x, 95. See lawful and forbidden occupations. "By selling flesh, lac, and salt, a Brāhmaṇa at once becomes an outcaste; by selling milk, he becomes degraded to the position of a Śūdra in three days." (*Vasishṭha*, ii, 27.)

[68] *Vasishṭha*, xix, 7; *Āpastamba*, ii, 10, 12–16; *Gautama*, xi, 31.

[69] *Yo lobhāt adhamo jātyā jīvedutkrishṭakarmabhih* |
Tam rājā nirdhanam kritvā kshiprameva pravāsayet ||

[70] *Dialogues*, i, 120.

[71] *Vasishṭha*, ii, 22; *Vishṇu*, ii, 15.

[72] *Epigraphia Indica*, vii. Tālagunda Pillar Inscription, vv. 10 and 11.

[73] *Vishṇu*, xvi, 8–14, for example. Māgadha is a merchant in Manu and Āyogava, a carpenter.

[74] Watters: *Yuan Chwang*, i, 147. For example, in the *Jātaka* we find that the Chaṇḍālas, "the lowest race that go upon two feet . . . meanest men on earth, dwelt away from the city in Chaṇḍāla settlements" (*Jātaka*, iv, 397, 200, 376).

[75] *Manu*, iv, 80; *Vasishṭha*, xviii, 14.

[76] *Āpastamba*, i, 5, 16, 22, and i, 17, 1. See *Aprayatena tu Śūdreṇa upahritam abhojyam* | *yatra Śūdra upasprišet* and commentary.

[77] *Jātaka*, 497; iv, p. 242. Camb. tr., iv, 388. [78] *Āpastamba*, ii, 2, 3, 4.

[79] Ibid., i, 6, 18, 10, 14.

[80] *Śukranīti*, vv. 54 and 56.

Bhrityam parikshayet nityam viśvāsyam viśvasettadā |
Naiva jātih na cha kulam kevalam lakshayedapi ||
Vivāhe bhojane nityam kulajātivivechanam |

[81] *Vishṇu*, lxi, 50 f.

[82] *Bhag. Gītā*, xvii, 8, 9, 10.

Āyussatvabalārogyasukhaprītivivardhanāh |
Rasyāh snigdhāh sthirāh hridyā āhārāh sātvikapriyāh ||
Kaṭvamla lavaṇātyushṇa tīkshṇa rūksha vidāhinah |
Āhārā rājasasyeshṭā duhkhaśokāmayapradāh ||
Yātayāmam gatarasam pūti paryushitam cha yat |
Ucchishṭamapi chāmedhyam bhojanam tāmasapriyam ||

[83] *Vishṇu*, 51, 78. [84] Ibid., 51, 62.

[85] *Cch. Up.*, x, 5; *Mahābhārata*, Śānti, 141.

[86] The Veda forgotten may be learnt again. but the Brāhmaṇa loses his character if he is not of good conduct (*Kuṟal*, 134).

[87] Ibid., 51, 76. [88] *A.V.*, xii, 4, 5.

[89] *Mahābhārata*, Udyoga Parva, 34, 47.

[90] *Cch. Up.*, iii, 17, 4.

[90a] Quoted in *JRAS.* for 1894, p. 360.

[90b] See Bournouf: *Introduction*, p. 205.

[90c] Smith's *Aśoka* in *Rulers of India* Series.

[91] Smith, *Early Hist. of India*, p. 345. There is ample evidence of the religious toleration of South Indian kings. We read in the *Śangam* works that the temples at Kāverippaṭṭaṇam, the Chōḷa capital, were dedicated to Śiva, Subrahmaṇya, Baladeva, Krishṇa, and Indra. (*Silappadikāram*, v, ll. 169–75.) See also *Maṇimekalai*, i, ll. 54–7. *Puṟam*, 56, has the same gods, except Indra. Later kings in South Indian History were also tolerant, as the inscriptions of the Chōḷas, Pāṇḍyas, and Pallavas clearly show.

[92] See Bhandarkar: *Vaishṇavism, Śaivism*, etc., p. 153. The story is referred to in the Govindapūr Stone Inscription (*Ep. Ind.*, ii, 338).

[93] *Manu*, x, 43, 44.

[94] *Vishṇu Purāṇa*, iv, 16; *Padma Purāṇa*, vi, 250, 1 and 2.

[95] *Rāmāyaṇa*, Āraṇya Kāṇḍa, 13, 48.

[96] McCrindle, *Ancient India*, as described by Megasthenes and Arrian.

[97] *Puṟanāṉūṟu*, stanza 58, l. 8, also *Kauriyan* in *Śil.* 15, 2. The Chōḷa king is thus addressed in *Puṟanāṉūṟu*, 37. "Thou scion of the Chōḷa line who saved the dove from woe." "Descendant of him who to save a dove from grief did'st enter the weighing scale." (*Puṟanāṉūṟu*, 39.) These refer to the story of Śibi *Chakravarti* having sacrificed his own flesh to satisfy the eagle that had seized the dove and would not leave it.

[98] *Aśoka*, p. 41.

[99] See Bālakāṇḍa of the *Rāmāyaṇa* for the Aryan ancestry of non-Aryas like the Rākshasas and Vānaras.

[100] See M. Srinivasa Aiyangar: *Tamil Studies*, p. 61.

[101] *Matsya Purāṇa*, 48, 24–48; *Vāyu*, 99, 27.

[102] *R.V.*, iii, 43, 3; iv, 16, 9; v, 31, 7; vi, 20, 4; vii, 1, 10.

[103] *Cch. Up.*, iv, 17, 2; *Jātaka*, 539; *Manu*, xi, 33; ii, 230; *Arthaśāstra*, p. 7; *Ait. Br.*, v, 32; *Sat. Br.*, iv, 6, 7, 13; *Br. Up.*, i, 5, 5.

[104] *Atharvabhiḥ Upāyaiḥ* in *Arthaśāstra*, p. 15.

[105] See Hopkins, *The Great Epic of India*, p. 38.

[106] *I'tsing* (Takakasu's Tr.), chaps. 23, 32.

[107] Smith, *Early Hist. of Ind.*, p. 302.

[108] *Encyclopaedia of Religion and Ethics*, viii, 331.

[109] Farquhar, *Outline of the religious Literature of India*, p. 113.

[110] *Jātaka*, 31, 154. Professor Macdonell writes: "There is reason to believe that when the Aryans spread over India, the land of serpents, they found the cult diffused among the barbarians and borrowed it from them" (*Hist. of Sans. Lit.*, 111). But Max Müller says: "There can be no doubt that a belief in serpents had its origin in the Veda" (*Contr. to the Sc. of My.*, ii, 598 f.). The latter view is more correct as there are references to *sarpa* and *sarpabali* in the *Yajur-Veda*.

Tree Worship.—The sacredness of certain trees was recognized in the Vedic age, e.g. the Aśvattha, the Udumbara, and Palāśa. There is the prayer to Araṇyāni (the forest deity) in *R.V.*, x, 146. Aśvattha in i, 135, 8; x, 97, 5, is used for making the sacred fire. The worship of it is indicated in *A.V.*, v, 4, 3.

and vi, 11, 1. The gods are said to sit under it in the third heaven. Aśvattha is the seat of the gods in *A.V.*, v, 4, 3; vi, 95, 1. There is a prayer to the tree in *A.V.*, iii, 6. See also *Cch. Up.*, viii, 5, 3.

In the *Tait. Br.*, Aśvattha is so called because to it was tied the horse, and Agni resided in the tree for one year.

Tree worship is mentioned along with the worship of rivers in the *Rāmāyaṇa*, the latter, perhaps, based on the worship of the rivers in the hymn x, 75, and x, 9, 1–3, of the *R.V.* (See *Rāmāyaṇa*, Ayod. Kānd., 55, 24, and 55, 20 f.)

The Buddha appears several times in the *Jātaka* as a tree-god; e.g. *Jātaka*, 520.

Worship of the Guardians of the Quarters in *Rāmāyaṇa*, e.g. Ayod. Kāṇḍ., 16, 24.

111 *Encyclopaedia of Religion and Ethics*, see *Aiyanār*.

112 We do not find Subrahmaṇya in the early religious works. The earliest occurrence of the word is in the Brāhmaṇas in the sense of a "priest". The first mention of Subrahmaṇya as a god is in the Epics, where he is *Skanda* the son of *Rudra*. See *Rāmāyaṇa*, Bālakāṇḍa, 38; *Mahābhārata*, Vana Parva, 227 and 228. In North India the name Subrahmaṇya is unknown.

113 The various names of Śiva's consort appear in *Tait. Āraṇ.*, Ambikā (x, 18); Durgā (x, 1); Kātyāyanī and Kanyākumārī (x, 1); Umā in *Kenopanishad*, iii, 25; Kālī and Karālī in *Muṇḍ. Up.*, i, 2, 4.

114 Getty, *The Gods of Northern Buddhism*, p. 111.

115 *Rudrayāmala Tantra*, xviii; *Brahmayāmala Tantra*, i–iii, in *Mahāchīnāchāra Tantra* in *Tārā Tantram* (Gauḍaratna Mālā Series, No. 2).

116 *Śat. Br.*, ix, 3, 4, 8. 117 *Āpast. Śr. Sūtra*, xx, 1, 1.

118 *Camb. Hist. of India*, i, 107.

119 Shama Sastri, *The Evolution of Indian Polity*, p. 27.

120 Kirāta girls are mentioned as sellers of the Soma in *Atharva-Veda*. I am indebted for this suggestion to Dr Sten Konow.

121 *Pañchaviṁśa Brāhmaṇa*, xvi, 6, 7; *Kauś. Br.*, 25, 15.

122 e.g., *Vishṇu*, v, 51, 61. 123 *Mahābhārata*, Āśvamedhika Parva.

124 *Samyutta*, Pāli Text Society's ed., p. 102. *The Book of Kindred Sayings*, tr. by Rhys Davids.

125 *Mahābhārata*, Āśvamedhika Parva. 126 Ibid.

127 e.g., *Manusmriti*, v, 36, 38, and 52.

128 *Mahābhārata*, Vana Parva, 80, vv. 14 and 17.

Na te śakyā daridreṇa yajñāḥ prāptum mahīpate |
Tīrthābhigamanam puṇyam yajñairapi viśishyate ||

129 *Āryāvartam tasmin ya āchāraḥ sa pramāṇam.* (*Baudhāyana*, i, 25.)

130 *Totemism and Exogamy*, iv, 14.

131 *R.V.*, i, 51, 3; ii, 17, 1; iii, 39, 4.

132 Śānti, 296, 17–18. *Mūlagotrāṇi chatvāri samutpannāni Pārthiva* | *Angirā Kaśyapaśchaiva Vasishtho Bhrgureva cha* ||

133 *Cch. Up.*, iv, 4, 1; *Āś. Gr. Sūt.*, iv, 4.

134 *Baudhāyana*, *Saptānām Rishīṇām Agastyāshṭamānām Yadapatyam tadgotram* |

135 Pāṇini has, *Apatyam pautraprabhriti gotram* |

136 *Āpastamba*, ii, 5, 11, 15 and 16; *Gobhila Gr. Sūtra*, iii, 4, 4.

137 *Asamprajñātabandhuḥ Āchāryāmushyāyaṇamanuprabravīta* (*Pravaramañjarī*).

138 See *Baudhāyana*,

Yānutpādayate yānupanayate yānadhyāpayate yānyājayate te tasya putrāḥ bhavanti |

139 In Egypt there was the institution of the marriage of brothers and sisters. "Such unions of brothers and sisters were the rule, not the exception, in

Ancient Egypt, a simple and effective expedient for keeping the property in the family, which, if the sister had married another, would pass to the latter." Frazer, *Adonis, Attis, Osiris*, pp. 394–7.

140 *Manusmriti*, v, 56.

141 Hopkins, *The Great Epic of India*, 379.

142 *Manusmriti*, xi, 33. See Professions forbidden for Brāhmans.

143 *Arthaśāstra*, p. 343.

144 *Mahābhārata*, Ādi Parva, 142 f.

145 *Baudhāyana*, i, 1, 2, 4.

146 Ibid., i, 1, 2, 3. Cousin marriage "has been, as a rule, permitted, and even favoured, among all races except the Aryan". Frazer, *Folklore of the Old Testament*, ii, 134.

147 Shama Sastri, *Evolution of Indian Polity*, p. 9.

148 *R.V.*, x, 40, 2. *Ko vāmśayutrā vidhaveva devaram maryam na yoshā krṇute sadastha ā* |

149 Keith, *Hist. of Sans. Lit.*, in "Heritage of India", p. 91.

150 *Memoirs of the Archæological Survey of India*, No. 4, p. 119.

151 Lüders, *List of Brahmi Inscriptions*, No. 6.

152 *Viśvabhārati Quarterly* for January, 1925.

153 *India, What can it teach us*, p. 82.

154 Keith, *Sansk. Lit.*, op. cit., p. 20.

155 See Appendix E for Sanskrit borrowings in the *Śilappadikāram*.

156 Havell, *The History of Aryan Rule in India*, p. 107. See Sir J. Marshall's *Guide to Sanchi*.

157 Rawlinson, *Cuneiform Inscriptions*, i, 312.

158 Gerini, *Researches on Ptolemy's Geography*, p. 122 f.

159 *Hist. of Ar. Rule in Ind.*, op. cit., p. 238.

160 *Hist. of Ind. and East. Archit.*, p. 272.

161 *Maṇimekalai*, 19, ll. 107–9. *Magadavinañjarum Marāṭṭakkammarum Avantikkollarum Yavanattaccharum taṇḍamiḻ vinaiñjar*, etc.

162 *Provinces of the Roman Empire*, ii, 301.

163 Heeren, *Historical Researches*, ii, 426.

164 *Periplus of the Erythrean Sea*, pp. 39, 45, 47, 88.

165 Vincent, *Commerce and Navigation of the Ancients*, ii, 404.

166 Cunningham, *Ancient Geography of India*, p. 339.

167 *Pattuppāṭṭu* : *Paṭṭiṇappālai*, p. 294, ll. 187–91.

Vaṭamalaippiranta maṇiyum ponnum
Kuḍamalaippiranta vāramum agilum
Tenkaḍal muttum Kuṇakaḍarrukirum
Kankai vāriyum Kāvirippayanum
Iḻattuṇavum Kāḻakattākkamum |

Kāḻakam may perhaps be identified with Kaḍāram, which is taken to be Burma. Or, may it be identified with the island Kāradwipa in the Malay Archipelago, which the sage Agastya is said to have colonized?

168 e.g., *Baveru Jātaka*, No. 339.

169 *Periplus of the Erythrean Sea*, para. 56, p. 222.

170 *Arthaśāstra*, p. 94.

171 The *Suśśoṇḍi Jātaka*, No. 360. Suvaṇṇabhumi is one of the countries in the north-east, according to Varāhamihira. Alberuni speaks of the Suvarṇadvīpa, an eastern group of islands in the Indian Ocean. He calls it Zabaj, as does Suleiman. Can this be the same as Celebes or Śrī Bhoja?

172 McCrindle, *Ktesias*, p. 86.

173 *Arthaśāstra*, p. 298.

174 McCrindle, *Megasthenes*, Frag. 34.

175 *Arthaśāstra*, p. 298.

176 *Manusmriti*, iii, 158.

[177] *Arthaśāstra*, ii, 28 (Nāvādhyaksha). There were Royal ships (*Rājānaubhih* in *Arthaśāstra*, p. 126). See *Strabo*, xv, 46.

[178] *Arthaśāstra*, p. 126 f.

[179] *Arch. Sur. of India*, New Series, xv, 29; vol. vi, Madras, plate xii, coins Nos. 52–4.

[180] *Jātaka*, ii, 128; iv, 138.

[181] "Sea Power in Early South Indian History," in the *Journal of the Mythic Society, Bangalore*, for 1926.

[182] *Periplus*, p. 46.

[183] *Manusmriti*, x, 84.

Krishim sādhviti manyante sā vrittih sadvigarhitā |
Bhūmim bhumiśayān chaiva hanti kāshṭam ayomukham ||

[184] M. Senart on "Caste" in *Ind. Ant.*, January, 1912, p. 133.

[185] *Tree and Serpent Worship*, p. 78.

[186] *Rāmāyaṇa*, Yud. Kāṇḍa, 81.

The paintings at Ajanta, it is clear, were inspired and patronized by Dravidian princes. They are perhaps Dravidian in nature and origin, and certainly so by their situation. The same may be said of those at Sigiriya in Ceylon. Yakshas and Nāgas are said to be the custodians of these paintings, and these two represent perhaps the two distinct schools of the art prevalent in South India.

The circumstances leading to the marriage of Ushā, the daughter of the Asura king Bāṇa, and Aniruddha, a grandson of Krishṇa, are perhaps illustrative of the high development that the art of painting had reached among the non-Aryas. Ushā had a dream of a beautiful youth who was accompanying her everywhere she went and was very solicitous to her. She confided the secret of her dream to her maid Chitralekhā (clever in painting). The latter agreed to produce before the princess paintings of all the lovely princes of the age, so that she might identify and mark out the subject of her dream. The figure of Aniruddha was recognized as the one that was haunting her mind. Later on the marriage of the two is said to have taken place.

[187] *R.V.*, vii, 104, 20, 22. [188] *Rāmāyaṇa*, Kish. Kāṇḍ., 25, 22 f.

[189] The order of the occupations by which they may gain sustenance is thus given: *Rita* (truth—the gleaning of corn), *amrita* (ambrosia—what is given unasked), *mrita* (food obtained by begging), *pramrita* (agriculture). Trade and money-lending are *satyānrta* (a mixture of truth and falsehood). Life as a farmer was far superior to that of the "truth and falsehood of trade" and to that of an artisan. *Manusmriti*, iv, 5 f. *Arthaśāstra*, p. 7.

[190] *Arthaśāstra*, book iv, chap. 1 (*Kārukalakshaṇam*).

[191] These correspond to miracle, mystery, tableau and pantomime.

[192] For illustrations see *Madras Ep. Rep.* for 1918.

[193] P. C. Ray, *History of Hindu Chemistry*, i, pp. 195–6.

PART V

CONCLUSION

CONCLUSION

A study of the ancient history of India reveals the fact that the divergent cults and creeds sank their prejudices and differences to realize the unity and the peace of her past. The higher spiritual intelligence of the Aryas with its great constructive genius gradually welded the non-Aryan civilization with its own, so that each contributed its best to the common stock, and both went hand in hand along the path of progress.[1] Though at first the advance of the Aryas could be accomplished only after long and arduous warfare with the aboriginal tribes, they readily achieved a political superiority, followed by religious ascendancy and social amalgamation. Aryan sages carried and spread their religious doctrines in the countries conquered and into the lands inhabited by the non-Aryan races. But the Aryas are seen to adopt and assimilate the beliefs and practices prevalent among the people with whom they came into contact, but which were alien to them, and were at first looked upon as uncivilized and barbarous. This blend of cultures was sometimes the result of conscious processes of admixture, while at other times the fusion was effected in a way unknown both to the Aryas and the non-Aryas.

The Aryan dominion in the Vedic age extended only as far as the Vindhya mountain, and beyond this range lay the vast extent of territory of the non-Aryas who contested at every step with the advancing Aryan invaders. Chief among the non-Aryan peoples were the Nāga, Nishada, Vānara and Rākshasa. There were, besides, many non-Aryan tribes on the outskirts of *Āryāvarta*, whose chieftains are said to have fought in the "Great War". The Epics and the Brāhmaṇas display a larger geographical knowledge, and the *Rāmāyaṇa* is perhaps the first work which discloses the migration of the Aryas of the North beyond the Vindhya mountain to colonize the lands inhabited by the non-Aryan tribes of the South. But we have also evidence of diplomatic alliances of a far-reaching nature between the two peoples, and in the lands already conquered a gradual process of fusion of the two cults is clearly visible. The social relations show considerable improvement over the previous epoch, for in the Epics, instances of interdining and intermarriage are more frequently met with. These resulted in a tendency towards confusion of castes. In religion also there is a gradual commingling of the beliefs and practices of the Aryas and the non-Aryas, and instances are not wanting of non-Aryan chiefs who were masters of the Vedic lore, Brāhmanical scriptures and philosophy. The social and connubial relationship thus established is followed by slowly evolving changes in language.

From about the sixth century B.C. the interaction of the institutions of the Aryas and the non-Aryas comes prominently into view. In this period were evolved some of the most remarkable results of the gradual processes of reconciliation that was going on in the society of the ancient Hindus. The Buddhist and Jaina records and the Hindu law-books and Purāṇas are clearly indicative of this fact. The ceremonies that were elaborated in the Brāhmaṇas were beyond the comprehension of the masses of the Hindu population, and a reaction began with the foundation of Buddhism which drew its numbers mostly from the non-Aryan classes. Efforts were made to question the validity of the teaching of the Veda on the ground that the force of reason and intellect must predominate over that of faith and revelation. The force of Brāhmanical tradition was thus gradually weakened, the caste system was condemned, and the efficacy of animal sacrifices questioned. "The great deed, socially and politically, of Buddha consists in the fact that he removed the clear-drawn distinction between esoteric and exoteric wisdom, and that . . . he proclaimed a gospel for all."[2]

As sacrifices were possible only for the rich and privileged classes in the society, the Brāhmans suggested a substitute for others that they may have salvation. The religious exercise which was within the easy reach of the poor and was as efficacious in effect as, if not more than, sacrifices was holy pilgrimage. This substitute arose out of the spirit of conciliation and compromise that characterized the relations of the two peoples. As pilgrimages were made for worship of the aspects of the Divine present in the places of pilgrimage, they presupposed intense devotion, and hence was evolved the doctrine of *Bhakti*.

Two New Features: 1. Pilgrimage

Pilgrimage to holy places acts as a great social, religious and educative factor. It brings into close contact people from different and distant parts of the country, and makes their acquaintance more and more easy. Caste rubs shoulders with caste and prejudice with prejudice in places of pilgrimage. By following a policy of "give and take", the pilgrims are made to realize the oneness of the country of which they are members, and a feeling of unity pervades in the land. The centres of religion, besides offering stepping-stones for the pilgrim on his progress towards the realization of the spiritual goal, are seen to be of considerable educative value. They open up new grounds for a study of new phases of life, foster a contact with new creeds and cultures, and engender a wholesome feeling of unity and patriotism without which there could be no real education.

The immense benefits accruing to the society from pilgrimages and travels appear to have been understood by the ancient Hindus. "There is no happiness for him who does not travel; living in the society of men there is scope for even the best and the most virtuous to commit sins. Indra is a friend of the traveller, therefore travel in the country."[3] "All mountains, rivers, holy lakes, places of pilgrimage, the abode of the *rishis*, cowpens, and temples of gods are places that destroy sin."[4]

2. Bhakti

Another important feature of modern Hinduism closely allied to holy pilgrimages is the *Bhakti* cult, the origin of which may be assigned to this period. The *Bhakti* cult [5] rested on three cardinal points, viz., symbols or forms, God-names on which to concentrate one's attention (*mantras*), and God-men who had taken it as a voluntary duty to preach and practise the highest principles by which to evolve and perfect the inner self. These last were the *Avatāras* who appeared at times of great crises. The *Bhakti mārga* appears as a substitute for costly sacrifices on the one hand and the metaphysical *Jñāna mārga* on the other. It is popular religion, the religion of the masses. It enunciates the principle that every being of God's creation may get release from perpetual bondage by concentrated and devoted worship of any of the important manifestations of the Divine. *Pūja* is one of the essential concomitants of *Bhakti*.

The doctrine of *Bhakti* in its clear and modern form may be said to have its beginning in the *Bhagavat-Gītā* where Śrī-Krishṇa says,[6] "I take with great grace what is offered with intense devotion, be it a leaf, a flower, a fruit, or even water." From the age of the *Gītā* began the Krishṇa cult. As time went on, the religion of the Aryas, of which the *homa* which meant oblations to Fire and through Fire as a messenger to the other Gods, with offerings animate and inanimate, became transformed to include as the vital factor in worship *Bhakti* or devotion and *Pūja* or offerings of sixteen kinds (*shoḍaśopachāra*).[7] The religion of the Hindus developed in a novel way, and the cult of *Pāñcharātra* arose.

The origin and nature of the *Bhakti* cult and of the *Pāñcharātra* are thus dwelt upon by Professor Garbe [8]: "About two centuries before Buddha the warrior-chief of the Yādava clan, who was also a religious teacher, but not of the Brāhmanic schools, founded a moral religion of monotheism, God being in his system called simply Bhagavān . . . The founder of the religion was himself identified with the God he taught, so that the son of Vasudeva became God. . . . This was the form of the Vāsudeva religion recognized in the fourth century B.C. by Pāṇini, and the doctrine of *Bhakti* belonged to it. But for a century or more after this, Krishṇaism still lay outside the Brāhmanism."

The view set forth above seems to have been based on a misapprehension. The *Bhakti* cult as it was propounded by Krishṇa in the *Gītā* was certainly not heterodox. Śankara in his *Sūtra bhāshya* calls the *Gītā*, *samasta Vedārthasārasangraha-bhūtam*,[9] "the very essence in abridged form of the meaning of all the Vedas." What the *Gītāchārya* suggested was only an easy method of devotion to those who were perplexed by the difficulties of the Vedic scriptures and doctrines. The passage *traiguṇyavishayā Vedāh nistraiguṇyo bhavārjuna* has been assumed to indicate that the teacher of the *Gītā* was not satisfied with the Vedic practices, and so cut away from them.[10] It is a false assumption leading perhaps to a misinterpretation of the evolution of Hindu religious and social life. The passage in question was intended only for one who was fit to become a *Jñāni* and *Sannyāsi*, and to inculcate what every Hindu was ultimately to aspire for. Śrī Krishṇa teaches Arjuna the superiority of the *Jñāna mārga* to the *Karma mārga*. In the words of Sir R. G. Bhandarkar,[11] "About the time when the systems of religion . . . arose, there was a tendency amongst the people which often worked itself out, as is evident from the Pāḷi birth-stories, to give up worldly life and to betake themselves to residence in forests or mountains. Even Buddhism, Jainism and other like systems considered an ascetic life to be a *sine qua non* of religious elevation. There is reason to believe that Śramaṇas existed before the rise of Buddhism. The religious systems that had sprung up were mostly atheistic. The Indian mind had become prone to indulge in mere moral discourses and thoughts on moral exaltation, unassociated with a theistic faith as appears clear from Buddhism and other systems, and also very dry moral dissertations of which the *Mahābhārata* is full. Such a system as that of the *Bhagavat-Gītā* was therefore necessary to counteract these tendencies.

Theistic ideas were so scattered in the Upanishads, that it was necessary for practical purposes to work them up into a system of redemption capable of being grasped easily. These appeared to be the conditions under which the *Gītā* came into existence."

The *Pāñcharātra* which grew out of this *Bhakti* cult developed certain features and peculiarities which perhaps have not found sanction in the Vedas. Hence it is that Śankara says in his commentary,[12] "Śāṇḍilya is said to have promulgated the *Pāñcharātra* doctrine because he did not find a sure basis for the highest welfare of man in the Veda and its auxiliary disciplines." Similarly, Kumārila [13] holds tne view that the *Pāñcharātra* was "opposed to the Veda" and "was not honoured by those who know the Vedas". The *Bhakti* of the *Gītā* should not be taken to be identical with the *Pāñcharātra* as it was developed by Śāṇḍilya and in later times. One of the most important points of difference lies in the formulation of the *vyūhas* in the latter cult. These are Pradyumna, Aniruddha, Sankarshaṇa and Vāsudeva. In the opinion of the late Sir R. G. Bhandarkar,[14] "it may be taken for granted that the two *vyūhas*, Vāsudeva and Sankarshaṇa, only were known up to the time of the earliest inscription which is to be referred to about the beginning of the first century before the Christian era, so that the system of four *vyūhas* was not fully developed up to that time."

The worship of the deities that came to be taken as the forms of the quarternity of *Purushottama* was prevalent in India from very early times. The worship of Vāsudeva and Baladeva is mentioned in a passage of the *Niddeśa*. Vāsudeva is mentioned as God by Patañjali. The Besnagar column, the *Garuḍa-dhwaja*, was constructed by a Yavana envoy "in honour of Vasudeva the God of Gods". As it has been noted, the Ghosūṇḍi inscription refers to the setting up of a stone for worship of the *Bhagavāns* Sankarshaṇa and Vāsudeva.

The *Bhagavat Gītā* does not speak of the *vyūhas*, but mentions

Vāsudeva, *not* among the *vyūhas*, however, but among the *Vrishṇis*. The worship of Sankarṣhaṇa is mentioned in the *Arthaśāstra*.[15] But it may be seen that nowhere in these cases is the worship of any of the *vyūhas* referred to as the same as that of Vāsudeva. For example, we have the distinct worship of Sankarshaṇa and Vāsudeva, of Vāsudeva and Baladeva, and of Vāsudeva. If the idea of the *vyūhas* had been prevalent in the age when these gods were worshipped, separate mention should not have been made of Sankarshaṇa or Baladeva from Vāsudeva. These were distinct gods for whom separate worship was offered, and it was only later that they came to be looked on as the aspects of the same God. The position taken by Bhandarkar seems therefore to be substantially correct.

The mistake lies in the identification of the *Bhakti* of the *Gītā* and the *Pāñcharātra* which is a later development. It might be that Śāṇḍilya's doctrines came to be looked upon as unorthodox, but there is nothing to warrant the opinion that the *Bhakti* of the *Gītā* was similarly unorthodox from the Vedic standpoint.

Thus the Aryas were ever prepared to make a compromise. They recognized the canonical character of the religious beliefs of the non-Aryas and admitted them into the Aryan religious and social system. Some of the practices contained in the *Atharva* collection were apparently carried to perfection by the non-Aryas, for they do not seem to have been at first accepted by the Aryas. The period also witnesses certain changes in the languages of the two peoples evolved by the slow processes of admixture, and the formation of the Prākrits and the various vernaculars in the land.

By the close of the Buddhist period there had been a gradual fusion of the Aryan and the non-Aryan alike in social and economic life and in religion and language. Socially, the non-Aryan classes found their way into the Aryan caste system, and the Smritis disclose the dangers that had resulted from the admixture that was taking place in the society. Due to intermarriage and intermingling of occupations a large number of mixed castes had been formed. *Varṇa* or colour had ceased to be a criterion, and the new castes were based on occupation and birth, and the Smritis fixed the occupations of these. Another criterion of caste or class-formation was geographical or regional. Certain classes of the population came to be identified with certain localities, and these became endogamous groups.

Pollution and untouchability resulted primarily out of hygienic, physiological, sentimental and ethical objections. Those castes were declared to be polluting as were accustomed to certain interdicted practices, such as the eating of meat and the drinking of liquor. Such of the lower castes as shunned these practices were, of course, considered to cause less pollution. It may be noted here, in passing, that ideas of pollution by touching have gained greater currency in the South than anywhere else in India, for South India has preserved Brāhmanical traditions and practices more close than the other parts of the country. Castes in Malabar strike the observer as a bewildering phenomenon. There are in that district various grades of castes and sub-castes from the proud and orthodox Nambūdiri Brāhmaṇa on the one hand to the lowest Nāyāḍi on the other. The degree of pollution depends on the distance. There are some castes which are looked on by the Nambūdiri as causing pollution only by touching, e.g. the foreign Brāhmaṇa settlers; some cause pollution if they come within five or six feet, e.g. the artisan class; distance of about a hundred feet is necessary in the case of the Īzhava, the professional toddy-tapper; his purity is unimpaired only if twice the distance is kept with the cow-killing Pariah; while the Nāyāḍi, perhaps the last according to the social stratification in Malabar, will have to stand furlongs off, and should cry out from the distance as the Asuras of olden times were supposed to do. Pollution by approach finds ample illustration in Malabar. It is in evidence in other parts of India, too, and should not be looked upon as of quite recent growth. Unapproachability in India is a custom as old at least as the third or fourth century A.D. The Chinese travellers Fa-Hien and I'tsing say, "Those who clear away filth have to strike sticks while going about in token of their approach.[16] When one by mistake touches them, he washes himself and garments thoroughly." It was perhaps older. The Jātakas consider the Chaṇḍāḷas as unclean, and contact with them was pollution. In one Jātaka a Seṭṭhi woman starts out early in the morning for fetching water, but sees on her way a Chaṇḍāḷa. At once she says, "I have witnessed to-day something inauspicious," and washes her eyes. So much was the dread of the pollution. The very sight of the Chaṇḍāḷa was a precursor of ill-luck. In another story a Brāhmaṇa from West India in his rambles comes by a Chaṇḍāḷa woman, and finds himself unclean for her mere approach.[17]

As a result of the restrictions contained in the law-codes regarding marriage, occupations, and touching, taken with the new criteria of caste-formation, Brāhmans came to be of many classes their nature and character being dependent on birth, knowledge of the Veda, and good and righteous deeds. Besides, there were different classes of Brāhmans belonging to particular localities. As Mr Atkinson observes in his *Primitive Law*, mere local contiguity constituted the sense of relationship. Exogamy appeared in its local form, i.e. all within the same locality were relations and all outside it were strangers free in marriage.[18]

The Kshatriyas had ceased to exist in their purity owing to various causes. The admixture of the blood of the foreigners with the fighting clans of North India resulted in the creation of new classes of people who took rank with the old Kshatriyas. These had only the fighting and martial spirit to deserve the name. The term Kshatriya became synonymous with a soldier, and the Kshatriyas were looked upon as mere fighting clans like the Rajputs. Many of the Kshatriya line of kings had been superseded by the foreign monarchs in North India, and by the rapid growth of non-Aryan and Dravidian kingdoms in the Centre and the South. The Kshatriya kings of old were great patrons of Brāhmanical ceremonies. Now that it was recognized that sacrifices which entailed great suffering and expenditure were not very efficacious, they gradually fell into disuse; and the kings of ancient India lost much of their power and prestige in consequence. Lastly, the Hindus with their philosophical bent of mind submitted "in patient, deep disdain" to the successive waves of invaders. The internal tranquillity of the Hindu could not be shaken by shots of bullets or the blaze of powder. The Hindus, especially the Kshatriyas, therefore lost their elemental strength, valour and martial spirit. This led eventually to the decay of the caste as such.

The Vaiśya occupations of agriculture,[19] cattle-breeding, trade and money-lending passed primarily to the Śūdra classes in the society. There were more frequent marriages between the two last castes. The fact that all the classes in the social strata tacitly followed the *anuloma* custom shows that the social wounds in the society had been already healed, but the loss to the social system on account of the relegation of the military and the economic aspects of life to the lower orders in the society reacted upon the stability of the social edifice as a whole.[20] Hindu society may well stand comparison with ancient Roman and mediaeval English, as regards the presence and preservation of the middle classes connecting the Brāhmaṇa above and the audi-Drāviḍa below by a series of buffers to prevent each social stratum from coming into collision with that immediately above and below it. There is hardly any evidence of the struggle of the social classes until new-fangled notions of social and political life led to the dismemberment of the Mahaṛāṭṭa Confederacy, because the great lesson of ancient India had been forgotten. The result was that Hindu society as it was constituted even in the period of the Muhammadan invasions showed only the two broad divisions, Brāhmaṇa and Śūdra, with a large number of imperceptible grades in both.

As regards religion, the Hindu pantheon shows that the Gods were partly adapted from the non-Aryas, and the religious customs and observances were the result of influences, Aryan as well as non-Aryan. Thus, the non-Aryan peoples had come "to be more and more completely under Hindu influences with the result of a great extension in the caste-system and the concurrent reflex action of tribal and non-Aryan religious beliefs and practices on orthodox Hinduism. The counter-influence of the higher classes of non-Aryan intellect, like that of the main Dravidian peoples, became insistent, and all the new influences between them changed Hinduism greatly from its former general aspect. In ritual there was the decay of the old Vedic pantheistic sacrificial worship, which was replaced by worship at temples, public festivals, animal sacrifices and cults of new divinities, while other forms of religious practice, far removed outwardly at least from the Vedic and old Brāhmanism, became prominent. Highly organized sects increased indefinitely, sect marks (*tilaka*) which were really specialized diagrams of magic power (*yantra*), sect education and initiation (*diksha*), with worship of sectarian teachers (*Guru*), sect watchwords (*mantra*), and sect symbols (*tantra*) also became characteristic."[31] Hindu religion evolved to be a tapestry of endless variety of hues and shapes.

In the fields of Indian arts, industries and commerce the two appear to have mingled likewise. "Dravidian art and architecture were wholly impregnated with Vedic idealism and the craftsmen referred all their traditions to Vedic teachers." Some of the features of art seem to have been absorbed and conserved more fully in South India than in the North. But non-Aryan influences are also easily detected, and the importation of foreign features into Indian art appears to have been due to Dravidian enterprise. The Indian agricultural system owes to both Aryan and non-Aryan influences while the sea-voyages and commercial relations with foreign countries were undertaken by the latter.

Politically, there arose some powerful non-Aryan states and the Aryan dominion was contracted at the beginning of the Christian era by the assertion of non-Aryan influence in the east in Aṇga, Vaṇga, and Kalinga, and the permanent settlements of Śaka, Yavana and other alien powers in the West. Side by side with these kingdoms in North India is seen the steady rise in the South of the Dravidian kingdoms which find clear mention in the inscriptions of Aśoka. But a spirit of conciliation and compromise seems to have pervaded the relations of the various peoples of India even from the beginning of her history, and the Hinduism of later times was the result of this absorption and assimilation of elements, Aryan and non-Aryan. There is thus a thorough mingling of the two cultures in the early making of India, and this, it must be conceded, is a remarkable feature in the evolution of Hindu Culture.

> " Into the bosom of the one great sea
> Flow streams that come from hills on every side,
> Their names are various as their springs.
> And thus in every land do men bow down
> To one great God, though known by many names." [22]

NOTES TO PART V

[1] Havell, *History of Aryan Rule in India*, p. 15.
[2] Keyserling, i, p. 54.
[3] *Aitareya Brāhmaṇa*, vii, 15. [4] *Gautama*, xix, 14. *S.B.E.*, ii, 276.
[5] Bhakti is used by Pāṇini in the general sense of " love directed to God ". *Pāṇini*, iv, 3, 95.
[6] *Bhagavat Gītā*, ix.

Patram pushpam phalam toyam yo me bhaktyā prayaśchchati |
Tadaham bhaktyupahritam aśnāmi prayatātmanah ||

[7] The sixteen kinds of upachāra (reception) are : (1) Āvāhana (invocation), (2) Āsana (seating), (3) Pādya (cleansing the feet), (4) Arghya (offering of water), (5) Āchamana (sipping water), (6) Snāna (bath), (7) Vastra (clothing), (8) Uttarīya (upper cloth), (9) Gandha (sandal), (10) Pushpa (flowers), (11) Dhūpa (incense), (12) Dīpa (light), (13) Naivedya (offering of food), (14) Pradakshiṇa (going round the god), (15) Mantra-pushpa (final flower-offering), (16) Namaskāra (prostration).
[8] *JRAS.*, 1905, pp. 385 f.
[9] *Brahmasūtra Bhāshya*, ii, 2, 45. [10] *Bhagavat Gītā*, ii, 45.
[11] *Vaishṇavism, Śaivism and other Religious Systems*, pp. 3 f.
[12] *Brahmasūtra* (op. cit.). [13] *Tantravārtika*, Dr. Jha's tr., p. 165.
[14] *Vaishṇavism, Śaivism*, etc., p. 3. [15] *Arthaśāstra*, p. 401.
[16] *I'tsing*, Takakasu's tr., chap. 29. The lower classes made way for the higher castes in the streets. See *Śilappadikāram*, xvi, l. 107.
[17] *Jātaka*, ii, 83 ; iii, 233 ; iv, 376. Cited by Mr. N. S. Subba Rao in his *Social and Political Conditions in Ancient India.*
[18] *Primitive Law*, p. 289.
[19] The word that is now used to denote a trader is shet, shetti, chetti. These seem to be identical with seṭṭhi, having been derived from the latter. The word seṭṭhi is used in Jātaka to denote a merchant. *Jātaka*, i, 120 f. ; iii, 49 f. Seṭṭhi was a leading millionaire merchant of Rājagriha (*Vinaya* in *S.B.E.*, xx, 180).
[20] " We whose boast it is we that kindled the flame of the world's civilization alone are defrauded of our privilege and have become cowards by compulsion, unfit to answer the world's challenge to our manhood, unable to maintain the sanctity of our homes and shrines." Mrs. Sarojini Naidu, *Presidential Address to Indian National Congress*, 1926.
[21] R. C. Temple, *The words of Lalla, the Prophetess*, p. 64.
[22] Gover, *The Folk-Songs of Southern India*, p. 165.

APPENDICES

APPENDIX A

1. The Battle of the Ten Kings

Durādhyo u' Aditim śrevayanto chetaso vijagribhre Parushṇīm |
Mahnāvivyak prithivīm patyamānah paśushkaviraśayachchāyamānah ||
Īyurardham nanyardham Parushṇīm āśuśchanedabhipitvam jagāma |
Sudāsa' Indrah sutukām amitrānarandhayan mānushevādhrivāchah ||
Ekam cha yo vimśatim cha śravasyāvaikarṇayorjanān rājānyastah |
Dasmo na sadmanniśisātibarhih śūrah sargamakriṇodindra eshām ||
Nigavyavonavo Druhyavaścha shashṭih śatasushupuh shaḍsahasrā |
Shashṭih vīrāso adhishaḍ ḍuvoyu viśvedindrasya vīryakritāni ||
Ādhreṇa chittadvekam chakāra simhyam chitpetvenājaghāna |
Avasraktīrveśyā vriśchadindrah prayachchad viśvā bhojanā Sudāse || (*R.V.*, vii, 18, 8, 9, 11, 14 and 17.)

Yuvāmhavantā' ubhayāsa' ājishvinḍram cha vasvo Varuṇam cha sātaye |
Yatra rājabhih daśabhih nibādhitam pra Sudāsam āvatam Tritsubhissaha ||
Daśarājānah samitā' ayajyavah Sudāsam Indra Varuṇānyuyudhuh |
Satyānriṇāmadmasatām upastutih deva' eshāmabhavan devahūtishu || (*R.V.*, vii, 83, 6 and 7.)

2. Sarama and the Paṇis

P. Kimichchantī Saramā prēdamānaṭ durē hyadhvājagurih parāchaih |
Kāsmehitih kā paritakmyāsīt katham Rasāyā' atarah payāmsi ||

S. Indrasya dūtih ishitā charāmi mahā' ichchantī Paṇayo nidhīnvah |
Atishkatobhiyatāsanna' āvat tathā Rasāyā' ataram payāmsi ||

P. Kīdrik Indrah Sarame kādriśī kāyasyedam dūtīrasarah parākāt |
Āchagachchānmitramenādadhāma athājavām gopatih no bhavāti ||

S. Nāham tam veda dabhyam dabhatsa yasyedam dūtīrasaram parākāt |
Na tam gūhanti sṛavato gabhīrāhatā' Indreṇa Paṇa yaśśayadhve ||

P. Imā gāvah Sarame yā aichchah paridivo antāntsubhage patanti |
Kasta' enā' avasrijāt ayudhvyuta asmākam āyudhāssanti tigmā ||

S. Asenāvah Paṇayo vachāmsyanishavyāstanvah santu pāpīh |
Adrishṭo va' etava' astu panthā Brihaspatirva' ubhayānamriḷāt ||

P. Ayam nidhih Sarame' adribudhno gobhiraśvebhih vasubhirnyvishṭah |
Rakshanti tam Paṇayo eshu ɡopārekupadamalakamājagantha ||

S. Ehagamanṛishayah somaśitā' ayāsyo' Angirasonavagvāh |
Ta etamūrvam vibhajanta gonām athaitadvachchah Paṇayo vamannit ||

P. Evāchatvam Saramā' ājagantha prabādhitā sahasā daivyena |
Svasāram tvā kriṇavaimāpunargā' apate gavām subhage bhajāna ||

8. Nāham veda bhrātritvam no svasritvam Indro viduh Angirasaścha ghorāh |
gokāmā me' achchadayanyadāyamapāta' ita Paṇayo varīyah ||
Dūramita Paṇayo varīya' udgāvoyantu minatirṛitena |
Brihaspatiryā' avindannigūhlāh somogrāvāṇa rishayaścha viprāh ||

3. Vedic Agriculture

Kshetrasya patinā vayam hiteneva jayāmasi |
Gāmaśvam poshayitnvāsano mriḷatīdriśe ||
Kshetrasya pate madhumantamūrmin dhenurivāpayo' asmā dhukshva |
Madhuśchutam ghritamiva supūtam ṛitacya nah patayo mṛiḷayantu ||
Śunam vāhāh śunam narah śunam kṛishatu lāngalam |
Śunam varatrābadhyantām śunimashṭāmudimgaya ||
Śunāsīravimām vācham jushethām yaddivi chakrathuh payah |
Tenemām upasiñchatam ||
Ar-āchī subhage bhava sīte vandāmahe tvā |
Yathā nah subhagāsasi yathā nah suphalāsasi ||
Indrah sītām nigriṇhātu tām Pūshā'nuyachchatu |
Sā nah payasvatī duhām uttarām uttarām sa mām ||

(*R.V.*, iv, 57, 1, 2, 4, 5, 6, 7.)

Yunakta Sīrā viyugātanudhvam krite yonau vapateh bījam |
Gira cha śrushṭih sabharā' asanno nedīya'itṛiṇyah pakvameyāt ||
Nirvāhāvān kriṇotana samvaratrāt adhātana |
Siñchāmahā' avatamudriṇam vayam sushekamanupakshitam ||
Prīṇitāśvān hitañjayātha svastivāham rathamitkriṇuddhvam |
Droṇāhāvamavatam aśmachakram amsatra kośam siñchatā nṛipāṇam ||

(*R.V.*, x, 101, 3, 5, 7.)

4. The Voyage of Bhujyu

Tugroha Bhujyum Aśvinodamekhe rayim na kaśchin mamṛivām avāhāh |
Tamūhathuh naubhih ātmanvatībhih antarikshaprudbhirapodakābhih ||
Tisrah kshapah trirahātivrajadbhir Nāsatya Bhujyum ūhathuh patangaih |
Samudrasya dhanvan ārdrasya pāre tribhī rathaih śatapadbhih shaḍaśvaih ||
Anārambhaṇetad avīrayethāmanāsthane agrabhaṇe Samudre |
Yadaśvinā ūhathuh Bhujyum astamśatāritrām nāvam ātasthivāmsam ||

(*R.V.*, i, 116, 3 f.)

5. The Story of Vena and the Origin of the Nishadas

Mrityostu duhitā Rājan Sunīthā nāma nāmatah |
Prakhyātā trishu lokeshu yā sā Venam ajījanat ||
Mamanthuh dakshiṇam cho'rum rishayastasya Bhārata |
Tatosya vikrito jajñe hrasvakah purusho'śuchih ||
Dagdhasthūṇapratīkāśo raktākshah kṛishṇamūrdhajah |
Nishedetyevam ūchuh tam rishayo Brahmavādinah ||
Tasmānnishādāh sambhūtāh krūrāh śailavanāśrayāh |
Ye chānye Vindhyanilayā Mlechchāh śatasahasraśah ||

(*Mahābhārata*, Śānti, 58, 100–5.)

6. Vibhīshaṇa's Advice to Rāvaṇa

Ayaśasyam anāyushyam paradārābhimarśanam |
Arthakshayakaram ghoram pāpasya cha punarbhavam ||
Etannimittam Vaidehībhayam nah sumahatbhavet |
Āhritā sā parityājyā kalahārthena tena kim ||
Na nah kshamam vīryavatā tena dharmānuvartinā |

Vairam nirarthakam kartum dīyatāmasya Maithilī ||
Yāvanna sagajām sāśvām bahuratnasamākulām |
Purīm dārayate bāṇaih dīyatāmasya Maithilī ||
Yāvatsughorā mahatī durdharshā harivāhinī |
Nāvaskandati no Lankām dīyatāmasya Maithilī ||
Vinaśyanti purī Lankā śūrāh sarve cha Rākshasāh |
Rāmasya dayitā patnī svayam yadi na dīyate ||
Prasādaye tvām bandhutvāt kurushva vachanam mama |
Hitam tathyam aham brūmi dīyatāmasya Maithilī ||
Purā śaratsūryamarīchisannibhān navān supunghān sudriḍhān nripātmajah |
Srijatyamoghān viśighān vadhāya te pradīyatām Dāśarathāya Maithilī ||
Tyajasva kopam sukhadharmanāśanam bhajasva dharmam matikīrtivardhanam |
Prasīda jīvema saputrabāndhavāh pradīyatām Dāśarathāya Maithilī ||

(*Rāmāyaṇa*, Yud. Kāṇḍ., 16 and 17.)

7. Food and its Influence on Man's Physical and Mental Qualities

Sa ya ichchet putrah me śuklo jāyeta Vedamanubruvīta sarvamāyuriyāditi kshīrodanam pāchayitvā sarpishmantam aśnīyātāmīśvarau janayitavai |

Atha ya ichchet putro me kapilah pingalo jāyeta dvau Vedāvanubruvīta sarvamāyuriyāditi dadhyodanam pāchayitvā sarpishmantamaśnīyātām īśvarau janayitavai |

Atha ya ichchet putro me śyāmah lohitaksho jāyeta trīn Vedān anubruvīta sarvamāyuriyāditi odanam pāchayitvā sarpishmantamaśnīyātām īśvarau janayitavai |

Atha ya ichchet duhitā me paṇḍitā jāyeta sarvamāyuriyāditi tilaudanam pāchayitvā sarpishmantamaśnīyātām īśvarau janayitavai |

Atha ya ichchet putro me paṇḍitah vigītah samitingamah śuśrūshitām vācham bhāshitā jāyeta sarvān Vedān anubruvīta sarvamāyuriyāditi māmsaudanam pāchayitvā sarpishmantam aśnīyātām īśvarau janayitavai |

(*Brihadāraṇyaka Upanishad*, vi, 4, 14–18.)

8. Nahusha and Yudhishṭhira—Definition of Brāhmaṇa

N. Brāhmaṇah ko bhavet Rājan |
Y. Satyam dānam kshamā śīlam anṛiśamsyam tapoghriṇā |
Driśyante yatra Nāgendra se Brāhmaṇa iti smritah ||
N. Chāturvarṇyam pramāṇam cha satyam ched Brahma chaiva hi |
Śūdreshvapi cha satyam syād dānamakrodha eva cha ||
Y. Śūdre tu yadbhavet lakshma dvije taccha na vidyate |
Na vai Śūdro bhavet Śūdro Brāhmaṇo na cha Brāhmaṇah |
Yatraitat lakshyate sarpa vṛittam sa Brāhmaṇa smṛitah
Yatraitān na bhavet sarpa tam Śūdram iti nirdiśet ||
Jātiratra mahāsarpa manushyatve mahāmate
Sankarāt sarvavarṇānām dushparīkshyeti me matih

(*Mahābhārata*, Vana, 182, 21, 21 and 32.)

9. Drupada and Yudhishṭhira on Polyandry

D. Ekasya bahvyo vihitā mashishyah Kurunandana |
Naikasyā bahavah pumsah śrūyante patayah kvachit ||
Soyam na loke Vede vā jātu dharmah praśasyati |
Lokavedaviruddham tvam nādharmam dharmavid śuchih ||
Kartumarhasi Kaunteya kasmāt te buddhih idriśī ||
Y. Sūkshmo dharmo mahārāja nāsya vidmo vayam gatim |
Pūrveshāmānupūrvyeṇa yātam vartmānuyāmahe ||
Na me vāganṛitam prāha nādharme dhīyate matih |
Evam chaiva vadatyambā mama chaitanmanogatam ||

Āśrame Rudranirdishṭāt Vyāsāt etanmayā śrutam |
Esha dharmo dhruvo Rājan chara enam avichārayan ||
Mā cha śankā tatra te syāt kathanchit api Pārthiva ||
(*Mahābhārata*, Ādi, 210, 27–31.)

10. Hanumān's Description of Rāvaṇa

. . . Suptam Rākshasaśārdūlam prekshate'sma mahākapih |
Kāñchanāngadanaddhau cha dadarśa sa mahātmanah |
Vikshiptau Rākshasendrasya Bhujau Indradhvajōpamau ||
Airāvatavishāṇāgraih āpīḍanakṛitavṛaṇau |
Pīnau samasujātāmsau samhatau balasamyutau ||
Samhatau parighākārau vṛittau karikaropamau |
Chandanena parārghyeṇa svanuliptau svalankritau ||
Tābhyām sa paripūrṇābhyām bhujābhyām Rākshaseśvarah |
Śuśubhe'chala sankāśah śringābhyāmiva mandarah ||
Muktāmaṇivichitreṇa kāñchanena virājitam |
Mukuṭenāpavṛittena kuṇḍalojvalitānanam || etc.
(*Rāmāyaṇa*, Sund. Kāṇḍa, 10, 9–30.)

11. The *Bhagavat Gītā* on "Sacrifices"

Brahmārpaṇam Brahmahavih Brahmāgnau Brahmaṇāhutam |
Brahmaiva tena gantavyam Brahmakarmasamādhinā ||
Daivamevāpare yajñam yoginah paryupāsate |
Brahmāgnau apare yajñam yajnenaivopajuhvati ||
Śrotrādīnindriyāṇyanye samyamāgnishu juhvati |
Śabdādīn vishayān anye indriyāgnishu juhvati ||
Sarvāṇīndriyakarmāṇi prāṇakarmaṇi chāpare |
Ātmasamyamayogāgnau juhvati jñānadīpite ||
Dravyayajñastapoyajña yogayajñāstathāpare |
Svādhyāyajñānayajñāścha yatayah samśitavratāh ||
Śreyān dravyamayād yajñād jñānayajñah parantapa |
(iv, 24–28 and 33.)

12. The Eight Kinds of Marriage

Āchchādya cha archayitvā cha śrutiśīlavate svayam |
Āhūya dānam kanyā ya *Brāhmo* dharmah prakīrtitah ||
Yajñe tu vitate samyak ṛitvije karma kurvate |
Alankritya sutādānam *Daivaṃ* dharmam prachakshati ||
Ekam gomidhunam dve vā varādādāya dharmatah |
Kanyāpradānam vidhivat *Ārsho* dharmah sa uchyate ||
Sahobhau charatām dharmam iti vāchānubhāshya cha |
Kanyāpradānam abhyarchya *Prājāpatyo* vidhih smritah ||
Jñātibhyo draviṇam datvā kanyāyai chaiva śaktitah |
Kanyāpradānam svācchyandyāt *Āsuro* dharma uchyate ||
Ichchayānyonyasamyogah kanyāyāścha varasya cha |
Gāndharvah sa tu vijñeyo maithunyah kāmasambhavah ||
Hatvā cchitvā cha bhitvā cha krośantīm rudatīm grihāt |
Prasahya kanyāharaṇam *Rākshaso* vidhiruchyate ||
Suptām mattām pramattām vā raho yatrōpagacchate |
Sa pāpishṭho vivāhānam *Paiśācha*śchāshṭamo' dhamah ||
(*Manusmriti*, iii, 27–34.)

13. Daiva and Asura

Abhayam satvasamśuddhih jñānayogavyavasthitih |
Dānam damaścha yajñaścha svādhyāyastapa ārjavam ||
Ahimsā satyam akrodhah tyāgah śāntih apaiśunam |
Dayā bhūteshu aloluptvam mārdavam hrīrachāpalam ||
Tejah kshamā dhritih śaucham adroho nātimānitā |
Bhavanti sampadam *Daivīm* abhijātasya Bhārata ||
Dambho darpo abhimānaścha krodhah pārushyam eva cha |
Ajñānam chābhijātasya Pārtha sampadam *Āsurīm* ||

APPENDIX B

(GENEALOGICAL TABLES)

I. The Line of Purūravas

Brahma

1 Atri
2 Soma
3 Budha (married No. 8)

4 Daksha
5 Aditi
6 Vivasvat
7 Manu
8 Iḷā (married to No. 3)

Purūravas (son of Nos. 3 and 8)

II. The Line of the Yādavas

A

Yadu
Kroshṭu
Yudhajit

1 Vrishṇi
2 Śvaphalka
3 Akrūra (married No. 7)

4 Andhaka
5 Āhuka
6 Ugrasena
7 Sugātrī (married to No. 3)

B

1 Yadu
2 Kroshṭu

3 Yudhajit
4 Andhaka
5 Āhuka
6 Devaka
7 Devakī (married to No. 10)

8 Devamīḍhusha
9 Śūrasena
10 Vasudeva (married No. 7)

APPENDIX C

I. Union of Castes—*Anuloma*

Man	Woman	Manu	Vasishṭha	Baudhāyana	Gautama	Vishṇu	Others [1]
Br.	Br.	Br.	Br.	Br.	Br.	Br.	Br.
Br.	Ksh.	[2]	Ambashṭha	Brāhmaṇa [3]	Ambashṭha	Ksh.	Mūrdhāvasikta
Br.	Vaiś.	Ambashṭha	—	Ambashṭha	Daushyanta	Vai.	Bhrijjukaṇṭaka
Br.	Śūd.	Nishāda, Pāraśava	Pāraśava	Nishāda, Pāraśava	Nishāda	Śūd.	Pāraśava
Ksh.	Ksh.	Ksh.	Ksh.	Ksh.	Ksh.	Ksh.	Ksh.
Ksh.	Vai.	—	Ugra	Kshatriya [3]	Ugra	Vai.	Māhishya
Ksh.	Śūd.	Ugra	—	Ugra	Pāraśava	Śūd.	Yavana
Vai.	Vai.	Vai.	Vai.	Vai.	Vai.	Vai.	Vai.
Vai	Śūd.	—	Nishāda	Rathakāra	—	Śūd.	Karaṇa
Śūd.	Śūd.	Śūd.	Śūd.	Śūd.	Śūd.	Śūd.	Śūd.

II. Union of Castes—*Pratiloma*

Man	Woman	Manu	Vasishṭha	Baudhāyana	Gautama	Vishṇu	Others
Śūd.	Br.	Chaṇḍāla	Chaṇḍāla	Chaṇḍāla	Chaṇḍāla	Chaṇḍāla	Chaṇḍāla
Śūd.	Ksh.	Kshatta	Vaiṇa	Kshatta	Kshatta	Māgadha	Pulkasa
Śūd.	Vai.	Āyogava	Antyāvasāyin	Māgadha	Āyogava	Āyogava	Vaidehaka
Vai.	Br.	Vaideha	Rāmaka	Vaideha	Vaideha	Vaideha	Māgadha
Vai.	Ksh.	Magadha	Pulkasa	Āyogava	Māgadha	Pulkasa	Dhīvara
Ksh.	Br.	Sūta	Sūta	Sūta	Sūta	Sūta	Sūta

[1] According to Gautama. Kauṭilya (*Arthaśāstra*, p. 165) calls the offspring of a Vaiśya by a Kshatriya woman Vaidehaka, and of a Vaiśya by a Brāhmaṇa woman Māgadha.

[2] In the *anuloma* form of marriage the offspring of a "twice-born" man and a "twice-born" woman entitles the issue to acquire the qualities of the father (*Pitrsadriśa*), but not his caste (*Pitrsajāti*). They acquire castes intermediary between that of the father and of the mother—lower than that of the father, but higher than that of the mother. Yājñavalkya and others give them the names Mūrdhāvasikta, Māhishya, and Karaṇa. Manu does not give any specific name to such offspring. He says :—

Strishvanantarajātāsu dvijairutpāditān sutān |
Sadrśāneva tānāhuh mātrdoshavigarhitān (Manu., x, 6).

[3] We read in *Baudhāyana Smriti* :—

Brāhmaṇād Kshatriyāyām Brāhmaṇah |
Kshatriyād Vaiśyāyām Kshatriyah |

The sense in which the words Brāhmaṇa and Kshatriya are used will become clear from the preceding passage from the commer *Manusmriti*, x, 6.

III. Mixed-Caste Unions with the Main Castes

Man.	*Woman.*	*Caste of the offspring.*
Brāhmaṇa	Ugra	Āvrita (Manu)
Do.	Ambashṭha	Ābhīra (Manu)
Do.	Āyogava	Dhigvaṇa (Manu)
Nishada	Śūdra	Pukkasa (Manu)
Do.	Vaiśya	Do. (Baudhāyana)
Śūdra	Nishada	Kukkuṭaka (Manu)
Vaiśya	Nishada	Do. (Baudhāyana)
Pukkasa	Do.	
Ambashṭha	Brāhmaṇa	Śvapāka (Baudhāyana)
Ugra	Kshatriya	Vaiṇa (Baudhāyana)

IV. Union of Mixed-Castes

Man.	*Woman.*	*Caste of the offspring.*
Vaidehaka	Āyogava	Maitreyaka (Manu)
Nishada	Vaidehaka	Kārāvara (Manu) Āhiṇḍika
Chaṇḍāla	Do.	Pāṇḍusopāka (Manu)
Kshatta	Ugra	Śvapāka (Manu)
Nishada	Āyogava	Mārgava, Dāsa, or Kaivarta (Manu)
Chaṇḍāla	Pukkasa	Sopāka (Manu)
Do.	Nishada	Antyāvasāyin (Manu)
Vaidehaka	Ambashṭha	Veṇa (Manu) Vaiṇa (Baudhāyana)
Ugra	Kshatta	Śvapāka (Baudhāyana)

Note.—Baudhāyana says that Kshatta is superior in caste to Vaidehaka; and Ambashṭha is superior to Ugra.

APPENDIX D

SOUTH INDIA AND INDO-CHINA [1]

Indo-Chinese traditions, inscriptions and architecture disclose the close connexion between South India and the countries in the East.

Ligor, one of the provinces of Indo-China, is supposed to have been founded by a certain Dantakumāra who is said to have fled from the Godavari District and got shipwrecked off the coast of the Malaya peninsula (Gerini, p. 107). The kings of Funan or Cambodia were descended from a Brāhmaṇa Kauṇḍinya,[2] apparently of South India, who was addressed by a supernatural voice "to go and reign in Funan". Kauṇḍinya was rejoiced at the vision, landed on the shores of Indo-China, married a Nāga maiden Somā, and was enthusiastically accepted as king by the people of Funan. The later kings of Indo-China styled themselves as "Varman", and this custom may have been a borrowing from the Pallavas of South India. The names met with are Bhadravarman, Śambhuvarman, Indravarman, Simhavarman, Rudravarman of the Amarāvati line of kings; Satyavarman of Pāṇḍuranga; Jayasimhavarman, Bhadravarman, and Indravarman of Champa; Chandravarman, Kauṇḍinyajayavarman, Bhāvavarman, Vīrayarman, Mahendravarman, Śrutavarman, Śreshṭhavarman, Jayavarman, Indravarman, Yaśovarman, Rājendravarman and Sūryavarman of Cambodia. Many of these names look like borrowings from Pallava genealogy, and a few of these happen to be names appearing in the latter.[3]

In the province of South Annam at a village called Vo-Canh "has been discovered a block of granite on which is engraved the oldest Indo-Chinese record"[4], "comparable indeed in many respects to the famous inscription of Rudradāman at Girnar . . . or to the contemporary inscriptions of Sātakarṇi Vāsishṭhīputra at Kanheri." The writing on this stone represents "a stage which cannot possibly date later than the third century A.D., and it seems to have fairly closely followed the developments and even the temporary fashions of the writing in southern India".

The inscription seems to be very important as it contains the name of the king Śrī Māra. It runs as a gift of movable and immovable property, gold, silver and grains, by

"*Śrī Mārarāja kulavaṃśa vibhūshaṇena*
Śrī Māra Lokanripatih kulanandanena".

The king Śrī Māra (second century A.D.) mentioned in the epigraph is said to be the ornament of the clan and family of Śrī Māra Rāja. He was the founder of the Hindu dynasty at Champa. It is interesting to note that Māra is a title or name assumed by the Pāṇḍya kings of South India, and it is possible that the title of Māra for the king of Champa was borrowed from that of the Pāṇḍyas. Among the traditions of Cambodia is mentioned an embassy which was sent by one of her kings to the king of India at about 240 A.D. The name of the latter is given as Mulun. This word is rendered by Dr Sylvain Levi as Muruṇḍa. It seems more appropriate to take the word to be identical with Māran, perhaps one of the early Pāṇḍya kings of the *Śangam* period.

Among the gods worshipped in Indo-China Śiva is mentioned as the most powerful. In Amarāvati, one of the provinces of Indo-China, which reminds us of Amarāvati, in South India, the seat for some time of the Andhra line of kings, is the famous temple of Bhadreśvara. The origin of this temple is thus given: "According to tradition, the *linga* Bhadreśwara had been shaped by Śiva himself, and handed over by him to the *rishi* Bhrigu who gave it over to Uroja, the founder of the royal dynasty of Champa." It may be remarked in this connexion that the relation of Bhrigu, the father of Paraśurāma, and Indian cultural expansion over Indo-China is noticeable in the tradition of the latter country. Similarly, the stories of the colonization of Camboja by Agastya, "the sage of the South," as it is evident in an inscription at Ankor Vat as well as the origin of a dynasty of kings in the province, seem to indicate that the culture of Indo-China may have migrated from South India.

But the kings seem to have been tolerant. The temples in Annam "are tower-shaped, built of strong bricks, patiently and most artistically carved, and their inner recesses contain wonderful sculptures of gods and goddesses, not the least important among them being some, peculiarly South Indian: Śiva, Vishṇu, Umā, Lakshmī, Skanda, Gaṇeśa and Nandi, Buddha and Lokeśwara".[4] Indravarman, one of the kings of Cambodia, is spoken of as an adept in Śaivapāśupata kalpa, which is apparently the same as the Śaiva Siddhānta of the Tamils.[5]

One of the ports of Southern Annam, Nhatrung, is towered by a brick shrine dedicated to Bhagavatī. The Bhagavatī cult is peculiar to Malabar, and is said to have been introduced there by Bhārgava Paraśurāma, who has the axe as his favourite weapon. The district where the temple was built was also known as Kauṭhāra, derived from *kuṭhāra*, which means the axe. This corresponds to the epithet *Paraśurāma kshetra* given to the Malabar coast. From these pieces of evidence it becomes clear that Indo-China should have received large cultural influences from the west coast of India.[6]

NOTES TO APPENDIX D

[1] This short note is based on the researches published in the *Bulletin de l'Ecole Francaise d'Extreme-Orient* (*B.E.F.E.O.*) and the *Journal Asiatique*. These are now being summarized and translated by Dr L. Finot in the *Indian Historical Quarterly* of Calcutta. I have also used the comprehensive study of Buddhism and Hinduism by Sir Charles Elliot, *Hinduism and Buddhism*, and Gerini's *Researches on Ptolemy's Geography*.

[2] Elliot says, "It may be affirmed with some certainty that Kauṇḍinya started from Mahābalipuram." *Hinduism and Buddhism*, p. 106.

[3] The four *yūpa* inscriptions of Mūlavarman in East Borneo referring to a sacrifice performed by Brāhmans are, according to Vogel, written in Pallava-Grantha characters.

[4] Three gods worshipped by the people of Champa are seen to be peculiarly South Indian, viz. Skanda or Subrahmaṇya, Śankaranārāyaṇa or Harihara, and Śiva in his dancing posture as Naṭarāja. The word *Śāstā* appears as the name of one of the gods of Camboja. Sir Charles Elliot is apparently uncertain about the derivation of this word, and says "*Śāstā* sounds like a title of Śākya Muni" (*Hinduism and Buddhism*, vol. iii, p. 120). This is not correct. *Śāstā* or *Dharma Śāstā* is the name under which Harihara or Ayyappan appears in Malabar. The reference in the inscription cited by Sir Charles Elliot is therefore to Harihara. An inscription of Ang-Pou reads thus and is in praise of Harihara:

> Jayato jagatām bhūtyai kritasandhī Harāchyutau |
> Pārvatīśrīpatitvena bhinnamūrtidharāvapi ||

(Victory be to Hara and Achyuta united into one for the welfare of the world, though they differ in their form as the lords of Pārvatī and Śrī).

[5] In the inscriptions at Sdok Kāk Thom it is stated that the King Jayavarman summoned a Brāhmaṇa Hiraṇyadāma from Janapada, for the latter was well versed in *Siddhavidyā*. Is it likely that Janapada is the same as Kāveripaṭṭaṇam ?

[6] Other evidences of South Indian cultural influences in Indo-China may be seen in certain practices prevalent in that country, e.g. inheritance through the female line (compare the *marumakkattāyam* law of inheritance in Malabar by which rights to property pass to the nephew (*marumakan*), and not to the son), and the practice of *satī* which was quite common among the people of South India in the period of the *Śangam*. In a few places Sir Charles Elliot brings out the close resemblance of the temples at Camboja to those at Pattadkal, Aihole, and Vatapi in the Bijapur District.

Kauṇḍinya Jaya Varman, one of the kings of Funan or Camboja, is said in Indo-Chinese tradition to have sent to China a Buddhist preacher by name Nāgasena, who took with him as presents a finely shaped gold image of the king of the dragons, an elephant carved in white sandal. and two *stūpas* of ivory. These are peculiarly South Indian products. Similarly, the mention of an image of sandalwood in a temple at Champa may also be taken to indicate the same point.

APPENDIX E

BORROWINGS FROM SANSKRIT IN THE TAMIL EPIC ŚILAPPADIKĀRAM[1]

A. *Themes*

II, 46 f.: *Amritamadhana* myth (churning of the ocean by the Gods).

III, 1–7: Mādhavi the courtezan is described as a descendant of Urvaśī, who was cursed to live her days on this earth by Agastya.

VI, 7–13: The story of King Muchukunda in the *Bhāgavata Purāṇa*.

VI, 39–65: The *nāṭya* (dancing) of South India is borrowed from the " ancient " Bharata *Nāṭya śāstra*.

XII, p. 322: Reference to the story of Kamsa, the uncle of Śrī Krishṇa, and the killing of *Śakaṭāsura*, a ruse set up by him. Cf. *Marudinaḷandu nin māman chey vañchavuṟuḷum śakaṭam uḷaittaruḷ*.

XIII, 631: Puhār without Kovalan and Kaṇṇaḳī is compared to Ayodhyā while Rāma and Sītā were in exile. This is a very favourite theme, like that of Krishṇa. Cf. *Yānkanumaraśe tañjamenṟarüngānaḍainda varuntiṟal pirinta Ayōtti pōle.*

XIV, 46 f.: Rāmāyaṇa story in *Tātai yēvalin māduṭan pōki kādali nīnga kaḍuntuyaruḷandōn vedamudalvar payandōn*, etc.

XIV, 50 f.: The story of Naḷa and Damayantī.

XV, 54 f.: Reference to the story of the Brāhmaṇa and the mungoose in *Piḷḷai nakulam perumpiṟitāka veḷḷiyamanaiyōḷinaintu pin chella*, etc.

The " northern sayings ", perhaps, *Aparīkshya na kartavyam kartavyam suparīkshitam | Paśchāt bhavati santāpam Brāhmaṇyā nakulam yathā* || is referred to in *Vaṭadiśaippeyarumāmaṟaiyāḷan . . . Vaṭamoḻivāchakam cheyda nallēḍu.*

XVI, 180: *Tantrakaraṇa*, a handbook of sorcery, and *Indiram* (grammar) are referred to in *Tantira karaṇamennuvarāyinindiram*, etc.

XVII, p. 448: Reference to the miraculous deeds of Śrī Krishṇa in childhood and the exploits of Trivikrama, God Vishṇu in one of his incarnations.

XXVI, 237: Senguṭṭuvan's conquests are compared to the conquest of Lanka by Rāma.

B. *Sanskrit Ideas*

I, 1, 4, 7: The worship of the Moon (*Tingaḷ*), Sun (*Nāyir*) and Varuṇa and Indra (*Māmaḷai*).

I, 24: Twelve years the age limit for the marriage of girls. Cf. *Īkaivān Koḍiyannāḷ īrāṟāṇḍakavaiyāḷ.*

I, 50–64: Marriage rites, Aryan in form.

II, 26: *Kusumaśara*, the God of Love, is referred to in *Viraimalar vāḷiyōḍu vēnilvīṟṟirukkum* (He who has the flowers for his arrows).

II, 44: *Uruvilāḷan oruperunkaruppuvil irukarumpuruvamāka* (brows resembling the two halves of a sugarcane, the bow of the formless God (*Ananga*), Tamil *Uruvilāḷan*).

[1] The references are to chapters and lines unless otherwise indicated. I was assisted in the study by my colleague Mr. R. Vasudeva Sarma, M.A., B.L.

V, 169–72 : Temples of Śiva, Shaṇmukha (Subrahmaṇya), Balarāma, and Kāma. See also xiv, 4, 7 f.
VIII, 64 : The sixty-four *kalās* in *Eṇṇeṇkalaiyum*.
IX, 29 : Vision in dreams here is apparently based on that of the dream of Bharata, when he was summoned to Ayodhyā after the death of Daśaratha. Cf. *Taittirīya Āraṇyaka*, part 3, on Dreams.
X, 196 f. : The 1008 names of Kāma corresponding to the 1008 of Vishṇu in *Kāmanai venrōn āyirattettu nāmam*.

The difficulties mentioned by Kōvalan, the hero, as besetting his way to Madura, so as to dissuade his wife from accompanying him, are similar to, and perhaps suggested by, the description of the troubles in the forest which Rāma recounts to his queen.

XII, 54–74 : The description of *Aiyai* or *Korravai* (goddess) similar to that of Kāḷī or Buddhist Tārā.
XII, p. 322 : *Śankarī, Yantarī, Nīlā, Jaṭāmuṭi, Chenkaṇṇaravu*, the other names of the Goddess, same as Sanskrit names of *Devi, Śankarī, Yantrī, Nīlā, Jaṭāmakuṭā, Raktalochanā*.
XIII, 110 : *Mūvakaittānattu*. Cf. three *Tānas* (musical tone).
XIII : Brāhmans act as envoys in accordance with Aryan practice, e.g. Kauśika acts for Mādhavī.
XIV, 94 : Indra is *Vajra vendar* (the God of *vajra*, thunderbolt).
XIV, 180 f. : Flaws in diamond, such as *kākapadam, kaḷankam, vindu, mekai*; cf. *Śukranīti* on the qualities of diamonds.
XIV, 201 : Different names of gold, such as *śātarūpam* (*jātarūpa*), *śāmbūnatam* (*jāmbūnada*).
XIV, p. 446 : Reference to the Divine music of Nārada in *Mutumaṛai ter Nāradanār muntaimuṛai narampuḷarvār*.
XV, 175–83 : Compare the incident where a God had half his body turned monkey-like, because of the charity of Śāyalan, with the story in the *Mahābhārata*, where the mungoose became golden in colour because of the efficacy of the self-sacrifice of the Brāhmaṇa family at Kurukshetra.
XX, 33 : Pāṇḍavas or *Panchavans*, from whom the ancestry is traced of the Pāṇḍyas.
XX, 53 : Kaṇṇakī's prayer to Fire-God that certain persons may not be affected by the fire at Madura is similar to that of Sītā when Lanka was on fire.
XXV, 162 : The repentance that Śeran Śenguṭṭuvan feels after the wars with his foes may have been suggested to the Author of the Epic by the great disgust and sorrow that overcame Aśoka after his conquest of Kalinga.

C. *Parallel Expressions*

Preface, 27 and 45 : The doctrine of *Karma* in *Vinai viḷai kāl vmādalin* (Reaping the results of one's past deeds).
II, 63–4 : *Maṛuvinmangala vaṇiyēyanṛiyum piṛitaṇiyappeṛṛadai yevankol*. Cf. *Kimiva hi madhurāṇām maṇḍanam nākritīnam* (What need for ornament for those naturally pretty, in *Śakuntaḷā*).
III, 109 : *Orumukaveḷiniyum porumukaveḷiniyum*, etc., cf. *yavanika* (curtain).
X, 28 : *Kalaiyilāḷan kāmar* (The god Kāma who is without form). Cf. *Ananga*.
XI : *Mālaikkaḍan*. Cf. *Daivamānhikam*.
XI, 100, 101 : *Pūrvajñāna* acquired by the sprinkling of water may be compared to the grant of *divyachakshus* to Arjuna in the *Bhagavat Gītā*. The duration of the fight between Śenguṭṭuvan and the Aryas was 18 *nāḷis* (a *nali* is 24 minutes), as in other cases it was 18 years, 18 months or days.
XXIV, p. 514, last line : Lightning is *Indira vil* (Indra's bow).

D. *Sanskrit Expressions borrowed and adapted*

Preface: Iḷangō *Aḍiyal*, cf. Āchārya *Pādāh*. Kōvalan, cf. Gopālan. *Vaṇiyan* (trader), cf. *Vaṇikjana*. *Adhikāram* in the title of the Epic *Śilappadikāram*, cf. *Adhikāra*, which is derived as *adhikritya kritam kāvyam*. *Śānti* to please the gods in *Śānti cheyya*.

II, 27: *Ramyasthala* (sporting place) in *Nirai nilai mādatlaramiyamēṛi*.

III, 25: *Āchārya* in *Āśān*.

III, 30: *Deśya* music in *Dēśikattiruvinōśai*.

III, 107: *Bhūtāh* in *Pūtarai yeḻuntu*.

III, 111: *Vitāna* in *Ōviya vitānattu* (Roofing).

III, 142 and 143: *Āmandrika* (a kind of bugle) in *Kūṭi ninṛiśaitta tāman dirikai* and *Āmandirikaiyōḍantaram*.

IV, 30: *Mekhala* (girdle) in *Mekalai aśainta*.

IV, 41: *Hāra* (garland) in *Parū ukkāḻāram*.

IV, 54: *Pravāḷa* (coral) in *Pavaḷa vāṇutal*.

IV, 44: *Manda mārutam* (gentle breeze).

V, 4: *Paṭa* (garment) in *Putaiyirut paḍā am*.

V, 15: *Nagara* and *Vīthi* (town and street).

V, 17: *Kāruka* (smith).

V, 28: *Kāmsya* (copper) in *Kāñjakara*.

V, 44: *Āyurveda* and *Gaṇita* (medicine and astrology) in *Āyuḷ vedarum Kālakkaṇitarum*.

V, 48: *Sūta*, *Māgadha*, and *Vetāḷika*.

V, 78: *Balipiṭha* (the seat of offering) in *Muḻuppalipiṭikai*.

V, 153: *Pūrṇa kumbha* (pot full of water for reception) and *Pālika* (rearing of tender sprouts) in *Pūraṇakumbattu ppoḷinta pālikai*.

V, 180: *Puṇyasthāna* (sacred seat) in *Puṇṇiyattānam*.

VI, 11: *Vañcham peyarta mā perumpūtam*. Cf. *Kūṭayuddhā hi Rākshasāh* in the *Rāmāyaṇa*. *Vañcha* (ruse).

VI, 84: *Nūpuram* (anklet).

VI, 89: *Kaṇṭika* (neck ornament).

VI, 91: *Mastakamaṇi* (jewel on the forehead) and *vajra* (diamond) in *Mattakamaṇiyōḍu vairam kaṭṭiya*.

VI, 103: *Indranīla* (a precious stone).

VI, 106: *Daivokti* (an ornament) in *Daiva vuttiyōḍu*.

VI, 131: *Veḷāvāluka* (sands of the sea-shore) in *Vēḷai vālukattu*.

VI, 150: *Ketaki flower* in *Kaitai vēli*.

VIII, 45: Flowers *champaka*, *mādhavi*, *tamālam*, especially the last.

VIII, 54: *Alaktaka* (vegetable dye).

VIII, 94: *Aḷaka* (curls on the forehead).

VIII, 95: *Taṭa* (level spot).

IX, 21: *Ḍākini* (demon) in *Iduṇinam tinnum Iḍākinippai* (Iḍākini that eats carcasses).

IX, 69: *Jaladhi* (ocean) in *śaladiyōḍāḍi*.

X, 14: *Indravihāra* (temple of Indra) in *Indira vikāra*.

X, 13: *Antarachārika* (those that wander in the sky) in *Antaraśārikaḷ*.

X, 18: *Arhat sthāna* (seat of a Buddhist monk) in *Aivakai ninṛa Arukattānattu*.

X, 25: *Śilātalam* (cool spot).

X, 28: *Malaya mārutam* (the wind from the Malaya mountain).

X, 46: *Rūpa* and *kula* in *Uruvum kulanum* (form and clan).

X, 144: *Āhūti* (offering to the Fire) in *Marayōrākkiya vāvuti narumpukai*.

X, 161: *Atiśayam* (heap).

XI, 92: *Bila* (cave) in *Perumāl keṭukkum pilam*.

XI, 94 and 95: The names of the lakes *Puṇyaśaravaṇa*, *Bhāvakāriṇi*, and *Ishṭasiddhi*.
XIII, 123: Sweets (*mōdaka*).
XIII, 140: *Muraja* (drum) in *muraśa*.
XIII, 151 f.: The flowers *Kurava*, *vakula*, *śenpaka*, *pāṭala*, *tāla*, and *kuṭaja*.
XIV, 81: *Malayaja* (the produce of the Malaya) in *Malayaśa*.
XIV, 90: *Kunkumavarṇa*.
XIV, 127: *Udyāna* (flower garden) in *Uyyāna*.
XIV, 155: *Tūrya* (bugle) in *tōriya*.
XIV, 169: *Kavacham* (shield).
XXV, 15: *Yojana* in *yōśanai* (= 8 miles).
XXVI, 138: *Kañchuki* (Chamberlain).
XXVII, 179: *Tāpasa Vesha* in *Tāpada veḍa* (the guise of a saint).

Other Sanskrit names appearing in this Epic are Parāśara, Kauśika, Dakshiṇāmūrti, Kārtika, Vasu, Kumāra, Bharata, Kanaka, Vijaya, Sanjaya, Indra, Jayanta, Vasantamālā, etc.

INDEX